Fast-Forward

Fast-Forward Urbanism

Rethinking Architecture's Engagement with the City

Dana Cuff and Roger Sherman, editors

Princeton Architectural Press

Contents

Recycling Ecologies

Essays

Rerouting Infrastructure

Essays

Regenerating Economies

Essays

Projects

Projects

Projects

Published by
Princeton Architectural Press
37 East Seventh Street
New York, New York 10003

For a free catalog of books, call 1.800.722.6657.
Visit our website at www.papress.com.

Editor: Becca Casbon
Designer: Jan Haux

Special thanks to: Bree Anne Apperley, Sara Bader, Nicola Bednarek
Brouwer, Janet Behning, Megan Carey, Carina Cha, Tom Cho, Penny (Yuen
Pik) Chu, Russell Fernandez, Pete Fitzpatrick, Linda Lee, John Myers,
Katharine Myers, Dan Simon, Andrew Stepanian, Jennifer Thompson, Paul
Wagner, Joseph Weston, and Deb Wood of Princeton Architectural Press
—Kevin C. Lippert, publisher

Library of Congress Cataloging-in-Publication Data

Fast-forward urbanism : rethinking architecture's engagement with the
city / Dana Cuff and Roger Sherman, editors. — 1st ed.
p. cm.
Includes index.
ISBN 978-1-56898-977-8 (alk. paper)
1. City planning—Social aspects. 2. City planning—Evaluation.
3. Architects and community. 4. Architecture and society. I. Cuff, Dana,
1953– II. Sherman, Roger, 1958– III. Title: Rethinking architecture's
engagement with the city.
NA9050.F37 2011
711'.4—dc22

2010017033

To Sarah Jane Lind,

a generous source of insight, energy, and creativity

Published with generous support from:

School of Architecture, Princeton University

School of Architecture, Rice University

John H. Daniels Faculty of Architecture, Landscape and Design,
        University of Toronto

Department of Architecture and Urban Design, UCLA

Foreword

This collection of essays and ideas has been brewing since we founded cityLAB, our now-established think tank based in the Department of Architecture and Urban Design at UCLA. In spring 2006, we organized a symposium and invited a group of architects and thinkers to spend two days with us to generate the seeds for a new school of thought. This book is a testament to that group's provocative launch into terrain that we expect will grow more well-defined over the coming years. The group consisted of: Hitoshi Abe, Stan Allen, Penelope Dean, Michael Dear, Mario Gandelsonas, Ed Mitchell, Albert Pope, R. E. Somol, and Interboro (Georgeen Theodore, Tobias Armborst, and Daniel D'Oca). We want to single out Bob Somol, who organized the symposium with us. Over the years, our collaborations—particularly in the History Channel competition for LA 2106—have produced a shared set of ideas about the next generation of urbanism in the United States.

Through cityLAB at UCLA, we have built a consortium of institutions that are actively engaged in their own design investigations of the contemporary metropolis. These include Rice University's School of Architecture under Lars Lerup and present Dean Sarah Whiting, the School of Architecture at Princeton University under Dean Stan Allen, and the University of Toronto's John H. Daniels Faculty of Architecture, Landscape, and Design, led by Dean Richard Sommer. The generosity of these schools supported the color reproductions in *Fast-Forward Urbanism*.

Many people deserve our gratitude, for without them this volume is unlikely to have materialized. Sarah Jane Lind supported cityLAB, both intellectually and financially, when it was just an idea. Her unwavering enthusiasm has given the center an essential momentum for all its undertakings. At UCLA, support from Dean Chris Waterman and Chair Sylvia Lavin, followed by Chair Hitoshi Abe, has been critical. Sylvia gave us the opportunity to organize a lecture series around our very early thoughts about new forms of city-making. Chris and Hitoshi, along with Pat Baxter, offered institutional support whenever they had the means to do so. Bianca Siegl helped set the tone when she was part of cityLAB in its early days.

A number of graduate students worked with us from the organizing of the symposium to the mailing of the manuscript. Per-Johan Dahl, Ari Seligmann, Amelia Wong, Linda Samuels, Nate Vanderlaan, and Claudia Ziegler each contributed reliable help as well as intellectual spark to our efforts. We also appreciate the capable editors at Princeton Architectural Press—Kevin Lippert, who became involved in the book at its earliest phase, and Becca Casbon, who ushered it through its later phases. Their patience and intelligence is greatly valued. Lastly, we gained a new colleague, Harrison Timothy Higgins, at cityLAB in December 2008 as associate director and academic researcher. Tim's smart reading of the projects and the essays, his persistence in bringing the book to closure, and his incredible management skills were all necessary to complete *Fast-Forward Urbanism*.

Between the two of us, our own families deserve our deepest appreciation. At Dana's house, the architectural intelligence of Kevin Daly is pervasive, so it's impossible to distinguish the origins of any good idea. Our kids, Amelia and Julian, have grown into constructive, insightful critics. Around the corner, Roger's gang of three—Jennifer Schab, Olive, and Lucy—knowingly and unknowingly provided keen insights into the city we live in as a set of underlying practices and logics waiting to be capitalized upon by the architect-entrepreneur. Thanks again to them all.

Dana Cuff and Roger Sherman
Santa Monica, California

Introduction

Dana Cuff and Roger Sherman

At this historical juncture, it is imperative that architecture seek new means to engage urbanism. Since 9-11 and Hurricane Katrina, the two greatest American urban catastrophes in memory, architecture's failings have been broadcast on the front pages of the daily news. Our greatest successes, at Bilbao or Las Vegas (however different these may be), are not apparently relevant to the multiple crises contemporary cities face. The frenzy of urbanization occurring across the globe has made us more aware than ever that the architecture, landscape, and planning disciplines are unable to manage the process. Our models of design practice have come up short; the profession's definition of design is inadequate.

Be it Los Angeles's Grand Avenue, Biloxi, or Lower Manhattan, the city appears as a stop-action frame: nothing happens for interminable periods, when suddenly we arrive at built results seemingly by fast-forward, with no clear grasp of how we got there. Like a series of discontinuous jump-cuts, the landscape transforms in a sequence of disorienting new frames where the destabilization is never complete, since some things have stayed the same. Today, the indifferent backdrop of the city evolves organically, taking the small steps that everyday urbanism endorses. Urban theory has a harder time absorbing the more radical jump-cuts, where architecture tends to thrive. Only in retrospect, when pieced together into a legible, historical narrative, does urbanism account for the eruptions that punctuate a city's transformation. By contrast, fast-forward urbanism is projective; it grapples with the big leaps, seeking to explain them, design them, and launch them.

Following the disasters that New York City and New Orleans endured, another tragedy ensued: neither city has triumphed over its ordeal. The long-standing narrative of recovery that has characterized post-crisis cities will be broken.[1] In the Gulf Coast, the only group of architects organized enough to respond were the New Urbanists, hundreds of whom assembled to assist the rebuilding effort. In New York, public outcry turned back conventional preliminary proposals in favor of bold, new design solutions. Both efforts failed. While there are many explanations of these failures, we argue they were unsuccessful because architecture needs to rethink its relation to the city. In other words, we need new theory—not because our formal operations are themselves inadequate, but because they remain independent of our understanding of urban change. While modernist master plans were at once colonizing and eternal, the contemporary city responds most favorably to change that is like a virus to a host. Weak spots and holes are occasions not for projects, per se, but for systemic interventions that can reproduce elsewhere. Fast-forward urbanism mobilizes the rethinking of architecture's relation to the city, specifically in terms of temporal, opportunistic, and strategic transformations.

If 9-11 and Katrina made architecture more aware that it missed the target, there are myriad indications that planning's misfires have also caused vast collateral damage. At the beginning of this millennium in America, there is pressure to reconceive the urban plan. With the end of sprawl finally in sight and an ailing national infrastructure, inner cities have deteriorated to the point of being uninhabitable, and disastrous environmental conditions prevail.[2] The current federal administration, like Roosevelt's in the Great Depression, targets revitalization of urban areas and infrastructure as a primary means to stimulate the national economy while investing in our material future. But just how to invent a robust infrastructure, whose design is as ambitious as its economic underpinnings, is a question that planning and architecture have not posed, let alone answered, from the sidelines.

In this urban century, when for the first time in history more than half the world's population lives in cities, we face an environmental crisis that has the potential to swamp all others. Architecture's green movement seeks to integrate environmental sciences and landscape into its portfolio, with strategies that emanate from eco-tech, biomimicry, and regionalism. Yet the promise in all these approaches is nearly suffocated by the twin forces of moralism and commercialism: architecture is branded with a heavy coat of greenwash, making it both good and marketable. The problem is not the branding, but the discipline's rejection of it as a medium for serious work.

To begin, our objective is to extend current discourse about urban transformation and architecture's role therein. The object of fast-forward urbanism is the city, or rather, that region where canonical distinctions retreat, because nature is a cultural construction and whole cities are suburban. This metroburbia accepts the possibilities offered by landscape urbanism, while simultaneously reconstituting architectural and urban design as a continuous field of operation.

At the onset of an era in which reconfiguring, revitalizing, and reimagining will increasingly dominate metropolitan practices, an architecture that engages what we used to call the city and the suburbs is required. In light of these new demands, architects, planners, and landscape designers have been concocting peculiar remedies from our old bag of tricks. Instead, we need new kinds of operations undertaken opportunistically that reference the existing urban work—the city as found. Not only are the urban circumstances definitive, but so are the urban operations, which involve a fundamental rethinking. The projects and essays in this volume—which stands on the shoulders of, and yet in contrast to, prior ways of referencing the city—speak to the opportunistic new ways of making cities.

North America's particular combination of market forces and public policy has generated alternative urbanisms that seem particularly improbable—most notably those of the "new" (the developments of traditional form) and the "everyday" (the voyeurism of emergent process). The first of these urbanisms ironically mirrors the positivism of the modernist movement whose legacy it seeks to remedy or even negate. In what could be viewed as the urban version of an Oedipus complex, New Urbanism substitutes one manifesto for another. Its vision and principles are equally unable to deal with the messiness of existing conditions and the market forces that control them. It indiscriminately borrows an urban imaginary from an earlier model of city life, and fails to recognize how the forces that produce cities today have radically changed—in the scale of increments of development, instruments of financing, audiences, and implicit lifestyles. For these reasons, it is not coincidental that New Urbanism has achieved its greatest successes, again ironically, not by strategically intervening in existing older urban cores, but on so-called greenfield sites, which are unencumbered by complications that would challenge the degree of control demanded by (their) master-planned designs.[3]

At the other end of the spectrum, the urbanism offered by the every-day possesses a critical complacence that all-too-readily relinquishes the role of the design disciplines to shape cities and stimulate their necessary transformation over time. It endorses a very particular valence of the status quo that gives agency to the bottom-up forces of the less empowered, while failing to grapple with the fact that the capital essential to urban develop-ment more often than not flows from the top down, whether from public or private coffers. The contribution that everyday urbanism has made relative to the work contained within this book must not go unacknowledged, in the field's establishment of the premise that working within the city as it is, and as it operates, is a productive research enterprise capable of unearth-ing practices hidden in plain sight, waiting to be exploited. As such, we see the existing city as a laboratory, incubator, and starting point for all future action. Where the present approach differs from everyday urbanism is in the latter's disregard of the crucial need for the architect-urbanist to assume a more complex role as a double agent whose interests alternate—and negotiate—between those of the client and the interests of those who will invariably be affected by their actions. It is precisely this interface, where the operating system of the existing city can embed design with a more strategic value, that links the various propositions in this volume.

Whether everyday or new, architecture has held a tenuous grasp on city-making, particularly when we examine the recent past. The New Urbanist approach to Katrina is characterized in the many final reports for towns engaged in the Mississippi Renewal Forum.[4] The recommendations involve what we would call "micromastering," or master planning with a fine-toothed comb, yet still its organizers admit three years later, "Every problem, and therefore every alternative solution, is more complex than we imagined."[5] From porch design to town plans, the form-based prescription for rebuilding met the expectable hurdles: nonconformists, developers with different ideas, town councils that had to operate expeditiously, homeown-ers who just wanted to get back to normal. At Ground Zero, by contrast, rebuilding rested upon the persona of the architectural hero, namely Daniel Libeskind. But there was little agreement among the multiple, powerful players involved, and Libeskind's magical hold crumbled. While it appeared that the architect's virtuoso performance, in terms of both the design and rhetoric surrounding the Freedom Tower, might provide enough momentum to carry his World Trade Center proposal to implementation, a fast-forward jump just one year after the competition found Libeskind "virtually neutralized by commercial forces" according to architectural critic Joseph Giovannini.[6] A March 2010 editorial in the *New York Times* jump-cuts to more recent events, demonstrating that even Libeskind's winning master plan—a ring of skyscrapers on the site—has little relevance to the changing development conditions in Manhattan.[7]

What resulted in both New Orleans and Lower Manhattan, even though they had almost nothing else in common, was the death of those proposals at the hands of local economic, political, and cultural practices. As such, the discipline of architecture (and with it, planning, urban design, and landscape architecture) has been blindsided. Neither the groundswell of well-articulated planning directives from New Urbanists, nor the bravado of creative genius from Libeskind, had substantial impact. The local political economy prevailed. It is worth stepping back into the recent history of architecture and urbanism to place this predicament in context.

Looking Backward

Within architecture, the city has always been something of a conundrum. As a context for architectural works, the city offers constraints that spawn both innovation and retrograde, historical mimicry. As a project, the city has proven to be too large, or at least too comprehensive, leading architects down the slippery slope of utopian thinking. As a political arena, building regulations may reflect stable public values, but the architect practices in the chaos of dynamic urban politics that oscillate between neighborhood activists and design review boards. And as a collective work, the city is too unruly to curate and yet too seductive (and important) not to try.

The paradox of the city is that it intrinsically demands design, yet inherently resists it. This can be viewed as the source of a number of architectural schools of thought about the city. In the modernist project, for example, architecture is intended to overcome the city's resistance. Analytic use-categories of residential, commercial, recreation, and transportation parse not only geography but life itself. Grounded on ideas emerging from structural anthropology, the urban condition is shared by the masses, whose basic needs are knowable and, with architects' help, solvable. Yet the modernist city is but one model; its postmodern offspring adopt new strategies. Rather than approach design from the top down, the city's resistance is substantially reduced if urban form derives from existing or past instantiations. Everyday urbanism, for instance, attacks the paradox differently, suggesting that the city does not demand design, at least not by professionals who see themselves as dictating form from the outside. Instead, the vitality of the city is shaped by everyday actors and practices, immune to our theories. Hence, no top-down design, no resistance.

The theorist-practitioners whose work appears in this volume use their research not as a basis for valorizing this conflict through its repro- duction, but as a means of realizing the new (life as it could be) via a more promising path than modernism's imposition of an entirely utopian vision (life as it should be). The propositions included here are extrapolative— learning from (a la Venturi), but also rejiggering existing phenomena and protocols in order to produce effects and logistical arrangements that, while familiar, are unprecedented. These approaches—landscape urban- ism, scripting, scenario planning, infrastructural urbanism, and the open city, to name a few—share the belief that contemporary metropolitan con- figurations themselves have become rich reservoirs of unformulated con- cepts. These loose concepts represent nascent forms of organization and identity capable of being invested with a level of as-yet-unrealized design intelligence.

Fast-Forward Urbanism was born of the frustration that—in response to the resistance encountered by the top-down to bottom-up norms and practices—architecture has, to a large extent, abandoned the city. Not only is its intelligentsia fond of seeing urbanism as extradisciplinary, but the city's principal players—be they developers or policy-makers—have come to see architecture as irrelevant. In the latter case, it is more accurate to say that the city has abandoned architecture, producing what Rem Koolhaas calls "junkspace."[8] Even there, what is retained is planning, institutionally as well as intellectually driven by a mixture of modern and postmodern ideas. In the early 1980s, an important progenitor of this volume, and perhaps for all contemporary theories of American urbanism, emerged: Colin Rowe's *Collage City*, which examines a role for architecture in the urban project that is not comprehensively utopian. Rowe describes modern architecture's ultimate conflict as being "between a retarded conception of science and a reluctant recognition of poetics."[9] He goes on to state that the science of modern urbanism was a myth obscuring the real problem of urban management, one better handled by the *bricoleur* than the engineer. In architecture, the myth of a reliable, knowable urban science of empirical fact has largely been abandoned since Rowe wrote his tract, but the question of management has hardly registered in professional discourse. Management, as politics and negotiation, is a critical topic of discussion in the present volume's theory of architecture-as-urbanism.

Rowe's second myth, poetics or "fantasies about freedom," alludes to all the larger progressive goals of modernism.[10] This humanitarian ideal, in its inevitable failure, led to a "tyranny of the 'majority,'" which ultimately marginalized the architect, fostering a kind of social guilt that continues to rear its head today.[11] *Fast-Forward Urbanism* builds upon *Collage City* insofar as it too seeks a path out of this paradox without abandoning modernism's virtues in toto. But unlike the other book, *Fast-Forward Urbanism* revolves around a common idea that has yet to be fully polemicized: that the contemporary (and particularly American) political economy both necessitates circumstantial revision of the modernist project and produces opportunities for moving it forward.

American Exception or Exemplar?

The conservative roots of American exceptionalism have been roundly criticized for ignoring the continuities and commonalities shared with other ideological and historical trajectories. The discomfort that this exceptionalism provokes is based on its political deployment. While urban processes are at heart political, they remain fundamentally spatial—and hence a legitimate question is raised about the spatiality of urban theory. Nevertheless, the murky water of the particularities of the American urban condition must be stepped into carefully. In this introduction we have sought to position ourselves within multiple traditions, from modernism to landscape urbanism, but this volume focuses almost exclusively on American urban practices and projects. That focus is justified not by what may be unique to the United States, but by what is highly legible there. For example, America has perfected—to the detriment of both cosmopolitanism and environmentalism—the suburban project, which it subsequently exported globally as a development, finance, and land-use model. The United States has witnessed historically contingent opportunities that are particular to its political economy. For example, American infrastructure is at a historically precarious point, as many of its roads, bridges, and services have significantly deteriorated to the point of requiring federal stimulus funding. There are certain conditions in the United States, then, that have fostered the cultivation of contemporary urbanity. These conditions are found in many different locales, and are at the same time unevenly distributed among regions. Still, they occur together often enough to serve note as a kind of characteristic condition within American urbanism.

First, American urbanism is inherently opportunistic. It is founded on a creative tension between public acts and the private sector. The public sector in the United States has never been as strong as its European counterparts, and this has shaped a particular type of urban politics and finance based more on private gains than public goods. Benefactors, moguls, corporations, and energetic citizens alike can mobilize urban transformations.

Second, the American city, especially as one moves westward across the continent, is trapped by its generic tendencies. This is in contrast to the European city, which struggles against the gravitational pull of an exaggerated historic identity.[12] The postwar American city in particular is a city of space (as Albert Pope describes it on pp. 143–75), with outward expansion dominating the transformation of almost all locales, as Venturi, Izenour, and Scott-Brown were the first to situate as part of a larger discourse on urbanism in *Learning from Las Vegas*.[13]

Third, the American city never cottoned to the master plan as its European counterparts did, in part because of its Tocquevillian participatory democracy and in part because of its Jeffersonian agricultural bias.

Eighteenth- and nineteenth-century cities—primarily in the East—were laid out as grids, but even these organizations were ad hoc and relatively rural in nature. City fathers had to realign streets after floods; a grid originating at a train station left no space for public buildings; towns radiated out from the commons, where livestock might be secured. The hierarchy of a central hub—which the Chicago School theorized as the organization of a concentric urban pattern—has been undone by inner-city abandonment, exurban growth, and municipal fragmentation. All these conditions make master planning too Herculean a task, leaving a more open set of game plans in its wake.

Fourth and last, the nature-culture binary is peculiarly contaminated and ambiguous in the United States. Culture as nature, nature as theme park, and landscape as culture are hardly contradictions there. It is not by chance that Los Angeles has provided such provocative urban theory in the past three decades. In displacing the classical center-periphery approach of the Chicago School, the less coherent but more challenging Los Angeles School forwards several key notions about the postmodern city being driven not by the core, but by the hinterlands (see Michael Dear's essay, pp. 226–41). The traditional duality of center-periphery (congested-to-dispersed, hot-to-cool) assumes a continuous gradient in terms of density, distances, speeds, accessibility, and financial production. This norm gives urbanism the value of radial hierarchy, a value that has been confused and undone through a seemingly never-ending string of natural disasters interwoven with cultural conflict.[14] However artificial or heroic, the paradoxical and peculiar orientation of American urbanity vis-à-vis nature serves for us as a set of operative principles, just as it provided alternatives for refiguring the city that designers from Frank Lloyd Wright to Frank Gehry have capitalized upon.

These conditions set up the American city as an exemplary paradigm rather than as an exception, where the multiple forces of contemporary urbanity are transparently but also instructively visible. As such, there are lessons worth extracting for practices that extend beyond the U.S. border. Far from complying or expressing any master narrative on control, cities like Los Angeles are more constructively understood as nexuses of various strands of thought that braid together into a condition that at the present moment can perhaps only be described as metroburban, forming an incomplete history for contemporary urbanism.

The Modern Project

In the spirit of "learning from," there is much to be gathered from the modern project, since its failures have been so noisily proclaimed that its lessons, in particular those for the American metropolis, have been obscured. At least since the 1960s, there has been ongoing critique of modernism, both in terms of architecture and in terms of the city. Simplified and vilified simultaneously, the failed modern project was an easy springboard from which to launch new ideas about design. Team X—made up of the younger members of CIAM (Congrès Internationaux d'Architecture Moderne)—was among the early critics, along with the more populist Jane Jacobs. Rather than lobbing yet another mortar, our particular view is that the master plan, as a quintessential emblem of the modern project, deserves scrutiny. Its inherent implications have crippled urban innovation, because master planning continues to predominate urban practices in spite of its widely recognized limitations. The master plan is dead. Long live the master plan.

To claim that the master plan is dead is hardly news. Substantial critique of the master plan came from its very progenitors in the 1960s, when CIAM members, led by architect José Luis Sert, attempted to revise the principles of the functional city to meet American urban conditions, where sprawl and inner-city slums resisted easy modernist applications. The historian Eric Mumford, in his exploration of the origins of the professional field of urban design, demonstrates that both modern urbanism at its most functional, abstract extreme—and its seeming opposite, postmodern traditional town planning—emerged from CIAM in the middle of the twentieth century.[15] It was CIAM's evolution in the U.S. context, according to Mumford, that transcended Le Corbusier's reliance on the tabula rasa and became the motivation for it to engage existing urban settings. The metroburban approach represented in the pages that follow are thus deeply tied to CIAM's American heirs.

If the limits of the modernist master plan have become clichés, it is worth approaching the topic in a new way, to better understand the qualities that have kept the master plan from dying its ultimate death and to recuperate what may have been inadvisably rejected along the way. Contemporary circumstances complicate the modernist contradiction that Rowe named, between science/management and poetics/social ideals: in the United States today (and yesterday as well), there is no master to do the planning. The city and state are inseparable from the consumer economy, leading to a corporate capitalism that turns citizens into shareholders. While the moral attack on comprehensive urban planning (that the master plan is elitist and indefensibly utopian) remains unchanged, the pragmatist critique must be elaborated. Hence, this book.

In his historical analysis of modernist state planning in the United States, Robert Beauregard argues that master planning schemes arose to rationally arrange the chaotic land use of newly industrializing cities in the late nineteenth century.[16] The master plan is and always has been an attempt to control the process that is the city in terms of functional and economic factors that could be spatially organized. The futility of this task has had strangely little impact on the enthusiasm with which such plans are adopted. At worst, the master plan is a fiction, a document that demonstrates ideals that no one imagines will be realized. In that sense, the master plan is a utopian instrument. At best, a master plan is an ideal type, in the Weberian sense that it represents an assembled, positive norm or a synthesis of possible phenomena, but not some perfect condition. Yet the master plan, in practice, exists as a static document to which particular actions are compared. Even if we agree in theory that it is more guideline than map, it is deployed as a portrait of the future. There is a certain confidence imparted by the plan—in the form of a standard—that keeps it in play long after its substantive worth has been discredited.

Our perspective admits the value of that confidence while seeking to convert false omniscience into working knowledge, replacing the master plan with tools and tactics of the trade. Within the world of planning, the important document for contemporary urban thought is not a static portrait of some single future condition, but the regulations that govern practices—that is, the focus is on the rules or codes by which the fast-forward transition is effected rather than the final frame. These codes underlie and operate to shape form. In legal theorist Lawrence Lessig's terminology, code is a form of law that creates the potential for choice and freedom, if designed correctly.[17] Like rules of the game that are intimately bound to the game board itself, an urban plan is to some extent predictable and to a significant extent at play.

It is worth examining a more specific situation to distinguish plan from code, a distinction that architectural theorist Françoise Choay has called the model and the rule.[18] Rules about urbanity, she argues, are the stuff of treatises, while the reproduction of models is a utopian form of spatial thought. Within the model (the master plan), circulation is the most relevant realm for rethinking the city (versus the other modernist elements of commercial, residential, and recreational space). Although occasionally taking the form of a linear building, as in Le Corbusier's viaduct in the Plan Obus for Algiers, the circulation of goods and people is always considered an important (if not the most important) function of the city. Transportation and mobility with their necessary efficiencies were emphasized rather than what might have been viewed as circulatory infrastructure, because like Le Corbusier's viaduct, circulation was a form-based entity and not just a hidden system of services. Contemporary city-making is focused on formally realized infrastructures, but considers the engineered service systems an opportunity to grab even more real estate. That so much infrastructure has remained purely instrumental and singular in function (power lines, storm-water channels, sewer-line easements, railways, highways) is a new point of entry for design. Infrastructure, as it is used here, implies going beyond function to create more complex and robust systems.[19]

It was Reyner Banham in Los Angeles, unsurprisingly, who considered transportation beyond its modern function of circulation as a form of art and entertainment. Though we might acknowledge the practices of early designers like Frederick Law Olmsted (or Thomas Vint and Stanley Abbott), who turned roadways into pleasure boulevards, it was really Banham who brought the road into the realm of performative infrastructure. Driving, for Banham, was a research method as well as an indulgence, and he divided the immense, unintelligible space of Los Angeles into ecologies that had as much to do with access as geography. Banham's road as a space of entertainment, culture, recreation, orientation, and identity—as well as mobility—is the way contemporary urbanity refigures infrastructure in a more interactive and relational context.

Kazys Varnelis pulls Banham's view into contemporary focus, looking at Los Angeles as a site of networked ecologies: "A series of codependent systems of environmental mitigation, land-use organization, communication and service delivery."[20] This type of infrastructure follows circumstantial events like laws, environmental constraints, and political pressure, rather than master plans. And while networked infrastructures have spatial registers, those of greatest interest here present design opportunities, with manifest ecologies. As Stan Allen has observed, "Urbanization today is not only a global phenomenon of physical and cultural restructuring, it has itself become a spatial effect of the distributed networks of communication, resources, finance, and migration that characterize contemporary life. The city today is everywhere and nowhere."[21]

From the machinic ideal of a city with a limited number of working parts, one part—that of circulation—is emblematic of the evolution leading to the metroburban project. Now, instead of modernism's efficient, single-use transportation systems, contemporary urbanities capitalize upon infrastructure to create entertaining, functional hybrid ecologies that in turn set into motion the next set of operations.

The Dutch Distinction

An additional, influential connection, both historically and conceptually, comes from current work and discourse in the Netherlands, led by theorists, practitioners, and firms such as Koolhaas/OMA, MVRDV, UNStudio, West 8, Roemer van Toorn, and Wouter Vanstiphout. Through institutions there such as the NAi and the Berlage, as well as by means of cultural policy, commissions, and direct subsidy, the Dutch government has supported architects' involvement and engagement in urban production.[22] It is a long-standing Dutch tradition to invent new urban form within existing conditions, given particularities in the Netherlands.

Despite the fact that the very pragmatism espoused by the Dutch had its philosophical, if not practical, origins in the United States—namely in the writings of John Dewey and William James—its political economy stands in stark contrast to the American one, the subject of which was to a large degree the source of inspiration for Koolhaas's *Delirious New York*. While that work—in which Koolhaas caught the architectural openness of New York (the arbitrary program, the real estate motive, the generic urbanism)—stands in stark contrast to Dutch design, it cannot be a model for U.S. urbanism. Patently distinct, determining forces exist, including the American city's conjugal ties to the market, its expansionist history and parallel disdain for density, and its privileged positioning of the individual over the collective.

Landscape Urbanism

The present approach to city-making, as explained above, has developed from a number of sources that include modernism and Dutch urbanism. However, the most direct progenitor and touchstone is landscape urbanism. It offers a third option to the false dichotomy of the top down (New Urbanism) versus bottom up (everyday urbanism) by strategically relating control and disorganization. It seeks to retroactively make sense of how things work in order to redirect them. In this sense, landscape urbanism's approach to design is one that is to be deployed when appropriate, as opposed to comprehensively; it is more strategic than systematic. Consequently, effect and atmosphere matter more than the plan/planning, specifically by employing the following tools:

> —surface (graphics, decoration)
>
> —programmatic indeterminacy
>
> —information (data, GIS)
>
> —change over time
>
> —form as a unit of organization, as having catalytic agency

This characterization of landscape urbanism is described by Stan Allen (see his essay on pp. 36–61), who notes that even though the contemporary field condition of cities is particularly well-suited to a landscape urbanist approach, its strategies have been successfully deployed not in cities, but in parks. As R. E. Somol points out in his essay "Urbanism Without Architecture," such an approach also tends to resist architecture as an autonomous object, resulting instead in something between figure and ground.[23] Landscape urbanism resists the politics of ownership in devious ways, permitting a kind of transgressive urban form and social behavior—rethinking the front lawn, the corporate plaza, and the vacant lot as potentially nonproprietary spaces or "landscapes." The fact that both landscape and infrastructure tend to resist market forces lends them particular urban status.

Landscape urbanism's strength is apparent in projects where the literal landscape elements (vegetal growth) and the ground plane dominate. It is weakest when applied to architectural projects in which the object is clear and there is little field that can be identified. Strategies and tactics of agglomeration are needed. Landscape urbanism, thus far, has been more successful at providing solutions to landscape rather than urban problems, making it perhaps not the strongest foundation for new urban theory. Nevertheless, we suggest this volume represents the next evolutionary state of landscape urbanism, one that embeds architecture into its theory and practice. That adaptation fundamentally alters landscape urbanism, while retaining some of its core elements. The principles below lay out this new urban terrain.

Eight Legs

As a starting gambit in the play for new theory and practices, the following eight principles of practice are offered in place of both the anarchy of laissez-faire urbanization and the containment project of prescriptive traditionalists.[24] We hope these principles cultivate new strategies for architects, landscape designers, and planners to work in the risky, accident-prone contemporary city. The eight constructs are reference points—the fast-forward urbanism we wish to introduce. When climate, economy, technology, and culture are all undergoing unpredictable but inevitable transformations, such principles are needed now more than ever.

1. The Radical Increment

Design strategy that utilizes accumulation as a means of catalyzing change, while producing urban character and identity in the process, works through what can be called radical incrementalism. This is to be distinguished from the advocacy of an aesthetics of accumulation (emblematized in the Metabolist project of the 1960s and 1970s and repopularized by several contemporary Dutch architects), in which increments are solely an expressive device, absent of an evolutionary development strategy. In this model, incrementalism is deployed within the project only, rather than as part of a larger typological strategy of urban assimilation and distribution. By contrast, radical incrementalism recognizes and takes advantage of the fact that the real estate speculators who are responsible for financing most of the buildings that constitute the fabric of the American city are creatures of habit. In contrast to the utopian vision of modernism, whose instrument was the aegis of the master plan (more recently in the New Urbanist guise of a false organicism), radical increments can be deployed strategically and with the purpose of developing a singularity of urban character, not its opposite. This is accomplished by the introduction of new typologies that others will adopt because they offer new norms to solve both current and older urban problems. Nothing breeds proliferation like the success of a new business plan, one that offers the architect an opportunity to transform the life and imageability of the city through entrepreneurship.

2. In Vivo rather than In Vitro

Design strategies achieve newness by harnessing and rejiggering existing (political, economic, cultural) behaviors and protocols rather than concocting extrinsic ones. This is not a traditional contextual argument. It moves away from the easy but false choice of the top down versus the bottom up, toward the creation of urban experiences that are familiar yet projective, popular yet critical, and informal yet orchestrated. This involves research that is applied rather than theoretical, and leads beyond a mere inventorying of existing conditions to an extrapolation of design methods that can adjust to changes in circumstance (see principle 7). Contemporary metroburban configurations themselves represent rich reservoirs of unformulated concepts and invisible practices waiting to be exploited. The in vivo pays close attention to the feedback loop that exists between new models and their performance in the field. Yet even if a model fails at one time or in one context, it can hold the seeds of success in another—a delayed or even inadvertent form of trial-and-error that stands in marked contrast with the now-or-never reliance on the "premiere" of the original that the in vitro demands. The in vivo argues that new forms of urbanity begin with learning how things work and why—not with the intent of expressing or fetishizing them, but in order to think about how else things might work.

3. Identity and Experience

The opposition of public versus private provides urbanism the traditional values of identity and difference. Today, however, identity has become over-developed: we have gone from the civic ideal of e *pluribus unum* to the individual profiling of *pluribus maximus*. The pyramid and bell curve have been turned on their side. The atmosphere of the contemporary city reflects this, consisting of defined overlay zones, or "O-Zones," indifferently distributed across a residual field and delimited by policies of exclusion and disinvestment.[25] The undeniable popular success of these enclaves (or, for that matter, less exclusive popular attractions such as Las Vegas or the so-called festival marketplaces that populate so many major American cities) is testimony to the same undeniable draw that the city as a whole once held: namely, the opportunity to become part of something unique, in a way that activates surprising forms of pleasure. Today, urbanism is driven by the realization that urban experience (not the same as the city of which it may be a part) has become commoditized. Rather than summarily decry this fact, it is more productive to accept that O-Zones are becoming our future communities of affiliation by capitalizing upon this fact, and exploit the opportunity they present to establish new platforms for collective life. In order to accomplish this, Somol argues for the need to merge the formerly distinct terrains of urban design (the planner) and experience design (the imagineer), believing that it is possible for architecture to be both critical *and* commercial, and perhaps become more urban in the process. The instruments of control of such a hybrid approach, which he calls "entertainment planning," are directed at emphasizing the orchestration of new operating systems and effects rather than (as is the convention) form and conditions (the bias of form-based zoning; the use of traditional tools such as the figure-ground, for instance, is irrelevant when working with contemporary cities like Los Angeles, where buildings cover less than 25 percent of the terrain).[26] In this way, it is possible to eschew the increasingly reductive narratives of theme in favor of the cunning arrangement of materials and logistics that are directed at cutting across traditional affiliations like age, income, and ethnicity. Rather than being driven by the marketplace and special interests, such an architecture-as-urbanism looks for ways to politicize the economic sphere and thus alter its spatial repercussions, cultivating new collectives that undermine the old politics of exclusion.

4. Recasting the Performative

Architecture-as-urbanism moves away from modernism's definition of performance as the optimization and expression of function in favor of another valence of the term that relates it to political economy. The *pro*formative, as it might be called, is entrepreneurial rather than indexical; it recognizes the catalytic agency of form, which builds value by purposefully tapping into a cultural psyche. Its implications for architecture are threefold. First, signification is seen as a form of performance: embedded with the intelligence of a branding strategy, the semiotic value of form attracts audiences and investment. Second, toward the same end, the proformative renegotiates architecture's relation to program by restaging accepted logistical patterns and protocols in a manner that ties it to identity through the medium of experience/doing. This new proformativity is best emblematized in the Trojan horse, whose form neither literally nor directly expresses its function. Indeed, to do so would disclose its plan (bait and switch) and doom it to failure. Instead, the Trojan horse is more cunningly conceived: designed to elicit a certain receptivity (signifying a gift), it accommodates its other intent (infiltration) sufficiently but not optimally. In the same way, it is possible for architecture to be commercial *and* critical, economically driven *and* political. The third facet of proformativity, explained in detail below (see principle 5), calls for architecture to eschew its current role in the city. That is, urban architecture must reject the false choice between acting either as a stand-alone "icon" (as with most institutions) or as infill (real estate)—in effect, having to choose to "perform" as architecture or urbanism, but not both. Allen points out that the thick two-dimensionality of today's city presents the opportunity for architecture to perform a more complex role, one traditionally assigned to infrastructure—namely, becoming an instrument and space of connectivity for the city-in-the-making.[27]

5. Infrastructure as Catalytic

In the American city today, infrastructure has become more qualified in its public role: increasingly limited in the degree of service it provides, as well as more localized in its reach (one need only move and try to ascertain utility service providers to discover this). Whereas traditionally the metropolitan grid provided a clear and dominant system of connectivity among private interventions, the continuity of that once-extensive network has been progressively undermined and fractured by the emergence of closed, privatized developments as the dominant figure of urban organization. At the same time, these communities—access to whose utilities are as limited as to its grounds—use the same services in a more localized but also customized way (the cable vs. satellite vs. broadband choice being one among many examples of this). In this brave new world of private governance off the grid, the potential of infrastructure as an instrument by which to lend character and a logic of organization to such places stands in marked contrast to its conventional status as an element of pure necessity, hidden in plain sight. Even in its accepted capacity as a planning instrument, however, infrastructure can be deployed in ways that suggest new logistical arrangements (discussed in principle 3) and strategies of agglomeration, provoked by shifts in the availability of material resources (see principle 6). Finally, it is possible to imagine that the natural extension of the same tendency toward localization will eventually lead (if it hasn't already) to its eventual application at an architectural scale (see principle 4). This will blur the time-honored distinction between "served" and "serviced" in a way that could offer opportunities to radicalize long-held conventions regarding the relationship between public and private, individual and collective space.

6. Plastic Ecologies

The relationship of the urban to the so-called natural landscape today is ambiguous, as landscape urbanism reminds us. But it is also paradoxical, providing fertile ground for design exploration—as suggested by the evolution in meaning of the term "ecology" itself, which no longer distinguishes between natural and artificial. Rather than try to "naturalize" development (as some in the green movement would have it), it is more enlightening to view nature through the lens of culture: namely, to understand nature as a product of political economy, evidenced in the complex associations that the color and term "green" itself has come to acquire. What has been called the postsuburban, or metroburban, necessarily calls for new combinations of natural and artificial, green and silver, landscape and infrastructure. These plastic ecologies are to be distinguished from the widespread interest within the design academy in biomimicry, which because it exploits only the semiotic dimension of culture-as-nature, resists deeper questions and misses more profound implications for architecture-as-urbanism. These include the effects of living with limited material resources, which itself suggests the emergence of distinct social arrangements organized around certain resources at the expense of others. In contrast to the literal form of plasticity offered by the biomorphic, ecological plasticity refers to the ability of urban environments to attract unlikely combinations of audiences through the radical combination and arrangement of materials and activities. Just as metroburbia promotes a varied field of social and cultural experiments, it equally promotes a sampling of resources in various combinations. If the world of unequal distribution also affords total access, people might be as likely to go in search of certain resources rather than expect small amounts of all resources to come to them. In place of the ecologies that have traditionally given identity to cities—energy, water, and cars, but also the single-family house and the shopping mall—new cultures, lifestyles, and natures can arise, activating surprising forms of pleasure and solidarity.

7. The Question of Contingency

Whether they are growing or shrinking, change is the only constant in cities today. Time is of the essence: design strategies must invariably address not just *what* unfolds in the future, but *how* it might (not will) unfold. Unlike the medium of landscape, where growth and evolution are assumed and where the effects of climate are relatively predictable, urban development is inherently volatile and, accordingly, calls for design strategies that do not merely embrace speculation but catalyze it. From the standpoint of architectural production, a central question in this atmosphere of risk is: Do we desire contingency, or do we have contingent desires? In other words, can contingency prove formally productive as an end in itself, leading to new configurations based on "if-then" diagrams of choice? Or is contingency more potent in reference to the provisional allegiances of metroburbanites, who move itinerantly from location to location over the course of a day, to the various "communities" of which they are members? Borrowing from practices like gaming, game theory, risk management, and arbitrage, such unpredictability is best dealt with not through defensively minded approaches geared to adapt to whatever may transpire, but instead through contingent strategies that nudge the future forward, "surfing" or leveraging given current cultural and economic tendencies, with the knowledge that they will invariably yield up the new.

8. Negotiating Discourses

Not since architect and delineator Hugh Ferriss's time has urban representation broken architecture's strictures to render the city's distinctions (see Albert Pope's drawings accompanying his essay in this volume, pp. 143–75). The final lesson of working in and on the contemporary American city concerns the inherent transformation of communications, both in terms of design representation and social negotiation, implied by the above seven points. Given the contingent and projective nature of design proposals today, new forms of visual expression—apparent in a number of the contributions to this volume—are critical. Architectural renderings depict imageability and end states, while diagrams portray ideas and processes, yet it is in between these two where new forms of architecture-as-urbanism are conjured. More than mere before-and-after depictions are necessary in order to suggest what is next. This pertains not just to questions of phasing, but also to alternative scenarios and readings of context. Not only is a more appropriate visual media set in motion, but communication between actors is fundamentally transformed and the interest of those beyond the traditional stakeholders is catalyzed through the choice of visual media. Markets, audiences, entrepreneurs, and managers displace citizens, designers, financers, and policy-makers, transforming the conventional dialogue concerning appropriateness to one about possibility—the urban future—without resorting to utopian visioning. Returning to Rowe's argument about science and poetics, the contemporary city calls for an awakening of the problem of management, in both politics and negotiation.

Looking Ahead

The school of thought captured between the covers of *Fast-Forward Urbanism* includes not only these eight strategies, which are reference points, but the essays and projects that follow. In the book, we have grouped the range of approaches to this future thinking about the next American city under three relevant urban operations, all of which refer—as evident in the "re-" prefix—to processes of both salvage and experimentation. "Recycling Ecologies" concerns ways to convert the interwoven systems of collectivities, their artifacts, and their environments into thriving contemporary cities. "Regenerating Economies" implies that the markets and efficiencies, as well as value, that comprise the city can be prodded into higher levels of performance. And lastly, "Rerouting Infrastructures" acknowledges that the utilitarian systems and functional networks that serve our cities need to be redirected toward more interwoven, complex, and potent ends. We offer this book to all those urban thinkers and practitioners who will lead the American city into its next spatial formation. While *Fast-Forward Urbanism* is by no means exhaustive, it will serve as a reference, for it contains works that are the seeds of a new urban generation.

1   Lawrence J. Vale and Thomas J. Campanella, eds., *The Resilient City: How Modern Cities Recover from Disaster* (New York: Oxford University Press, 2005).

2   Southern California Studies Center and the Brookings Institution Center on Urban and Metropolitan Policy, *Sprawl Hits the Wall* (Los Angeles: University of Southern California, 2001).

3   We are indebted to earlier versions of this perspective that were constructed in collaboration with R. E. Somol. A particularly astute formulation, in which Somol's role was primary, was our entry to the History Channel's City of the Future competition in Los Angeles in 2006, for which we collectively created *O-Z.LA*, an unpublished manuscript accompanying our design entry that is heavily drawn upon here. Roger Sherman, Dana Cuff, and R. E. Somol, *O-Z.LA* (12 Dec. 2006), http://www.citylab.aud.ucla.edu/la2106.html.

4   Less than two months after Hurricane Katrina struck the Gulf Coast, the Mississippi Renewal Forum was convened among more than two hundred professionals and civic leaders to find ways to rebuild in the wake of disaster. For more information, see http://mississippirenewal.com/.

5   Mississippi Renewal Forum, "Getting to the Future First: Lessons for America in Mississippi's Storm Recovery?" http://mississippirenewal.com/ (accessed 25 Aug. 2009).

6   Joseph Giovannini, "Disappearing Act," *New York Magazine*, 20 Oct. 2003, http://nymag.com/nymetro/arts/architecture/reviews/n_9348/ (accessed 15 Apr. 2010).

7   Staff editorial, "What Ground Zero Needs," the *New York Times*, 11 Mar. 2010, section A30 (New York edition).

8   Rem Koolhaas, "Junkspace," *October* 100, Obsolescence (Spring 2002): 175–90.

9   Colin Rowe and Fred Koetter, *Collage City* (Cambridge, MA: MIT Press, 1978), 3.

10   Ibid., 4.

11   Ibid., 6.

12   See Rem Koolhaas, "The Generic City," in *S,M,L,XL*, Rem Koolhaas and Bruce Mau (New York: Monacelli Press, 1995), 1238–64.

13   Robert Venturi, Denise Scott Brown, and Steven Izenour, *Learning from Las Vegas* (Cambridge, MA: MIT Press, 1972). See also Aldo Rossi, *The Architecture of the City* (New York: Oppositions Books, 1984).

14   See Mike Davis, *Ecology of Fear: Los Angeles and the Imagination of Disaster* (New York: Metropolitan Books-Henry Holt, 1998).

15   Eric Mumford, *Defining Urban Design* (New Haven, CT: Yale University Press, 2009).

16   Robert Beauregard, "Between Modernity and Postmodernity: The Ambiguous Position of U.S. Planning," in *Readings in Planning Theory*, ed. Scott Campbell and Susan S. Fainstein (Malden, MA: Blackwell Publishers, 2003), 108–24.

17   Lawrence Lessig, *Code and Other Laws of Cyberspace* (New York: Basic Books, 1999).

18   Françoise Choay, *The Rule and the Model* (Cambridge, MA: MIT Press, 1997).

19   cityLAB's open design competition in 2009, WPA 2.0, was an exploration of infrastructure's revitalization in terms of a more public, robust way of thinking. See http://wpa2.aud.ucla.edu.

20   Kazys Varnelis, *The Infrastructural City: Networked Ecologies in Los Angeles* (New York: Actar, 2009), 15.

21   Introduction to the Center for Architecture, Urbanism + Infrastructure at the School of Architecture, Princeton University, http://caui.princeton.edu/introduction (accessed 1 Aug. 2009).

22   State support of Dutch design and designers has dropped substantially over the past years. For an overview, see Hestia Bavelaar, "A brief history of the cultural policy in The Netherlands," http://www.designdenhaag.eu/en/background (accessed 15 Aug. 2009).

23   R. E. Somol, "Urbanism without Architecture," in *Points + Lines: Diagrams and Projects for the City* (New York: Princeton Architectural Press, 1999), 138–53.

24   Many of these principles arose from discussion during the Fast Forward symposium held at UCLA's Department of Architecture and Urban Design in May 2007. Participants at that symposium included many of the authors in this volume. Specifically, Albert Pope raised the distinction between in vivo and in vitro; ideas about collective identity and ambiance over form come from R. E. Somol's work; and Stan Allen championed the idea of connective infrastructure. Discussions about collective identities emanated from the *O-Z.LA* project (see note 3). While the present work relies on these contributions, we accept full responsibility for their formulation here.

25   Sherman, Cuff, and Somol, *O-Z.LA* (see note 3).

26   See, for example, R. E. Somol, "Join the Club: Golf Space, the New Town Square has 18 Holes," *Wired* 11, no 6 (June 2003), http://www.wired.com/wired/archive/11.06/golf_spc.html (accessed 8 Apr. 2010).

27   Stan Allen, "The Thick 2-D: Mat-Building in the Contemporary City," in *Practice: Architecture Technique + Representation*, revised edition (New York: Routledge, 2009).

Recycling Ecologies
Essays

Urbanisms in the Plural:
The Information Thread

Stan Allen

fig. 1 ››   Still from Jacques Tati's *Traffic,* 1971

The Waning of Affect

The metropolis puts an incongruous mix of beings into circulation…it is a place of experimentation, where new operational
propositions can be made concerning current practices.

–Anne Querrien

What *Gravity's Rainbow* tells us better than any other text is how
World War II was above all an operation of modernization: how
it was the necessary crucible for the obliteration of outdated territories, languages, filiations, of any boundaries or forms that
impeded the installation of cybernetics as the model for the
remaking of the world as pure instrumentality.

–Jonathan Crary

The late twentieth century saw the emergence of a radically horizontal, fieldlike urbanism: an interconnected fabric driven by the freeway, flexible capital accumulation, and the suburban ideal of private housing. A new city form has emerged, marked not so much by conflict, but by zones of intensity and exchange: nodes within the shallow section of the contemporary city. The pattern of massive decentralization established in the postwar United States—driven by the construction of an interstate highway infrastructure and new expectations with regard to housing and community—has been exported worldwide, moving cities away from density, diluting their complex mixtures, and minimizing conflict. This new city form is founded on mobility, and is dispersed and porous to the natural landscape. These cities (edge cities, generic cities, sprinkler cities) are often organized around the soft technologies of communication and ideas, and tend to arise independent of an older hub, complicating the conventional model of city and suburb. The sense of density, conflict, and disjunction associated with the early-twentieth-century metropolis has been evened out and smoothed over; the "culture of congestion" gives way to a dispersed field condition.

Associated with these new urban patterns is a sense of loss, a view that the traditional values of urbanity—whether understood as a place of experimentation and personal freedom or as a repository of collective memory—have been replaced by an entropic, global urban ooze, indifferent to place and history, spreading from Singapore to Frankfurt to San Jose. But these lapsarian narratives are always overstated; the new city emerges alongside and sometimes within the traditional city. Local differences persist, and they create complex new mixtures when they come into contact with changing technologies. The paradigm shift is never total. The classical urbanisms of Rome and Paris persist alongside the urbanisms of Los Angeles and Las Vegas; Tokyo, New York, and Shanghai; Lagos and Dubai; São Paulo, Atlanta, or Houston. Changing technologies, economies, and populations transform existing cities as much as they create new city forms. Our idea of the city today needs to encompass the procedures and protocols of popular culture, digital technologies, urban infrastructure, datascaping, scenario planning, the mixture of emerging and traditional typologies, edge cities, generic cities, shopping malls, minority subcultures, and nomad populations. It needs to include both hard and soft technologies: all of the very real effects of the urban, suburban, and posturban spaces proliferating today.

One clear symptom of this sense of loss has been a shift in the artistic practices associated with the urban experience. In the early twentieth century the metropolis was closely linked to the avant-garde techniques of collage and montage. The new city is associated with the loss of difference that emerged as a trope in postmodern thought. Modernity's capacity to shock, along with its formal techniques of fragmentation, has given way to levelling effects: the substitution of surfaces and screens for experience in depth, and the dominance of images and abstract values. This is the "slackening" of intensity described by Jean-François Lyotard or the "waning of affect" that Fredric Jameson has identified as one of the central motifs of postmodernity.[1] Distraction, which in the early-twentieth-century metropolis implied a radical model for new subjectivities, becomes empty time and uninflected space: drive time and junk space. ›› fig. 2

Jameson's loss of depth or Lyotard's slackening have very real counterparts in contemporary urban experience. Just as the jostle of proximity in the metropolis functioned to disrupt previously stable subjectivities, modernist methodologies of collage and montage acquired force through the collision of distinct orders and the generation of tension across seams of difference. Today, the urban subject is protectively encapsulated in the car or segregated in the mall, the residential enclave, or the airport—all of the "non-places" described by contemporary urban theorists—receiving mediated information on a proliferating series of screens. Cities are shifting from economies of production to economies of reproduction, rendering the differences between things less

1   See Jean-François Lyotard, "Answering the Question: 'What is postmodernism?'" in *The Postmodern Condition* (Minnesota: University of Minnesota Press, 1986); Fredric Jameson, "Postmodernism, or the Cultural Logic of Late Capitalism," *New Left Review* 146 (1984): 53–92.

fig. 2 ››   Shinto priests blessing a fighter jet

significant than the potential similarity of images. The city today is experienced as a field of effects, suspended in an ether of signs. These signs differ from one another not in substance, but in semantics—it's all bits and strings of digital code. The disjunctive play of difference associated with metropolitan density has lost the power to shock.

One response to this condition has been to rethink architecture and urbanism as yet other media, their physical presence dissolved into a late-twentieth-century culture of endlessly proliferating signs, screens, and images. It may be possible to gain analytical insight by focusing on the circulation of images and texts, but for an architect—whose task is not only to describe or critique these new conditions, but to actively intervene and potentially transform this more fluid urban field—other strategies are required.

Cities are the most intensive producers and consumers of new technologies. These technologies shape the city, but are also shaped by the needs and desires of the city itself. To work effectively in this dispersed, post-metropolitan city, we need new narratives and tools, pragmatic working tools that can begin to account for the always-present interplay of the real and the virtual in architecture and urbanism. Contemporary urbanism requires procedures and concepts capable of holding together coherence and discontinuity in productive new mixtures. It needs to engage the real complexity of the city today, as the technologies, politics, social life, and economic engines of urbanism continue to change. It needs to recognize the very real environmental crises of our time and to pay close attention to change and adaptation, recognizing all the dynamic complexity of the natural and social ecologies at work in the city. What is required is not a simple reassertion of architecture's physical presence, but a more nuanced theory that would account for both structure and effects, organization and information, weightless bits and dense matter.

Complex and Complicated

Merely to think about cities and get somewhere, one of the main things to know is what kind of problem cities pose, for all problems cannot be thought about in the same way.

–Jane Jacobs

Difference is the engine that drives urbanism. Cities bring public and private, open and closed, high and low, privileged and underprivileged into often uncomfortable proximity. The boundary between public space and private life in the metropolis is constantly in flux. Yet it is important to remember that the "culture of congestion" is not exclusively a product of the modern city. Historical accounts of life in both preindustrial and nineteenth-century cities record a churning mix of people and spaces in an atmosphere of barely controlled chaos. But if the city form of the late-twentieth and early-twenty-first centuries is characterized by a loss of difference, how can we recapture some sense of urban intensity in this new, dispersed field? Rem Koolhaas's formula of "congestion without density" (first proposed as a way of thinking about low-density cities such as Atlanta) is suggestive but difficult to sustain. What kinds of theories and techniques are available to work effectively with this new city?

New urban practices are emerging today at the intersection of geography, politics, ecology, architecture, and engineering. Among these practices, landscape urbanism in particular has acquired a privileged standing as the discipline capable of synthesizing expertise from a number of related fields.[2] Its ambition is large-scale and synthetic, often directed at distressed and marginal zones of the city. It is time-based and process-oriented, operating of necessity on a long-term horizon of implementation. Highly collaborative, landscape urbanism works almost exclusively in the public realm. Many of the variables associated with this form of practice—surface, change over time, and programmatic indeterminacy—are closely linked to the contemporary city. Landscape urbanism promises new strategies that are particularly well-suited to the dispersed field condition

2   "Because of its bigness—in both scale and scope—landscape serves as a metaphor for inclusive multiplicity and pluralism." James Corner, ed., "Recovering Landscape as a Cultural Practice," *Recovering Landscape* (New York: Princeton Architectural Press, 1999), 2; see also Charles Waldheim: "I coined the term 'landscape urbanism' in 1996 based on conversations with James Corner on the notion of 'landscape as urbanism.' The neologism formed the basis of a conference at the

Graham Foundation in Chicago (1997) and new academic programs in schools of architecture at the University of Illinois and the Architectural Association, London." Charles Waldheim, "Precedents for a North American Landscape Urbanism," *Center 14: On Landscape Urbanism* (November 2006): 303; see also David Grahame Shane, "The Emergence of Landscape Urbanism," *Harvard Design Magazine* 19 (Fall 2003/ Winter 2004); see also Charles Waldheim, "Landscape Urbanism: A Genealogy," *Praxis 4: Landscapes* (2002): 10–17.

of American cities, which (with the exception of the older cities of the Northeast) have always been low density and porous to the natural landscape. Despite—or, in some cases, because of—these advantages, landscape urbanism's impact has been limited. To date, the movement's significant projects have been urban parks; the city itself has remained untouched. Landscape urbanism has yet to propose tools to deal with dense urban conditions or to effectively integrate architecture and infrastructure.

In order to move forward, it is more productive to look on the one hand at some of the implicit theoretical underpinnings of landscape urbanism, in particular its connections to ecology and information theory, and on the other hand to posit landscape urbanism as one of many possible approaches to the city today: a necessary component in the toolbox, but not the only solution. The city is an intense locus of creativity and innovation, its collective energies always in advance of the disciplines of architecture or urbanism that attempt to control it. Architects and urban designers need to cultivate new ways of working that can respond to unanticipated but inevitable climatic, social, technological, programmatic, and economic changes: architecture and urbanism that parallel the evolving dynamic of the contemporary city. Ironically, this involves looking back to another conjunction of theory and urban change, beyond the associations of postmodern theory with contemporary urbanism, to the early 1960s and Jane Jacobs's provocative question: What kind of problem does the city pose?

Jacobs's answer to her own question is a counterintuitive one for a writer so closely identified with intimate scale, traditional street life, and community activism. In *The Death and Life of Great American Cities*, Jacobs writes, "Cities happen to be problems in organized complexity, like the life sciences."[3] She is referring to distinctions elaborated by scientist Warren Weaver a few years earlier. Weaver outlined three stages in the development of scientific thinking. In the first stage (from the seventeenth to the nineteenth centuries), the physical sciences developed analytical techniques for handling problems with a limited number of variables—the classical experiments of

3   Jane Jacobs, *The Death and Life of Great American Cities* (New York: Vintage, 1961), 433; see also Steven Johnson, *Emergence: The connected lives of ants, brains, cities, and software* (New York: Scribner, 2001). Johnson points out the connection between Jacobs and contemporary thinking about complexity.

motion, pressure, and temperature. "Simplicity," Weaver notes, "was a condition for progress at that stage of development of science." In the early part of the twentieth century, techniques were developed to solve problems characterized by a large number of variables—questions of probability and statistical mechanics that may not be predictable in individual instances, but that as a system possess orderly, average properties or patterns. Weaver calls these experiments "disorganized complexity." It was not until well into the twentieth century that a third class of problem began to be addressed seriously: those with a relatively small number of variables—small compared to the number of molecules, say, in a cylinder of gas, but larger than the two or three variables of classical physics. Moreover, in the life sciences, where these questions tend to appear, these variables are all organically interrelated. "These problems," Weaver notes,

> as contrasted with the disorganized situations with which statistics can cope, show the essential feature of organization. We shall therefore refer to this group of problems as those of organized complexity.... They are all problems which involve a sizable number of factors which are interrelated into an organic whole.[4]

4 Jacobs, *Death and Life*, 432.

These insights have subsequently been much more fully developed in a variety of scientific disciplines, but Weaver's formulation remains a concise definition.

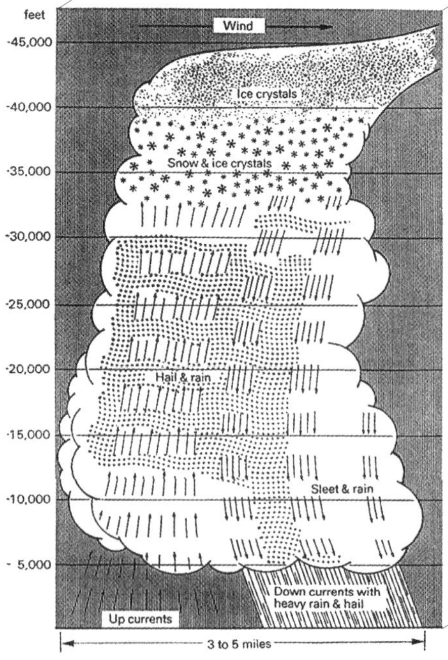

fig. 3 ›› Diagram, cloud formation

To propose that the city is a problem of organized complexity is highly suggestive and almost self-evident as a starting point. Complexity is a buzzword today, but to appeal to complexity as a metaphor does not get us too far. It is important to clarify that the organized complexity of the city is bottom-up and qualitative—where a relatively small number of interacting variables create complex effects—as opposed to the quantitative complexity of accretion, distortion, or deformation that is often associated with the concept in the architectural context. ›› fig. 3

Bruno Latour, for example, distinguishes between complex and complicated social formations:

> This opposition circumvents the traditional opposition between complexity and simplicity by focusing on two types of complexity. One, complication, deals with series of simple steps...the other, complexity, deals with the simultaneous irruption of many variables (as in primate interactions, for example). Contemporary societies may be more complicated but less complex than older ones.[5]

The engineering design of a complex piece of machinery (such as an automobile) is more accurately described as complicated: an assemblage of many parts, each one relatively simple. If any one of them breaks down, the entire system fails. Complex systems on the other hand, such as cities or natural ecologies, are robust and adaptive: they produce complex effects through the interaction of simple variables, incorporate feedback, and are capable of adjusting as conditions change. The current fascination with complexity in the architectural context is either purely formal, based on deformation, or process driven, based on an accumulation of many small parts or steps.

Jacobs had a strong intuition for the innate complexity of the city. For her, the city is uniquely able to mediate between change and consistency, and to hold local difference and overall regularity together in a relationship of dynamic stability. Her fascination with the intimate local scale is based on a sophisticated understanding of the city as a complex, interactive field condition:

> Under the seeming disorder of the old city...is a marvelous order for maintaining the safety of the streets and the freedom of the city. It is a complex order...composed of movement and change.... The ballet of the good city sidewalk never repeats itself from place to place, and in any one place is always replete with new improvisations.[6]

Although associated with populism and the small scale, it is a mistake to simply read Jacobs as opposing variation to order, endorsing the picturesque or the nostalgic proposals of New Urbanism. Surface variation and inclusive mixtures maintained in equilibrium by

5   Bruno Latour, *Pandora's Hope: Essays on the Reality of Science Studies* (Cambridge, MA: Harvard University Press, 1999), 304.

6   Jacobs, *Death and Life*, 50.

a sturdy yet concealed order are the characteristics of Jacobs's idea of organized complexity. Her description of the order of the city mirrors Gregory Bateson's account of the functioning of the natural ecology of a meadow, which he describes as

> a sort of dance, rather formal, say a minuet. And the purpose, functioning of this minuet is to detect and classify other patterns of dance. The meadow with its interacting multiplicity of species is unendingly dancing and thereby being bumped by information.[7]

The image of the city as a fluid, interactive system, "dancing" and being "bumped by information," is highly suggestive. It suggests a new and more flexible way of thinking about the city. But we still need a more rigorous working strategy and a means to translate these metaphors into working tools.

In the first instance, we need to pay close attention to the difficult and always variable order of the city itself. Future productive work will build upon—or radicalize—these insights from an earlier period and understand the city as a problem in organized complexity, that is to say, a dynamic system in which a relatively small number of variables interact in complex formations to create unexpected and only partially controllable wholes. In part this requires rethinking the limits of planning and design, recognizing the impossibility of predicting with any degree of certainty the future behavior of a complex, interactive system. Density and conflict can also be reimagined with iterative structures that incorporate change and difference into their fabric, rather than always registering difference as discontinuity.

7   Gregory Bateson, cited in Peter Harries-Jones, *A Recursive Vision: Gregory Bateson and Ecological Understanding* (Toronto: University of Toronto Press, 1995), 205.

Maxwell's Demon

> There are some diagrams or schemas, however, in which the form of the parts is of no importance, provided their connexions are properly shown. Of this kind are the diagrams of geometry which treats of the degrees of cyclosis, periphraxy, linkedness and knottedness.
> —James Clerk Maxwell

In *The Crying of Lot 49*, Thomas Pynchon sends his heroine, Mrs. Oedipa Maas, on a road trip, south to the outskirts of Los Angeles. For Pynchon, writing in 1965, the urban and suburban reality of Southern California was already not so much a physical place but a diagram of infrastructural, economic, administrative, and geographic forces: "San Narciso lay further south, near L.A. Like many named places in California it was less an identifiable city than *a grouping of concepts*—census tracts, special purpose bond-issue districts, shopping nuclei, all overlaid with access roads to its own freeway."[8] But if these exurban zones lack conventional identity, they are not completely formless. Even within the slack suburban fabric of Southern California, there is a sense of structure and anticipation, and a series of undecipherable forces at work in the diagram:

8   Thomas Pynchon, *The Crying of Lot 49* (1965; repr., New York: Harper and Rowe, 1986), 24, emphasis in quote mine. I believe it was K. Michael Hays who first pointed this passage out to me, and suggested its connections to ideas of infrastructure and organization.

She drove into San Narciso on a Sunday, in a rented Impala. Nothing was happening. She looked down a slope, needing to squint for the sunlight, onto a vast sprawl of houses, which had grown up all together, like a well-tended crop, from the dull brown earth; and she thought of the time she'd opened a transistor radio to replace a battery and seen her first printed circuit. The ordered swirl of houses and streets, from this high angle, sprang at her now with the same unexpected, astonishing clarity as the circuit card had. Though she knew even less about radios than about Southern Californians, there were to both outward patterns a hieroglyphic sense of concealed meaning, of intent to communicate. ›› fig. 4

Oedipa's aerial perspective of this sprawling exurban landscape reveals not chaos, but pattern and order: the "astonishing clarity" of a printed circuit. Pynchon's metaphor can hardly be accidental. The circuit card is a device to route flows of information; its architecture consists of pathways and nodes, and its functioning is determined by switches opening and closing. Its variables are neither formal nor semiotic, but organizational: what is connected to what, and through which

fig. 4 ›› Computer flow diagram

pathway. The metaphor suggests an idea of the city or the landscape as a map of information flows, feedback loops, and iterative processes.

This evocation of circuitry and electronics needs to be understood in the context of the novel's extended discussion of information, organization, and entropy, in particular the paradoxical thought experiment called Maxwell's Demon, proposed by the Scottish physicist James Clerk Maxwell and first published in 1871:

> Now let us suppose that…a vessel is divided into two portions, A and B, by a division in which there is a small hole, and that a being, who can see the individual molecules, opens and closes this hole, so as to allow only the swifter molecules to pass from A to B, and only the slower ones to pass from B to A. He will thus, without expenditure of work, raise the temperature of B and lower that of A, in contradiction to the second law of thermodynamics.[9]

When the concept of Maxwell's Demon is described to her, Oedipa has a quick comeback that encapsulates a century of scientific thinking: "Sorting isn't work? …Tell them down at the post office, you'll find yourself in a mailbag headed for Fairbanks, Alaska."[10] To a nineteenth-century thinker, sorting is not work, but twentieth-century concepts of information and entropy confirm that sorting—increasing the degree of organization in a system—is never cost-free.[11] It is indeed a kind of work, and the mathematical descriptions for thermodynamic entropy and information entropy closely mirror one another.[12] Pynchon anticipates the new realities of a postindustrial economy: a shift from work as physical labor to work as sorting: moving bits of data around. The paradoxes of Maxwell's Demon function as a productive conceptual hinge between abstract concepts of data and organization on the one hand, and physicality—forces, impacts, or changes in physical state—on the other. It is this interrelatedness between organization—understood as embedded information—and physical work that makes the Demon concept so suggestive in the urban context.

9   Cited in Anne Mangel, "Maxwell's Demon, Entropy, Information: *The Crying of Lot 49*," *TriQuarterly* 20 (Winter 1971): 195. Much of the discussion of Maxwell's Demon and entropy comes from J. Kerry Grant, *A Companion to The Crying of Lot 49* (Athens, GA: University of Georgia Press, 1994), 67–68.

10   Pynchon, *Crying*, 86.

11   Claude Shannon and Warren Weaver, *The Mathematical Theory of Communication* (Urbana: University of Illinois, 1949).

12   Grant, *Companion*, 88–91.

To envision the city structure as a printed circuit therefore is not so much to see it as a form of media, or as a text to be deciphered, but rather to see it as an organizational diagram with embedded structure: a network of paths and flows, the architecture of information exchange. For Pynchon, a former technical writer in the aerospace industry, the hieroglyphics of the city are unlikely to yield up specific or legible meanings. He sees the city as a technical device, and he wants to know how it works. More than its meaning, he is interested in the city's architecture: its internal structure, and its potential as a complex system capable of producing multiple meanings and unanticipated effects. As information theorist Claude Shannon notes, "The semantic aspects of communication are irrelevant to the engineering aspects."[13] Pynchon describes the city as a system of embedded information that makes possible a defined set of potentials: linkages yet to be made, circuits yet to be completed, all defined by the structure of the diagram itself.

Not only is the city, for Pynchon, a technical artifact first, it is also an artifact in which the peculiarly late-modern mixture of hard technologies—architecture and infrastructure—combines inescapably with the soft technologies of communication. The printed circuit is a component in a communication device (hardware): it makes communication possible, but in and of itself it has no meaning. It has nothing to do with media or semantics. It exists within a larger network, an infrastructure of frequencies, towers, receivers, broadcast networks, and regulatory agencies that mix the physical with the virtual. Specific, individual meanings or messages are less important than a more generalized intent to communicate. As Weaver has suggested, "A communication language must be designed (or developed) with a view to the totality of things that man may wish to say."[14] That is to say, in information theory as in the city itself, what matters is not the message sent, but the engineering of the network that makes it possible to send any number of messages at all.

13   Cited in Shannon and Weaver, *Mathematical Theory*, 8: "The word information, in this theory, is used in a special sense that must not be confused with its ordinary usage. In particular, information must not be confused with meaning." Elsewhere: "Information and meaning may prove to be something like a pair of canonically conjugate variables in quantum theory, they being subject to some joint restriction that condemns a person to the sacrifice of the one if he insists on having much of the other," 28; also cited in Umberto Eco, *The Open Work*, trans. Anna Cancogni (Cambridge, MA: Harvard University Press, 1989), 63.

14   Shannon and Weaver, *Mathematical Theory*, 27.

Artificial Ecologies

There is a principle specific to environmental ecology: it states
that anything is possible—the worst disasters or the most flexible
evolutions.

—Félix Guattari

As Pynchon's novel suggests, these exurban effects have come to be associated with the postwar landscape of Southern California, and Los Angeles has become a test case for the city as a low-density, artificial ecology.[15] Reyner Banham's *Los Angeles: The Architecture of Four Ecologies*, written a few years after *The Crying of Lot 49*, helped establish the idea of Los Angeles as the paradigmatic exurban city. Banham understood that the historian cannot stand outside and analyze this new city as an object, but must enter into it and become subject to the mobile forces of its fieldlike space: "The language of design, architecture and urbanism in Los Angeles is the language of movement...the city will never be fully understood by those who cannot move fluently through its diffuse urban texture."[16] The old (art historical) models do not work, and Banham looks for another unifying concept. What the notion of ecology offers him is a way of organizing the apparently random mix of "geography, climate, economics, demography, mechanics and culture" that Los Angeles displays. Ecologies are dynamic systems that maintain equilibrium through the interaction and feedback of multiple variables. In an ecological system, individual objects are less important than the interaction of multiple agents in the field. For Banham, it's a useful model to describe the architectural and spatial effects of the radically dispersed urbanism of Los Angeles in the late 1960s.

Natural ecologies exhibit complex, interconnective behaviors, developing unpredictable effects whose immediate cause is not always evident.[17] There is a particular kind of rippling, interconnected web of habitats, food supplies, behaviors, and resources that we have come to associate with ecology in nature.

15 I first used the term "artificial ecology" in an architectural context for an article on the work of MVRDV, published in 1997. Stan Allen, "Artificial Ecology," *Assemblage* 34 (Dec. 1997):107–9. At that time, my understanding of ecology was fairly intuitive; this interest led in turn to the work of Gregory Bateson, which has been the basis for the further elaboration of these early arguments.

16 Reyner Banham, *Los Angeles: The Architecture of Four Ecologies* (1971; repr., Los Angeles: University of California Press, 2001), 5.

17 Examples are easy to find, and always suggestive. Early in the 1990s, for example, Dr. James A. Estes, a marine ecologist at the U.S. Geological Survey, discovered an alarming drop in the population of sea otters on the Aleutian Islands. After investigating and rejecting typical explanations (disease, reproductive failure, and so on), Dr. Estes and his colleagues uncovered a complex web of cause and effect, where the triggering event was several steps removed from

the sea otters. Populations of nutritious foraging fish, such as ocean perch and herring, had declined sharply, and had been replaced by pollack, a less nutritious fish. As a result of this decline in their rich fish diet, the population of sea lions and seals also dropped. Orcas (killer whales), which had previously fed on the sea lions and seals, began to look elsewhere for food. Orcas and sea otters had coexisted for centuries, but with their traditional food supplies dwindling, the orcas modified their behavior, entered coastal waters, and began to eat the sea otters. In some places sea otter populations simply disappeared, while in others their numbers were diminished by up to 90 percent. This population decline could affect an entire coastal ecosystem. "A Mysterious Tear in the Web of Life," *New York Times*, 5 January 1999.

18   This is not necessarily a new idea; see, among others, M. J. Webber, *Information Theory and Urban Spatial Structure* (London: Croom Helm, 1979).

19   Gregory Bateson, cited in Félix Guattari, *The Three Ecologies*, trans. Ian Pindar and Paul Sutton (New York: Continuum, 2000), 27. The Bateson citation is from *Steps to an Ecology of Mind* (Chicago, IL: University of Chicago Press, 1972), 484.

20   Bateson, *Steps*, 457.

Cities too exhibit interconnectedness, mobilize multiple agents, and make complex demands on environments and resources.[18] Cities, like natural ecologies, emerge through recursive procedures. They are the cumulative result of countless individual operations repeated over time with slight variation. Difference is produced incrementally, as an effect of repetition and feedback. As an urbanistic model, an "artificial ecology" implies a complex choreography of agents, objects, and processes, where time is a key variable. To see the city as an artificial ecology is not to establish a loose analogy between the city and natural systems, but rather to take advantage of ecology as a powerful model for managing the city's inherent complexity. This approach further suggests that what architecture might learn from ecology is a more flexible form of practice itself: a series of working concepts flexible enough to accommodate the wildly improbable demands of the contemporary city.

The appeal to ecology here has little to do with sustainability, green architecture, or ecological design as currently practiced. Not all ecologies are green, and everything green is not ecological. There are ecologies of waste, development, pollution, or leisure, not to mention war, politics, or terrorism. Ecologies are by definition incompatible with fixed categories. They function through the interplay of complex variables, and nothing can be excluded. As Bateson puts it, "There is an ecology of bad ideas, just as there is an ecology of weeds."[19]

Rethinking the city as an artificial ecology might lead to a deeper ecology, one that doesn't work with the fixed categories of sustainable practices but questions the larger issues of natural and urban environments and takes full account of coevolution. "The organism which destroys its environment destroys itself," writes Bateson, noting the interconnection between species and context: "The unit of survival is a flexible organism-in-its-environment."[20] We need an ecology that includes conflict and change and that goes beyond the platitudes of harmony and nature in balance. If we think of cities as living entities, subject to the same laws as the rest of the natural world, we then have to pay attention to predation, violence, and extinction. The social ecology of the city is notoriously ruthless and indifferent: only those who can adapt and innovate survive. In addition to individuals, neighborhoods, districts, and entire cities grow and change and sometimes disappear altogether. ›› fig. 5

fig. 5 ›› Still from Michelangelo Antonioni's *Zabriskie Point*, 1970

In his book *Ecology of Fear*, social historian and critic Mike Davis turns to ecology not as a reassuring pastoral construct but for an image of nature as violent, unpredictable, and unforgiving. He writes,

This is not random disorder, but a hugely complicated system of feedback loops that channels powerful pulses of climatic or tectonic energy (disasters) into environmental work. The Southern California landscape epitomizes the principle of nonlinearity where small changes in driving variables or inputs—magnified by feedback—can produce disproportionate, or even discontinuous outcomes.[21]

21   Mike Davis, *Ecology of Fear: Los Angeles and the Imagination of Disaster* (New York: Henry Holt, 1998), 19.

Davis's book is subtitled *Los Angeles and the Imagination of Disaster*, and his is an ecology of conflict and catastrophic change. He juxtaposes a series of catastrophic natural events with the repeated imaginary of Los Angeles's destruction in movies and novels. By Davis's count, a fictional L.A. has been destroyed forty-nine times by nukes, twenty-eight times by earthquakes, and ten times each by invading hordes or monsters. At the other end of the scale, drought, blizzards, riots, fog, sandstorms, the Devil, Bermuda grass, and global warming each figure once. Nowhere are myths about nature so fundamental to a city's sense of itself than in L.A., and in the city's basin, humans have repeatedly put themselves in harm's way: building where they should never have built, destroying natural resources, and ignoring hints of disasters to come. For Davis, far from appealing to an arcadian idea of nature in balance, ecology is a social invention. It applies analytical models to understand the workings of natural systems and necessarily takes account of the man-made interventions.

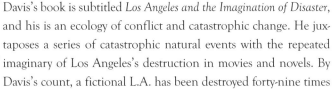

One of the most compelling points in Davis's book is his assertion that the norm of climate and geography in Los Angeles is one of extreme variation, incompatible with the "uniformist" models derived from pastoral Anglo-European landscapes. In extremist Los Angeles, norms and averages are a meaningless fiction. In the 127-year history of recorded rainfall in central L.A., for example, "Only 17 percent of years approach within 25 percent of the historical average. The actual norm tends to be seven- to twelve-year swings between dry and wet spells."[22] Instead of a landscape slowly evolved from a gradual accumulation of "low-intensity, high-frequency events," ecological change in Southern California takes place as "high-intensity, low-frequency events"—disasters, in other words. Furthermore, these events tend to occur in linked causal chains, making predictions from past experience nearly impossible. Southern California, Davis argues, is a "revolutionary, not a reformist landscape. It is Walden Pond on LSD."[23] Therefore, it is not surprising that in his discussions of tornadoes, rainstorms, earthquakes, and wildlife, Davis refers to chaos theory, fractal geometries, complexity, strange attractors, folding, and other nonlinear behaviors. To map and understand the unpredictable interactions of man-made and natural variables at work in these catastrophic events, the appeal to advanced mathematical modeling and nonlinear thinking is appropriate.

All this suggests that the mobile texture of the contemporary city could be understood as an assemblage of data and forces (social, economic, political, geographic, and infrastructural) operating in complex, interconnected webs that function very much like the climatic or tectonic forces Davis describes elsewhere in the book. The shifting map of L.A.'s social fabric, for example, resembles the folded topography of Southern California's seismic geology, with its hidden fault lines accumulating and suddenly releasing stress. Its network of infrastructures (roadways, water-supply, flood control, and so on) and their interlinked management structure involve the coordination of multiple variables and a high degree of uncertainty: all the complex life-in-time of the city itself. From freeway traffic to neighborhood demographics, from the

22   Ibid., 16.

23   Ibid.

real estate market to race riots, the late-twentieth-century city is a text-book array of nonlinear behaviors. Davis's appeal to ecological think-ing as an alternative explanatory framework, like Banham before him, is highly suggestive, but it remains at the level of metaphor. To work effectively in this new field, new tools and new ways of thinking about ecology will be required.

Information Landscapes

> The concept of information developed in this theory at first seems disappointing and bizarre…bizarre because it deals not with a single message but rather with the statistical character of a whole ensemble of messages, bizarre also because in these statistical terms the two words *information* and *uncertainty* find themselves to be partners.
> —Warren Weaver

"Ecological understanding," writes Bateson, "must be ecological." In other words, in order to understand any complex system, it is necessary to evolve a way of working and thinking that itself parallels the fluid-ity, adaptability, and recursion of natural life. Ecological systems, which tend to cross boundaries and exhibit complex, interconnected behav-iors, cannot be adequately apprehended from the perspective of fixed categories or separate disciplines. They cannot be reduced to objects or taken out of context. Bateson's tautological aphorism reinforces the idea that to appeal to ecology is not to appeal to a benign idea of nature and harmonious natural systems analyzed from a safe distance. It argues instead for a flexible ecological understanding that serves as a mental template to analyze any assemblage that exhibits the complex intercon-nected behavior and dynamic life-in-time of a natural ecology.

Bateson himself applied this "ecological" understanding to a diverse range of fields. Tribal structures, family dynamics, communica-tion theory, morphology, the interaction of species, and the evolution of natural form were all effectively reworked under a framework of complex interaction, feedback, and adaptation. Ecological systems—like the contemporary city—are always, in some fundamental way, out of control; and the observer is always part of the observed system. As Bateson has put it: "One of the major anti-human fallacies of the scientific community...is the premise that it is possible to have total control over an interactive system of which oneself is a part."[24] Instead of externalized relations of power, force, and competition, Bateson developed an epistemology of pattern, context, and form based on the exchange of information: "In principle, all metaphors derived from the physical world of impacts, forces, energy, etc. are unacceptable in explanations of events and processes in the biological world of information, purpose, context, organization, and meaning."[25]

[24] Bateson, *Letters*, 240–10b/1957, cited in Peter Harries-Jones, *A Recursive Vision: Ecological Understanding and Gregory Bateson* (Toronto: University of Toronto Press, 1995), 7.

[25] Ibid.

Information exchange seems counterintuitive as a model to understand the behavior of natural ecologies, but in fact this sometimes occurs in a very direct way, as in the exchange of nonverbal signals. More importantly for Bateson, and more suggestive in the architectural context, physical force is reconceived as information flow and organization redefined as embedded information. The force of a hammer's blow for instance, in Bateson's account, has little to do with energy and impacts, but is instead "news of a difference."[26] Agents and context are not separated out as figure and ground, but rather reconceived as interacting relations within a field condition. Survival is a question of "staying in the game." No special privilege is attached to power; as Bateson remarks, the tiger is only a part of the forest. ›› fig. 6

[26] Bateson, *Steps*, 460.

There is a final point that needs to be made with regard to the idea of an information landscape. We are used to thinking of information as a message or a signal, but for Bateson, the link

fig. 6 ›› Reindeer herd reacting to a helicopter overhead

between information, form, and ecology is more complex. Information, for Bateson, is not opposed to form (as form to content, for example), it is *form itself*. In a well-known statement, he defined information as "any difference that makes a difference in some prior event." That is to say, information is the perceivable difference between some present state and some prior state. It is not a physical signal, but (in his formulation) the "form of a form," made perceptible by comparison and contrast. Form is never static and meaning is never autonomous, because static, individual forms can never be perceived as different. Differences of configuration, pattern, or shape make sense only when put in play with a larger field of differences. Change is redefined as difference over time, and all form is relational, based on interval and change.

This is a broad notion of form, recognizing that behavior, response, and adaptation all take specific forms. "Static conditions can never be perceived," Bateson observes, concluding that "I'm afraid this means rewriting most of conventional ecology." The advantages of this account in the architectural context are self-evident; form understood as difference and information punctures the form/program dichotomy as it has been defined in architectural debates. Difference as the "form of a form" shifts attention to the performative agency of form itself and disentangles it from the discourses of meaning or formalism. Form as information implies organization: the degree to which specific structures are in place and their behavior in time. It equips the architect with a whole series of powerful conceptual and practical tools to work simultaneously on form and program through the agency of organization. If form is never static, and if it refers as much to the momentary patterns of a dynamic ecology as to the static configuration of an enclosing envelope, it becomes possible to approach program and event from the perspective of form and structure.

To rethink architecture, urbanism, or landscape architecture in terms of information exchange is counterintuitive but conceptually powerful. If we wanted to properly analyze a landscape like Central Park, for example, we would need a whole series of categories: traffic and movement, space and topography, program and event. We would have to touch on civil and environmental engineering, horticulture, urban and social history, geography, geology, architecture, landscape design, and gardening, not to mention finance, regulatory codes, and management. The park is an unruly mix of the physical (rocks, soil, paving) and the abstract (money, time, rules). Each of these categories can be rethought of as embedded information, and the interaction of their multiple variables in time recast as information exchange. Instead of thinking of traffic separation and circulation, the given structure of pathways can be considered as an organizational diagram (like Pynchon's printed circuit) that makes possible an open but not infinite series of movements and connections. A topographic surface sheds or retains water in a dynamic information exchange with rainfall; it enables program and event in a dynamic information exchange with users both animate and inanimate. Ecological theories of affordance (where species make tactical use of the particularities of landscape features—another kind of information exchange) can be useful here as well.[27] In interaction with climatic variables, soil chemistry and water distribution—the embedded characteristics of the landscape itself—determine what will and will not grow. The capacity of landscape to perform work—filtering water, processing organic matter, and so on—can be thought of as yet another type of information exchange over time. Even management structures—all the private and public agencies, and the apparatus of codes and regulations that are so important in the urban and landscape context—can be thought of as embedded information of a different sort, where organizational structure is also decisive. Information is indifferent to its material expression: it encompasses the abstractions of codes and management structures as easily as it does the physicality of a rock in the landscape.

> 27   James J. Gibson, "The Theory of Affordances," in *The Ecological Approach to Visual Perception* (Hillsdale, NJ: Lawrence Erlbaum Associates, 1986), 127–46.

Bateson's notion of information as consequential difference dissolves the false opposition between heavy, inert matter and immaterial, weightless bits. Form, for Bateson, is a diagram of forces, the result of information exchange between an organism and its environment. Bateson's approach would not distinguish between representational and material effects so much as it would shift attention to the performative effects of semiotic information, as well as to the material consequences of the information landscape. The pragmatic consequence in turn would be to pay close attention to all differences that make a difference: all of architecture's material effects and worldly consequences regardless of whether they derive from information or from matter.

From Landscape Ecology to Landscape Urbanism

> Landscape ecology considers the development and dynamics of spatial and temporal interactions and changes across heterogeneous landscapes, influences of spatial heterogeneity on biotic and abiotic processes, and the management of spatial heterogeneity.
> —Paul Risser, James Karr, and Richard T. T. Forman

As suggestive as the information landscape model is, it is difficult to transpose the ecological model directly to the design of city spaces without falling into loose metaphors. Architecture and urbanism always need a graphic apparatus to convert information into usable form. For this reason, the studies of landscape ecologist Richard T. T. Forman are a crucial intermediary.[28] Forman and his collaborators have taken the systematic methods of ecology and applied them to physical environments and large-scale landscapes. They have invented a series of categories and working concepts that make explicit the interactive natures of species and environments, while paying careful attention to spatial structure. Organizational and performative concepts such as patches, corridors, matrixes, and mosaics are among these useful working categories. The fundamentally horizontal interactions of landscape ecology—the thick mat of forest or meadow—are highly suggestive in the context of the spread-out architecture of the contemporary city. An extensive and sophisticated graphic apparatus suggests how time-based diagrams can be used to analyze and predict the behavior of landscape ecologies. » fig. 7

28   Paul Risser, James Karr, and Richard T. T. Forman, *Landscape Ecology* (New York: Wiley and Sons, 1986).

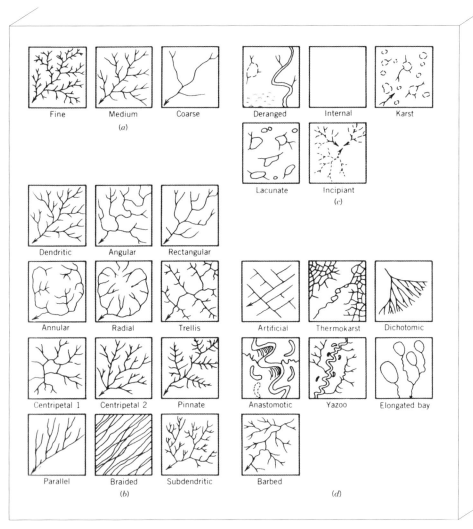

fig. 7 ›› Diagram by Richard T. T. Forman and Michel Godron of natural drainage densities and patterns, 1986

The principles of landscape ecology are not simply a formal model; more importantly, they serve as a model for process. Landscapes cannot be designed and controlled as a totality. Instead, they are projected and scripted or allowed to grow and evolve over time. Landscapes are diagrams subject to limited deregulation, more the products of management and cultivation than of design. Landscape ecology suggests an expanded urban agenda, going beyond master-planning to take account of the future life of the city. Going beyond form, an artificial ecology of the city would necessarily encompass structure (spatial and territorial organization), functioning (the day-to-day events and activities taking place on a site), and change (the evolution of the site over time). These are useful categories for the architect, who is—by training and habit—attentive to structure, nominally aware of function as a professional imperative, and not at all interested in change over time. Through careful attention to all three of these variables, there is a shift of emphasis from the form of the parts to their interaction in the field, and to the complex effects produced by that interaction. ›› figs. 8 + 9

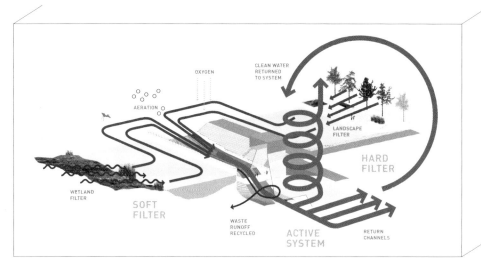

fig. 8 ›› Stan Allen Architect, Gwanggyo Pier Lakeside Park, 2008: Bio-Building operations diagram

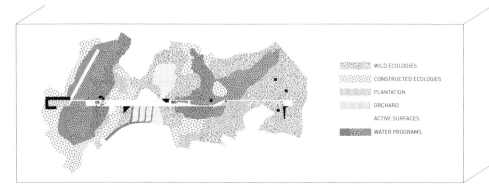

fig. 9 ›› Stan Allen Architect, Gwanggyo Pier Lakeside Park: Fields diagram

Landscape ecology and urbanism have a shared focus on large, hard-to-manage sites where many variables, natural and man-made, interact over time. The tools of landscape ecology are more analytical, but its close attention to diagrams, organization, and patterns of change over time suggests new working categories and graphic tools for projective work in landscape, architecture, and landscape urbanism. The specificity of the time-based diagrams and the examples from landscape ecology should also provoke skepticism about the too-easy embrace of emergence and self-organization in contemporary architecture and urbanism.

Emergence does not imply an indifferent architecture or an "anything goes" attitude. The conditions for emergence must be established through a precise architectural framework that allows change and evolution, and it is the organizational diagram that specifies these conditions. In an organizational schema, it is not only form or shape that counts, but performance and behavior as well. A branching system, for example, behaves differently from a networked system: it has to do with the numbers of available pathways and the pattern of the routing. Structure, configuration, and scale all play a part as architectural and organizational variables that can be designed and controlled with a high degree of specificity. This reflects a realism about what can be designed and what will change: a "thick" matrix with enough surplus information that it is open to being continually reworked and reengineered. An exacting design of initial conditions, coupled with an awareness of inevitable change, is a strategy to cultivate survival by adaptation and coevolution.

Synthetic Landscapes

To be sure, reading landscapes is not as easy as reading books, and for two reasons. First, the ordinary landscape seems messy and disorganized, like a book with pages missing, torn, and smudged....
Like books, landscapes can be read, but unlike books, they were not meant to be read.

–Peirce F. Lewis

The claim that architecture and urbanism could be productively rethought of as an artificial ecology might seem like a reiteration of the (by now) commonplace idea that all nature is constructed. The force of what is intended here is quite different. A useful point of departure is the recent Downsview Park competition, held in Toronto, Canada, in 2000.[29] The precepts of landscape urbanism were deeply embedded in the competition brief itself and were reflected in various degrees in all of the entries. Downsview also famously reprised some of the major players of the 1983 Parc de la Villette competition, held in Paris, France. If Parc de la Villette signaled the emergence of a speculative urbanism that understood nature as a cultural construct, and extended an architectural logic to landscape, Downsview marked a consolidation of landscape urbanism strategies, in which landscape strategies—and an attendant fascination with metaphors of emergence—were extended to architecture and urbanism. The radical claim of the 1980s was to extend architecture into the territory of landscape, to unmask the artificiality of landscape, and to install the regime of culture over that of nature. Today, at a time when the line between the artificial and the natural is increasingly blurred by developments in genetic engineering and changing biological paradigms, it is possible to rethink the strict division of natural and artificial in landscape through an information-based model of nature: a notion of landscape as synthetic nature. The nature/culture distinction, so important in the Parc de la Villette competition, has lost traction today. To claim that all nature is constructed no longer has critical force; it is simply a given, a starting point for a more complex synthesis.

The architects and landscape architects associated with landscape urbanism as it has emerged over the past decade make use of the logics of natural systems and the dynamics of ecological feedback, without the romantic attachment either to a pastoral idea of nature or to a critical model that feels the need to unpack the naturalness of nature. The synthetic landscapes proposed by designers today (like the city) are active rather than passive. Design has a transformative, activating agency. Synthetic landscapes are active, metabolic machines—natural operations

29 See the essays by R. E. Somol and Julia Czerniak in *CASE: Downsview Park Toronto*, ed. Julia Czerniak (Cambridge, MA: Harvard University Press; New York: Prestel, 2001).

that produce artificial, ambient effects. Nature—and, in particular, an information-based paradigm of biology—is the new lens through which culture and society—and by extension, architecture and urbanism—are viewed. When landscape is wholly synthetic, it is already disengaged from any pastoral idea of nature or its corollaries—the poetics of dereliction or the industrial picturesque. It doesn't need steel trees or plastic turf to announce its artificiality. Instead of treating nature as a scenic, benign force, designers today treat it as a slightly out-of-control raw material, a force capable of violent transformations and unanticipated mutations.

Under Cover of Green

Penelope Dean

> If science and technology march under the banner "everything
> is possible," design culture must know how to point out a path
> for these potential possibilities, a path that can be completely
> opposed to that which technological-scientific development has
> followed up to now.
> —Ezio Manzini

From the first moment that cities were thought to be amenable to rational solutions in the mid-nineteenth century, they were variously formu-
lated as "problems" of the hygienic, technical, or social kind, resulting in
urban paradigms ranging from the garden city to city beautiful to CIAM
to New Urbanism. Importantly, these disciplinary archetypes contained
both an ideology and a design agenda: the city beautiful movement
was dedicated to formal beautifications as a prerequisite for harmonious social order while modernist city plans—ranging from the metropolitan visions of Le Corbusier to the decentralization of Frank Lloyd
Wright's Broadacre City—were founded on calculation and/or zoning
as a reaction to congestion. More recently, New Urbanism recuperated
the modernist agenda with a new aesthetic and an organizing unit of the
"neighborhood"—in reaction to a perceived lack of community—strictly
codified with zoning parameters and pattern books. It is within this
canon that current calls for a "green urbanism" can be understood as yet
another formulation of the city as problem, this time under the rubric
of the "sustainable," where the problem constitutes a litany of environmental concerns, ranging from a general lack of nature in the city to air
and water pollution to contaminated soils and so on. In this latest redefinition, the ambitions of architecture and urbanism have shifted from
a modernist notion of being able to design the environment toward a
more subservient role of being part of a larger environment by design.

Yet what is curious in this recent reformulation of the city-as-problem is how the disciplinary prerequisites of ideology and design have become separated. For instance, the terms "green" and "sustainable" characterize numerous ideologies that range from the moralistic to the ecological to the social and appear within diverse disciplines from politics, economics, and science to the allied design fields, cutting across high and low discourses.[1] Within urbanism, however, these terms are yet to be associated with a coherent and explicit design agenda. Unlike earlier urban paradigms that synthesized ideology and design (i.e., vision with form) through the disciplinary focus of architecture, the continuing embrace of environmental reform has often resulted in an architecture and urbanism that rarely articulates a formal design project.

While two design attitudes can be generally identified in this context—one where building design generally defaults into a high-tech project and the other where the mapping of existing realities too often leads to a lack of design specificity (e.g., landscape urbanism)—neither have generated a substantial discourse where green aesthetics coupled with ideology can be seriously discussed in disciplinary terms. Indeed, both directions (high-tech and landscape urbanism) point toward a de-disciplining of architecture and urbanism.[2]

The high-tech route is now executed by a particular breed of architectural specialists, who, motivated by the natural sciences, have too-often reduced ideas to mere applications—either as off-the-shelf products (solar panels, rainwater tanks, and so on), as landscape elements (such as gratuitous plantings to embellish architecture), or as LEED paperwork (e.g., checklists for fast-tracked building permits)—to the extent that the words "green" and "sustainable" have become euphemisms, alibis, even, for not doing any design at all. Another perhaps more worrisome issue is that a plethora of technological solutions now takes priority over sociocultural ideas and continues to devolve a faction of the disciplines into a techno-scientific specialization.[3]

1   For a summary of some of the theoretical arguments and implications for architecture and design by a range of sustainability defenders, see Mark Jarzombek, "Sustainability: Fuzzy Systems and Wicked Problems," *Log* 8 (Summer 2006): 7–12. For a review of thirteen recent books covering ecology and design published between 1993 and 2001, see Richard Ingersoll, "A Post-Apocalyptic View of Ecology and Design," *Harvard Design Magazine* 18 (Spring/Summer 2003): 12–17.

2   This argument is elaborated in several of my essays. See "…never mind all that environmental rubbish, get on with your architecture," *Architectural Design: Energies: New Material Boundaries* 79, no. 3 (May/June 2009): 24–29; see also "Environment by Design," in *97ᵀᴴ ACSA Annual Proceedings: The Value of Design—Design is at the core of what we teach and practice*, ed. Phoebe Crisman and Mark Gillem (Washington, D.C.: ACSA Press, 2009), 198–206. Both essays are edited excerpts from chapter 8 of my PhD dissertation, "Delivery Without Discipline: Architecture in the Age of Design" (2008).

3   As an example of this aspect, see Ken Yeang's thesis on environmental design

in "Theory and Practice" and "Design Principles," in *Bioclimatic Skyscrapers* (London: Artemis, 1994), 16–31. For the casting of sustainability as a techno-functional problem in general, see Tony Fry, "The Sustainment and its Dialectic," in *Design Philosophy Papers* (Ravensbourne, Australia: Team D/E/S Publications, 2004), 33–45. For a compilation of recent projects that follow the "technology" trajectory, see Peter Buchanan, *Ten Shades of Green: Architecture and the Natural World* (New York: The Architectural League of New York, 2005).

4   While the progenitors of landscape urbanism have argued for its design possibilities—James Corner wrote that it "is first and last an imaginative project, a speculative thickening of the world of possibilities" and Charles Waldheim described it as a "cultural category" minimally offering "strategies of design" (See James Corner, "Terra Fluxus," and Charles Waldheim, "Landscape as Urbanism," in *The Landscape Urbanism Reader*, ed. Charles Waldheim [New York: Princeton Architectural Press, 2006], 32, 37)—Stan Allen more recently identified four "crutches" of landscape urbanism. The first involves its reliance on "surface," which, while suggesting formal connectivity, actually requires breaks. The second is programmatic indeterminacy, which has become an alibi for no design. The third is the excuse of "change," which has become an alibi for no specificity. And the fourth is its questionable ability to adequately address issues of "density" for new urban developments. These crutches were outlined in Allen's lecture

If the high-tech approach has traveled a path of specialization, the second route of landscape urbanism has gone the way of interdisciplinarity, toward invoking models of ecology for new design possibilities. It, too, has suffered from the lack of a formal design agenda, as its goals of programmatic "indeterminacy" and "flexibility" emerge as excuses for a lack of design specificity.[4] Just as techno-scientific applications threaten to de-discipline architecture into a specialization, the dissipation of architecture into landscape urbanism suggests another form of de-disciplining, where architecture—no longer considered enough on its own—is called upon to surrender its design specificity to "shared practices" via hybridization.[5]

The separation of an explicit design agenda from green ideology has not yet served to advance architecture or urbanism well. This division, coupled with a general absence of speculative ideas—the productive domain of architecture and urbanism during modernism—suggests that the disciplines have, to date, largely addressed environmental concerns with normative "problem-solving" attitudes. This reactionary mode of practice is all-too-subservient to the whims and paperwork of politicians and the market, and has largely followed industry and public policy rather than leading through design innovation. Yet in an age of consumer-driven environmental concerns—evident in products (from organic groceries to recycled materials), the lay media (in newspapers, style magazines, and TV documentaries), and A-list celebrity endorsements (from Brad Pitt to Bono)—it would seem that there are opportunities for architecture, and especially urbanism, to capitalize on the movement's pervasiveness for its discipline.[6] In other words, instead of asking what architecture and urbanism can do for green, it might be more productive to ask: What can green do for architecture and urbanism?

This politically incorrect question is not meant to dismiss green intentions, but rather draws attention to the fact that from within the disciplines of architecture and urbanism

"Objects and Fields: After Landscape Urbanism," at the School of Architecture, University of Illinois at Chicago, on 10 Nov. 2008.

5   This inadequacy was put forward by Charles Waldheim, who claimed: "Landscape urbanism offers an implicit critique of architecture's and urban design's inability to offer coherent, competent, and convincing explanations of contemporary urban conditions. In this context, the discourse surrounding landscape urbanism can be read as a disciplinary realignment in which landscape supplants architecture's historical role as the basic building block of urban design." See Waldheim, *Landscape Urbanism Reader*, 37.

6   A brief survey of the popular press's treatment of environmental concerns between 1970 and 2005 reveals the escalating coverage of this broader conversation. An exponential increase in the number of times the phrases "green design," "environment and design," and the "green consumer" appeared in print media from 1985 onwards demonstrates the popularization and proliferation of popular environmental thinking at a global scale. A LexisNexis Academic search of major world newspapers, magazines, and journals indicates that the number of articles that mentioned "green design" rose from 4 to 152 between 1985 and 2005. Similarly, the phrase "environment and design," appeared in 6 articles in 1970, 157 articles by 1980, and increased to more than 3,000 between 1985 and 2000. The words "green consumer" appeared in 4 articles in 1970, 166 articles by 1985, and 2,189 articles between

such issues have, to a large extent, been inadequately conceptualized. Two different possibilities for design might follow from this assumption. The first option advocates for the terms green and sustainability to advance solely as technological specializations, detached from architecture and urbanism.[7] This trajectory would support the abdication pointed out by Reyner Banham in his introductory "Unwarranted Apology" to *The Architecture of the Well-tempered Environment* (1969), where he grumbled that the separation of architecture from technology had led to "another culture" consisting of plumbers and engineers colonizing the environmental design of buildings.[8] In this scenario—then and now—sustainability would be understood as a subordinate obligation of architecture and urbanism, a task relegated to consultant practices (much like mechanical engineering is to architecture). Through a strategy of indifference, architecture and urbanism could be liberated to concentrate on other pursuits while seeking input from the green "experts." Even though this situation might allow for the necessary space to reorient the discipline's focus back toward modes of disciplinary production, it would not fully exploit the opportunities offered by the current popularity of green to generate a new prospect for design.

The second potential way for architecture to address sustainability—a "Join 'em if we can't beat 'em" scenario, as Banham remarked upon Buckminster Fuller's belated acceptance into the architecture profession—would pursue a more opportunistic path, one that aims to capitalize on the existence of a green movement.[9] In this more ambitious approach, green could be used as a Trojan horse to both recuperate a sociocultural design project for architecture and urbanism and to smuggle back into the disciplines those things that have ultimately been left behind after the wake of urban modernism: bigger ideas, polemics, and possible new worlds.[10] Adopting this path would require a significant mind-set change for the way in which green and sustainable issues have recently been addressed by design culture.

1985 and 2005. Finally, usage of the word "sustainability" exponentially increased in various articles from 235 in 1990 to over 3,000 in 2000. www.lexisnexis.com (accessed 28 Sept. 2008). As Wendy Meguro, a designer at environmental design consultancy Atelier Ten in New York, observed: "Recent media coverage of sustainability differs from environmental media in the past. There is a new, optimistic emphasis on personal responsibility to make choices that benefit the environment....As the principles of sustainable design are tied to occupant well-being and community responsibility, green buildings are becoming a valuable public relations tool." Quoted in Jordan Kauffman, "To LEED or Not to Lead," *Log* 8 (Summer 2006): 14.

7 This scenario is suggested in Jarzombek, "Sustainability," 12.

8 Reyner Banham, *The Architecture of the Well-tempered Environment* (1969; repr., London: The Architectural Press, 1984), 12. In answer to what he saw as a problematic separation between architecture and technology vis-à-vis the environment, Banham sought to reassert the importance of mechanical services and other environmental technologies at the center of the discipline. That was almost forty years ago. Since then, the rise of sustainable design and "green architecture" would appear to have closed Banham's gap on his own terms rather triumphantly, through the ongoing collapse of building- and enviro-technology. Yet what Banham once categorized as a disciplinary problem at the scale of architecture has since devolved into a generalized

Perhaps the most compelling case for environmental problems to generate an alternative intellectual and practical project for design comes from engineer and design theorist Ezio Manzini, who argues that the role of design culture is, above all, to advance and visualize a plurality of possibilities. Manzini writes:

At [the] level of activity, the designer is not so much a professional capable of solving given problems, as a cultural figure in the process of creatively linking the possible with the hoped-for in visible form. To take a specific example, the designer provides scenarios that visualize some aspects of how the world could be and, at the same time, presents it with characteristics that can be supported by complex ecological equilibria, which are acceptable socially and attractive culturally.[11]

In visualizing such scenarios, Manzini further suggests that such interventions require a top-down approach because they call into question sociocultural aspects, which are—by default—more readily associated with ideas. It is through the visualizing of ideas that Manzini argues that an "ecological reorientation" of the social imagination can occur through the attraction of new proposals of quality.[12] Understanding green as a problem of discipline as well as of the city, therefore, might just enable green to be opportunistically exploited for big ideas rather than small policies.

In the trajectory of reorienting green to advance a sociocultural project, it is initially useful to recast the term "green" itself, by way of a brief genealogy, as a corollary to the emergence of the modern city. Just as the city as problem came to be reformulated as a problem of the environment, definitions of green vis-à-vis the city can equally be seen to evolve over time when the term is provisionally understood through the cultural categories of nature and landscape.[13] Looking to the disappearance of nature in the United States over two hundred years— i.e., the erasure of green—as opposed to the appearance of the city, several changing perceptions of green can be identified and can serve to establish a background for how and why a revised

problem at the scale of the built environment.

9   Ibid., 268.

10   There is little literature addressing this trajectory in green urbanism. One exception at the time of this writing is James Wines's *Green Architecture* (Milan: Taschen, 2000), which attempts to reframe sustainable design through conceptual aspects. As Wines writes in his introduction: "While there are many publications today that cover the scientific and technological side of the eco-design revolution, this book approaches the subject from a conceptual, philosophical, and artistic perspective" (p. 9).

11   Ezio Manzini, "Prometheus of the Everyday: The Ecology of the Artificial and the Designer's Responsibility," *Design Issues* 9, no. 1 (Fall 1992): 19.

12   Ibid.

13   The categories of nature and landscape are seen as distinct from the field of landscape urbanism here.

14   The official federal designations and remediation programs started in 1980, when the Superfund legislation was passed. On remediation practices in Chicago, for example, see Ellen Grimes, "Fakes," *Log* 5 (Winter 2005): 15–20.

definition of green would eventually come to characterize the city as problem.

From the moment the U.S. Land Ordinance laid the foundations of land policy in 1785, the notion of green, previously understood through the category of nature, became recognized as habitable land, and later as arable land during the first half of the 1800s, with the introduction of farming and tree felling. In the late 1800s green came to be thought of as a form of cultivated recreation through parks and gardens, which were soon institutionalized with the founding of areas such as the Chicago Park District in 1934. During the first half of the 1900s, as cities continued to expand, green came to be understood as something to be preserved, initially indicated by the various forest preserves marked out during that period and finalized with the launch of the national Environmental Protection Agency (EPA) in 1970. Passing from interpretations of nature to land to garden to protected parks, the erasure (or disappearance) of landscape by means of the expansion of the city directed perceptions of green away from productive or recreational landscapes into a threatened environment. In other words, green came to be understood as a mutable conceptual or cultural category only as it became formalized as an urban part.

The agenda to "preserve" green during the 1970s marks a point of inflection between the disappearance of landscape and its subsequent reappearance inside the city. From around 1980 onwards, in the context of global environmental concerns, green came to be understood as something that needed to be added back in to the city, not exclusively as nature per se or as nineteenth-century parks (as will be discussed shortly), but curiously through new kinds of urban development. More recently, green additions have taken on various forms that continue to extend perceptions of the term: as a remediation problem, green is now perceived to be a clean-up-exercise, as toxic land in former industrial wastelands gets converted into wetlands;[14] as a beautification problem, street tree planting programs begin

15   See, for example,
Chicago's sowing of 200,000
trees as part of its Emerald
City agenda and New York
City's sowing of 23,700 trees
as part of its MillionTreesNYC
program and Mayor Michael
Bloomberg's PlaNYC 2030.

16   See, for example,
Chicago mayor Richard Daly's
launching of the Green roof
initiative in 2006.

to reintroduce landscape into the city;[15] and as a sustainable development problem, green buildings, green technology centers, and green roofs launch green as a techno-appliqué to architecture.[16] In total, this new accumulation of green often forms a set of tactics that operate in the absence of an overarching plan—the historic erasure of landscape having spurred an ad hoc strategy of green prosthetics. While the expansion of the modern city once erased green, it is now urban development that paradoxically returns green (as either landscape or building) to the city. Yet what is fundamentally different about this form of green urbanism from earlier urban paradigms is that its content is rarely driven by an explicit plan at the scale of the city. Instead, the city apparently becomes greener through what might best be described as a piecemeal approach, where random and unevenly distributed interventions occur at the instigation of politicians and city officials. Such an approach confirms the paradigmatic shift from architects' and urbanists' designing of the environment during modernism to their problem-solving policy for the environment today.

While the recent return of green to the city presents a potentially promising new terrain for architecture and urbanism, it is not the first time green was introduced into the city through urban development. When green—historically constructed as nature and landscape—was deployed in urban proposals from the late-nineteenth century to the mid-twentieth century, it was invariably understood as the design medium of bigger ideas. For example, during the city beautiful movement, Daniel Burnham's Chicago Plan (1909) introduced green by way of tree plantings and parks as part of a grander, aesthetically driven improvement scheme. Only a few years earlier, Ebenezer Howard's diagram for the Garden City (1898) had indicated green zoning as a medium of urban control, with new forests, fruit farms, allotment gardens, and cow pastures encircling and limiting the size of proposed towns. Just over twenty years later, Le Corbusier's Contemporary City of Three Million Inhabitants (1922) also deployed green as a "protected zone of woods and green fields" surrounding the hypothetical city, both in the interest of future development and also for civic health and peace: in other words, green as a therapeutic form of urbanism.[17] Le Corbusier advanced some of these ideas a decade later in his Ville Radieuse project (1933), also known as the *ville verte* (green city)—a proposal for a vertical garden city where the ground consisted of a public park with trees, paths, and pools, and where the rooftops were understood as a culture consisting of "sand beaches, clumps of shrubbery, and flowerbeds."[18] In this project Le Corbusier deployed greenery as "a basic material of city planning" to achieve a larger intent for decongested city lifestyles.[19] And almost concurrently, Frank Lloyd Wright's Broadacre City (1932) offered a notion of green as a productive agricultural landscape in his horizontal model for a disappearing city, affording decentralized lifestyles. While many of these projects were subsequently condemned for their top-down thinking and implausibility, they are important to recognize here precisely because they serve as an alternate genealogy for what green has previously done for architecture and urbanism.

With the passing of urban modernism and the subsequent denigration of large-scale thinking, the issue at present is how architects and urbanists might find a way to reassert their role as indispensable protagonists—"cultural figures," in Manzini's words—for producing and visualizing design scenarios for the city. If in the past green (through landscape and nature) served as a medium for larger ideas and scenarios, the question to ask today, perhaps, is whether the pervasiveness of an updated green design culture inversely offers the means through which to smuggle bigger, conceptual ambitions back into architecture and urbanism. In other words, can ideas and concepts make an appearance under the cover of green?[20]

In recent years, a few architects have begun to advance design speculations that not only address environmental problematics, but also manage, furtively, to deliver larger sociocultural agendas. Invariably deploying landscape as a medium of architecture, projects such as Emilio Ambasz's Green Town (1992),

17 Le Corbusier, *The City of To-morrow and its Planning* (Original French edition, 1924; repr., Cambridge, MA: The MIT Press, 1971), 167.

18 Le Corbusier, *The Radiant City* (Original French edition, 1933; repr., New York: The Orion Press, 1967), 109.

19 Ibid., 86.

20 Another future line of development would be to extrapolate bigger ideas from normative strategies to convert the current "content" status of green back into being a medium of a larger sociocultural project.

UrbanLab's competition entry Growing Water (2006), Toyo Ito and Associates' Parque de la Gavia (2003–current), and Atelier Bow-Wow's Void Metabolism competition entry (2007), just to name a few, reveal the disciplinary design potential of green for architecture and urbanism today. While by no means exhaustive, this nascent group begins to point out an alternate path for architecture and urbanism by extending and visualizing new directions for design.

Having spent much of his career creating a synergy between landscape and artifice, Argentinean architect Ambasz was recently quoted as saying, "I know it sounds presumptuous, but I lay claim to being the precursor of current architectural production concerned with environmental problems."[21] In a cunning repackaging of his oeuvre as green, after having largely dealt with vegetal matter in several projects, Ambasz has opportunistically capitalized on the current popularity of the green movement and the emergence of "green architecture" to resituate his work. This is most apparent in his 1992 Green Town proposal, where Ambasz expediently recycled a number of earlier projects to create a new city plan. Asking the formal color question "Why not green over grey?" and proposing a "soft over the hard" (vegetation over buildings) design agenda, Ambasz's scheme for twenty-five thousand to thirty thousand inhabitants aims to go "beyond the house in the garden" to achieve "the house and the garden."[22] Imagining the Green Town to consist of his earlier multitiered vertical garden planned for the Nishiyachiyo train station, his Fukuoka Prefectural International Hall covered with terraced gardens, and the belowground architecture of his Phoenix Museum of History, Ambasz relied on "a typological sampling, of the different types of buildings that would be needed to house the diverse needs of a new Green Town."[23] Collapsing landscape into architectural form, Ambasz puts forward a new definition of "man-made nature," where garden and building combine to "return to the city the very land it took away."[24] He writes, "Such a definition would have to incorporate and expand not only on the creation of

21   Quoted in Michael Sorkin, ed., "An Interview with Ambasz & Emilio," in *Analyzing Ambasz* (New York: The Monacelli Press, 2004), 205. Ambasz continues: "It has taken me thirty years to prove the practical advantages of my ideas….To see Renzo Piano, Jean Nouvel, Tadao Ando, and many others utilize vegetal matter in their projects makes me feel my mission is beginning to bear fruit."

22   Emilio Ambasz, "Why not the green over the gray," *Domus* 772 (June 1995): 83. This project was briefly covered in Emilio Ambasz, "Garden Architecture Goes to Town," *Architectural Record* (July 1991): 68–69.

23   Ambasz, "Why not the green," 83.

24   Ibid., 84.

gardens and public spaces but also on the creation of architecture which must be seen as one specialized aspect of the making of man-made nature."[25] Under a rubric of green, the idea advanced here is that the architectural object, now reconceived as an artificial landscape, provides a unit for urbanism. In contrast to the urban planning units of neighborhood (e.g., of New Urbanism or new towns) or the city-as-a-whole (e.g., the top-down scenarios of urban modernism), Ambasz's Green Town emerges through a collaged accumulation of architectural typologies. In a disciplinary project where landscape acts as the design medium to reinvent architecture, Ambasz slips in a form of typological urbanism that seeks to rethink both nature and artifice.

25   Ibid.

If Ambasz's Green Town suggests architecture and landscape as the planning unit for a new form of city, UrbanLab's Growing Water project for Chicago in 2106—a winning entry for the History Channel's 2006 City of the Future competition—offers a way to rethink the landscape strip as a generative strategy for urbanism. Envisioning that Chicago could evolve into a model city for cleaning water, principals Sarah Dunn and Martin Felsen propose a series of Eco-Boulevards "spread democratically throughout the city," east to west along the city grid.[26] These thin green bands—to consist of wetlands, forests, farms, gardens, recreation areas, and public space—array in parallel across Chicago's metropolitan area with the graphic signature of the Dutch polder landscape, and culminate in suburban Terminal Parks. While much of the project is predicated on the recycling of water—the operative purpose of the boulevards—it is the scale of the proposal that is of greater interest to disciplinary urbanism. Under the semblance of sustainability the project smuggles in a socio-cultural agenda at the scale of Burnham's 1909 Chicago plan: the desire for comprehensive democratic access to open-space amenities across the city.[27] Overlaying Chicago's "Emerald Necklace" of parks and green boulevards, first proposed in the nineteenth century with a new system of green bands, the project updates the urban vision of a park necklace into a twenty-first-century city-park network. Rethinking the bands as performative landscapes with high-density live

26   UrbanLab, *Growing Water: Chicago in 2106* (Chicago, IL: UrbanLab, 2007), 2.

27   Ibid., 4.

and work spaces at their edges, UrbanLab's Eco-Boulevards propose an implicit building and park agenda—boulevards potentially operating in much the same vein as what Frederick Law Olmsted conceived for Manhattan's Central Park. What is hidden within the project's environmental concern is the possibility for very big ideas to re-enter the disciplines of architecture and urbanism, and remain uncontested.[28]

Between Ambasz's architecture-landscape unit and UrbanLab's Eco-Boulevards, Toyo Ito and Associates' Parque de la Gavia proposal (2003–current) for a ninety-six-acre park in Vallecas, a suburb of Madrid, Spain, offers a third example of how the deployment of sustainable landscape criteria—in this case, water purification—can lead to design innovation for "a new concept of 'park.'"[29] By way of a very beautiful "trees of water" proposal, Ito creates "a variety of places" within the park, an approach that he claims is "identical to our thinking about architecture."[30] Reliant on techniques of energy recycling and waste processing, the project proposes two kinds of artificial "watertree" landforms—Ridge Watertrees and Valley Watertrees—whose plan-shapes have a fractal, treelike geometry and whose sections generate a system combining topography with water purification. Using the flow of water to generate a new formal vocabulary for the ground, Ito asserts an architectural design sensibility that, as can be seen in the project's various physical and conceptual models, combines the angular blue figures of the watertrees, the organic lines of topography, and an almost utopian field of greenery.[31] As the project's client, Francisco Rubio, remarked, the Parque de la Gavia is "a park without architecture, but where the architecture is inside the landscape itself."[32] In many ways, the illicit appearance of architecture in this proposal is what makes it so compelling. The project's hidden disciplinary agenda, as Ito points out, is the necessity to rethink both architecture and the park after modernism: "The public parks of 20th Century Modernism were laid out according to functional zoning. We can attest to the dull results in the parks of Tokyo suburbia, and architecture is

28 Aspects of this project are now being developed in Chicago as part of Mayor Daly's green initiative.

29 Francisco Rubio (director of the service for residential innovation, Municipal Housing Company) in Francisco Rubio, Mikiko Ishikawa, and Toyo Ito, "The Making of a Place: A New Park proposed for the 21st Century," *A+U* 5 (May 2004): 118.

30 Ito in Ibid., 115.

31 Ibid., 113.

32 Rubio in Ibid., 118.

conceived in exactly the same way. The dullness of architecture based on the concept of function is clearly visible. Can something be done to revitalize architecture and park?"[33] By using a brief to create a sustainable landscape, Ito manages not only to reinvent the park, but to also reclaim it for architecture through the disciplinary recolonization of landscape (as opposed to the hybridization of architecture into landscape urbanism).

Extending the possibilities of the aesthetics of green urbanism, Atelier Bow-Wow's Void Metabolism entry to the 2007 Great Pyramid contest—an urban planning competition for a 494-acre site in Dessau-Rosslau, Germany—proposes a ring of roads and a promenade of pavilions encircling a massive void, containing a pyramid at its epicenter. The building typologies, which occur at two scales—Leaf-Bedrooms (smaller) and Leaf-Facilities (bigger)—take the symbolic form of extruded leaf motifs—graphic ducks, in the Venturi/Scott Brown sense—and deliver, in the words of Atelier Bow-Wow, "A metaphor of the volumes that compose void metabolism: in fact, they could be any shape as the essence lies in the layout of detached elements generating a pattern of void spaces."[34] In total, the clustered arrangement of leaves forms a "Linear City" over time, which is connected to the pyramid via bifurcating "tree-paths" whose geometry generates a "variety of fields, from small cultivated gardens to agricultural crops to flower fields."[35] According to the architects, "Produce from the fields can be used in the linear city's restaurants, bakeries, and flower shops, creating a partially self-sufficient microcosmic ecosystem."[36] While Atelier Bow-Wow do not mention the terms green or sustainability anywhere in the project description, one cannot help but feel that they cash in on a sensibility of green via figurative graphic representation: color (exhausting the CMYK green palette), leaf outlines (extruded motifs and a William Morris-wallpaperlike array of leaf species), geometric branches in plan (the tree-paths), and agricultural textures (via Photoshop cut-and-paste). Operating in the disciplinary realm of architectural communication—after SITE Inc.'s Terrarium, Rainforest, and Forest Best showrooms (1978–80) made

33   Ito in Ibid., 114.

34   Atelier Bow-Wow, Void Metabolism project description, www.thegreatpyramid.org (accessed 11 Feb. 2009).

35   Ibid.

36   Ibid.

explicit use of live vegetation and soils as a medium of environmental communication—Atelier Bow-Wow's Void Metabolism makes explicit use of symbolic motifs to architecturalize nature and advance another alternative for green aesthetics. In so doing, the architects deliver an updated image of the historic linear city: from a literal formalizing of the line to the emergence of a loop composed of densities and patterns of signs.

As examples of what green can do for architecture and urbanism today, Ambasz's resituating of his work as green typologies, UrbanLab's smuggling in of a big urban idea for the city, Ito's reclaiming of the park for architectural design, and Atelier Bow-Wow's recuperation of symbolic aesthetics suggest that it is indeed possible for architecture and urbanism to advance a disciplinary project while visualizing possible new worlds in an era of environmental concern. Offering a way out from the design limitations of high-tech specialization and landscape urbanism's hybridization, the current popularity of green offers architects and urbanists the possibility to regain what their fields have ultimately given away: speculative ideas for the city. As green continues to return to the city under the current formulation of the city as problem, a central obligation for architects and urbanists is to be imaginative and opportunistic in soliciting what they can deploy to advance their disciplines.

Tabula Futura Imperfecta:
The Architecture of Disaster

Dana Cuff

fig. 1 ›› New Orleans's Lower Ninth Ward in its post-Katrina state

fig. 2 ›› Greensburg, Kansas, after the tornado in May, 2007

> If something cannot be created out of nothing, then, since there is something, it didn't come from nothing. And there never was a time when there was only nothing. If ever nothing was the natural state, which obtained, then something could never have arisen. But there is something. So nothingness is not the natural state; if there is a natural state, it is somethingness.
>
> —Robert Nozick

›› figs. 1 + 2 There is a distinct feeling of nothingness-displacing-some-thingness in post-catastrophe photographs. The depopulated streets of post-Katrina New Orleans's Lower Ninth Ward, the debris-cleared pit at Ground Zero after 9-11, the dusty street grid of the Kansas town of Greensburg after a May 2007 tornado leveled nearly all of its buildings—these images have a forlorn quality about them. In each, the ghost of some former life is barely visible. At other sites, like the empty lot in central St. Louis where the Pruitt-Igoe housing project stood before it was dynamited out of existence, not a trace remains. There, as with other urban renewal sites across the United States, it is as if philosopher Robert Nozick's thesis was exaggerated, but in the reverse. The some-thing that was once there is so forcefully absent that only nothingness, in the shape of vacant land or corporate plazas, can arise. Post-disaster sites and communities prefer the future perfect—we will have rebuilt by the time you return; in two more years, the present emptiness will have been filled with new life. The future perfect contains a projected past, an assurance that embedded in the present is a near future that will become visible in a more distant future. With or without a disaster, this is the quality that the city's existing context holds for the archi-tect; namely, the city frames a yet-to-be-determined something, vaguely visible yet undeniable, that will occupy a present empty space. Extant conditions do not project a specific thing, such as an agreed-upon archi-tectural style or character as historicists might like to imagine, but a future in which the present will have changed.

Architects have long imagined that a tabula rasa, a version of Nozick's nothing, was better than something. Le Corbusier in Chandigarh or Oscar Niemeyer in Brasilia—these places suggest archi-tecture can create urbanism magically, out of thin air. Such nothing-ness is not the same as the metaphysical nothingness that concerns Nozick and fellow philosophers at least as far back as Gottfried Leibniz.[1] But constructing parallels raises productive questions for urbanism. To the question "Could something arise from nothing?" Nozick answers in the negative. The corresponding question in urbanism is "Can a new city or piece of it be cre-ated in a void?" First, we could agree that even Chandigarh and Brasilia did not come from nothing. With so little context to frame those projects, a type of authorship as well as innovation was possible that couldn't be achieved in existing cities, teeming with all their somethingness. This something-nothing binary is misrepresented, of course; it is a continuum rather than a dichot-omy. The ghostly remains of a disaster's aftermath sit at the ful-crum, where both what was once present and what is now empty are apparent. This condition is productive, potentially, of its own

1   Robert Nozick, *Philosophical Explanations* (Cambridge, MA: Harvard University Press, 1981). This essay's opening quote can be found on page 125. In his 1697 essay "The Ultimate Origin of Things," Leibniz makes an analogy between creation and architecture. He argues that as each possible thing "strains towards existence," the one thing that exists has a certain perfection or essence—or max-imum effect at minimum cost—just as the rule for building on a particular site is to "construct the most pleasing building you can, with the rooms as numer-ous as the site can take and as elegant as possible." http://www.earlymoderntexts.com/pdf/leibuo.pdf, 2–3.

form of architectural and urban innovation. The two examples cited stand for more than innovation; they embody the utopian possibility that modernism brought to its tasks in India and Brazil at a particular historical moment. Each depicts a slice of public hope, the very quality sought after a crisis.

Clean Slates

Urbanism after catastrophe presents a peculiar, projective ground for considering architectural experimentation. There are, in such conditions, both the blank slate that is the modernist site of innovation and the existing context that has generated the heat of contemporary debate in urban politics. Post-disaster design holds the potential to retheorize modern and postmodern polemics.

Though associated with modernism, the tabula rasa has held a certain magnetism among architects—and philosophers—for much longer. It started with Aristotle's claim that a child's mind was a clean tablet, a kind of pure potential, with which John Locke agreed nearly two thousand years later.[2] The city grid represents the notion that urban form can be superimposed over an infinite, acquiescent landscape, from the ancient cities of Priene and Xi'an, to colonial towns laid out according to the Laws of the Indies, to nineteenth-century Philadelphia. But tabula rasa could be had not only in terra nova, but within existing cities as well. The clean slate could be an empty site, implying a lack of preconceptions and a freedom from constraints like program, context, regulation, and politics. Sites could be emptied of contaminants, wiped clean for purposes of urban "renewal," as if they could be made new again. Vital, poor communities of color were razed to achieve tabula rasa, often under a banner of hygiene and pathology that recommended excising an urban cancer. Cured but dead, the wastelands created in center cities could sit decades waiting for their second coming, only to be rebuilt as much-maligned corporate plazas, a kind of living dead. These intentional devastations (accompanied by unfulfilled utopian visions) are part of the family of disasters—natural or man-made—that forcefully

2   Aristotle, *On the Soul*, trans. J. A. Smith (Whitefish, MT: Kessinger Publishing, 2004); John Locke, *An Essay Concerning Human Understanding*, ed. Peter H. Nidditch (New York: Oxford University Press, 1979).

clean the urban slate: The Gulf Coast after Katrina, Rotterdam after World War II, Chicago after the Great Fire of 1871.

Once presented with a disaster's tabula rasa, the notion of recreating something that already exists (or existed) is hardly conceivable. At the World Trade Center site, there were proposals to rebuild the towers exactly as before, but these suggestions were not seriously entertained. Conventional wisdom suggests that creating a replica of the buildings destroyed would not represent a triumph of resilience or a fresh start. Alternatively, forms of historic reconstruction are favored by the public. Such solutions represent a nostalgic turn, a politically conservative retreat from the exigencies of a disaster that is likely to generate the least controversy. Nostalgic reconstruction, reminiscent of what was lost or a past that did not formerly exist, has grown less reassuring over the last few decades. The cliché version of New Urbanism, merely plastering historic referents onto the cheapest form of contemporary construction, is now thin and ubiquitous enough to seem false.[3]

3   This is not to discredit the New Urbanist goal of creating more pedestrian-oriented urban space, nor historic preservation.

Instead, this essay considers the post-catastrophic possibility that new architectural tactics could replace what went missing. By so doing, the site of destruction becomes a projective launch into the future, rather than a memorial to all that was lost. In a sense, catastrophe is a breeding ground for both conservation in response to the destruction (we can't forget the past) and, paradoxically, for an avant-garde. At the fulcrum where a full measure of the something that once was and the nothing that presently exists are in balance, new architectural work tips the balance toward an as-yet-undefined vision—the future imperfect. Since the blank slate that a catastrophe leaves in its wake forces the issue of starting fresh, the architectural bias toward the avant-garde is more capable of being expressed.[4]

4   Also, disasters call out the heroic attitude that characterizes a traditional avant-garde, even though this kind of paternalism or omniscience is rarely invoked in contemporary architecture. The role of design after disaster is thoughtfully considered in a series of articles in an issue of the journal Places that I co-edited. See "Recovering," special issue, Places 21, no. 1 (Spring 2009).

The tabula rasa of disaster, compared to philosophical nothingness or the conceptual clean slate, is profoundly tainted. While it demands a fresh start and permits a physical response unfettered by historic context, the violent erasure of history never leaves behind a blank slate, but a highly polemic one. Politics, memory, economic interests, and opportunity vie for power in the process of recovery. War-torn sites from Beirut to London depend not only on exigencies of recovery but on narratives of deliverance. Nowhere was this more convoluted than at the World Trade Center site, where many different groups—families of the victims, relatives of firefighters who died, Lower Manhattan advocates, a wide range of national and local politicos, and various parties with property claims—lobbied for their respective interests. With competing claims and varying degrees of public support, a mélange of solutions arose.[5]

If an important role cast for post-catastrophe architecture is to memorialize, it is oddly coupled with a desperate urgency to forget. The contradiction works against creative thinking about what might come next. Along with—or even dependent upon—active displays of recollection and amnesia comes recovery boosterism, producing a Freedom Tower whose optimistic rhetoric proclaimed victory over aggression. Soon after 9-11, future possibilities of marking the city's resilience were curbed by the bickering among interested parties and the normative forces of large-scale operators who held constant, such as the nation's largest retail developers, the Westfield Group, and architecture giant Skidmore, Owings and Merrill. As a result, a decade after the tragedy there was little construction aboveground at the site, and the promise of the resulting architecture had been severely eroded. Although Ground Zero's post–9-11 fate was sealed, there are counterexamples that prove other alternatives exist. Sometimes, as in the case of Chicago after the Great Fire, there is deliverance when new possibilities in architecture and the city arise. Radical architectural departures such as the steel frame and urban visions like the skyscraper are launched from the ashes of disaster.

Before considering several cases in greater depth, a test of their relevance is in order. The postmodern end of master narratives has sewn doubt into Daniel Burnham's dictum "make no little plans."[6] Instead, minor and fragmented utopias find fertile ground where comprehensive planning now falters. Not only is the construct of the master narrative discredited; in the case of the master plan,

5 No wonder then that the competition entries, including Daniel Libeskind's winning proposal, were the most provocative and promising in their early form, prior to being pushed and pulled in various political directions.

6 According to Paul Goldberger, there is little evidence that Burnham actually mouthed these words with which he is so often identified, but that he surely believed them. See "Toddlin' Town," the *New Yorker* (9 Mar. 2002), http://www.newyorker.com/ arts/critics/skyline/2009/ 03/09/090309crsk_skyline_ goldberger.

so is its instrumentality. Political scientist James C. Scott describes the abstract view from high above as "seeing like a state." The resultant overly simplified, remote solutions to problems are characteristic of high modernism.[7] Scott's analysis is particularly useful to thinking about post-disaster urbanism because his work is based on the politics of implemented, large-scale plans. His observations of both natural and social systems indicate that they fail when guided by the simplified, formulaic impositions of state power. While this analysis is incisive, the conclusions seem less so.

7   Scott in fact critiques Brasilia's high modernism, which he contrasts with Jane Jacobs's depiction of urbanism. James C. Scott, *Seeing Like a State* (New Haven, CT: Yale University Press, 1998).

Scott's own solutions to the problem of seeing simplistically—that is, like a state—are formulaic: take small steps, favor reversibility, plan on surprises, and plan on human inventiveness. If Scott's recommendations are abstract, it is because he makes them general rather than specific to a context or problem. In post-catastrophe reconstruction, specific actions (the small steps) define the solution. This is why architects and urbanists are so crucial to the rebuilding, since the design professions give material body to visions of possible futures. For designers after disasters, their normative task is explicit. Parallel to the Hippocratic Oath to do no harm, designers must do one better: do no harm and conceive of a future that is better than what exists. Rather than create something out of nothing, design is expected to create something better than the something we've got. This stops one degree short of comprehensive utopian planning, since it does not aim for perfection, but lands in a proximate realm.

The Devil You Know

The designer's predilection to invent minor utopias runs directly against the contemporary public's aversion to change. Conservatism dominates the reproduction of the built environment; that is, people tend to want more of what they have rather than something they've never had before. When confronted with the latter, the *habitus*—as social theorist Pierre Bourdieu terms the normative routines that govern our actions—has been broken.[8] Our habitual practices are codified in the built environment, through property and the claims we hold

8   Pierre Bourdieu, *The Logic of Practice* (Stanford, CA: Stanford University Press, 1990).

upon it, through regulation that has evolved to protect us from harm, through architectural form that absorbs daily life. Indeed, the space of the habitus is elaborated in architectural discourse. We refer to it as the urban "fabric," the background buildings that comprise the city, or the generic city—the state of distraction, where we need not focus our attention but can proceed in a routine manner. Logically, we could continue to reproduce the physical environment as background, if other parts of the social, political, and technological world remained static. Since they don't, though, we are constantly tinkering with the urban setting—trenching through the city to extend the subway, recladding facades, tearing down individual buildings to replace them with a higher, better use of their lot, or widening streets. These urban rifts through the background grab our attention and create the potential for the new.

When disaster strikes, the background disappears, and all those changes can be accomplished at once. This fact has not escaped opportunists of every stripe, from hungry architects to zealous politicians to unscrupulous entrepreneurs. It was this combination that descended upon the Gulf Coast as soon as the roads reopened. Halliburton jumped into reconstruction before there was a damage assessment (two months after Katrina struck, Halliburton had 125 million dollars in Gulf Coast contracts, even though they were under investigation for misuse of funds in Iraq), and 150 New Urbanists set up shop to sketch new Main Streets that this time around would incorporate Walmarts and casinos.[9] Halliburton's collusion with the federal response (subcontracting with FEMA, the Navy, and so on) is evidence of what leftist cultural critic Naomi Klein has called corporate capitalism's "shock doctrine."[10] This ready-in-the-wings strategy depends on the massive collective disorientation caused by disasters, which reduces public resistance to unpopular economic development policies. The state and its corporate bedfellows can then push through radical changes that restructure fundamental socioeconomic relations. Klein focuses on the way corporate invasions are triggered by crises, imposing a new set of economic relations on an unwilling population whose reactions are numbed by collective shock in the disaster's aftermath.

9 "Halliburton gets another $33 million for Hurricane Katrina clean-up," 12 Oct. 2005, http://www.halliburton-watch.org/news/katrina2.html.

10 Naomi Klein, *The Shock Doctrine* (New York: Metropolitan Books, 2007).

Klein's analysis is a good reminder to architects, in our enthusiasm for experimental reconstruction, that post-catastrophe opportunity can be exploited by any number of forces. Without doubt, urban crises break the habitual practices that resist change. But only sometimes do the results produce design invention. If there are patterns to innovative disaster recovery, architects and planners are presently unaware of them. To discover those patterns, it makes sense to engage case studies, since all disasters are by nature unique, and thus, anecdotal. I'd like to start by considering two historical cases: first, Chicago's Great Fire of 1871, and second, the national postwar housing crisis. While separated by more than half a century, by the type of emergency involved, and by the extent of destruction, these two very different disasters each produced innovative architectural forms in the United States. In the case of Chicago's fire, the steel-frame skyscraper resulted; in the postwar housing crisis, modernist public housing developments were built across the country.[11]

Since both disaster narratives are relatively well known, I will give but the briefest summary, instead focusing on the terms under which we could say that some design innovation took hold. Within the boundaries of such innovation, we include urban restructuring, redefinitions of program, formal effects, transformations of land use, technological advances, and architecture's advancement of its own disciplinary project as it simultaneously resolves the urban crisis at hand. » fig. 3

11   Even if these were not the first instances of skyscrapers or modern housing, the advancement and proliferation of each resulted from crisis.

fig. 3 » Postcard depicting Chicago's State Street in 1907, lined with the skyscrapers unleashed by the Great Fire of 1871

In just thirty-six hours, the Great Fire of 1871 reduced Chicago to ashen rubble. In contrast to the post-disaster discussions about whether New Orleans should be rebuilt at all (when the nation was treated to a lesson on "Why New Orleans Matters"), Chicago was the unquestioned economic center of the West.[12] Its recovery narratives were full of irrepressible entrepreneurial optimism, and reconstruction efforts got underway immediately. An immense insurgence of capital

12   This is the title of a book (by Tom Piazza, published by HarperCollins in 2005), but was also the subject of much debate between those seeking to rebuild in situ and others arguing that the city needed to move to higher ground to avoid future disaster.

13   Kevin Rozario, "Making Progress: Disaster Narratives and the Art of Optimism in Modern America," in *The Resilient City: How Modern Cities Recover from Disaster*, ed. Lawrence J. Vale and Thomas J. Campanella (New York: Oxford University Press, 2005), 27–54; see especially pp. 35–41.

14   Ross Miller, "Out of the Blue: The Great Chicago Fire of 1871," in *Out of Ground Zero*, ed. Joan Ockman (New York: Prestel Publishing, 2002), 46–62.

15   Siemens was the founder of what is now known as Siemens AG, the largest engineering firm in Europe. The electric elevator replaced previous hydraulic ones.

was available for rebuilding, which fueled the rise of a quick and dirty set of new buildings in Chicago. In its haste, the rebuilding effort took more lives than the fire, claiming as many as twelve construction workers in a single day.[13] This first post-fire ecology would itself be supplanted within a decade.

As recounted by scholar Ross Miller, Chicago's leaders saw tremendous, unprecedented opportunity in that rubble. A new building technology was available that would produce an urban mutation rather than a long, unfolding evolution. From Chicago's former small properties with wooden structures would emerge a new city of recently assembled large, steel-frame high-rises. The properties themselves could be aggregated, given the devastation and abandonment of the city center, and former residential uses were banished to the outskirts.[14] These changes instigated radical urban restructuring, even as the first material outgrowth was being jury-rigged back together.

It was on top of this initial temporary ecosystem that the long-lasting skyscraper ecology would be built. Work stopped on the first rebuilding effort due to a nationwide credit crisis that hit Chicago around 1873 and lasted until the end of the decade. That hiatus sparked further consolidation of buildable parcels, the refinement of high-rise building technologies, and the accumulation of investment capital. Siemens perfected an electric elevator in 1880.[15] Architectural fireproofing improved greatly, and the steel frame was ready to see widespread application. Miller points out that Chicago architects also invented "Chicago windows," wide fenestration that adapted to the larger sites, bringing light deeper into the core of thick buildings, along with a special raft foundation designed to stabilize tall buildings in the swampy Chicago soils. Thus, in the 1880s and 1890s, Chicago was rebuilt again, this time by capable architects like Burnham and Root, and Adler and Sullivan. It is this material legacy from two decades of recovery that remains from the 1871 fire. In turn, the restructuring of Chicago's urban pattern and practices set in motion a new group of possibilities in subsequent decades. For example, the superblock would be more likely to evolve in Chicago than other cities because some of its nineteenth-century constraints had already been removed.

There were several conditions that sparked a creative adaptive response to the fire's devastation:

1. A future perfect site: widespread devastation (nothing) displaced the former city (something), creating a future-perfect site
2. Public will: there was shared consensus on the city's resilience
3. New means: recent technological innovations became available
4. Design intelligence: a talented pool of architects and urbanists were on hand[16]
5. Restructuring: basic conditions of reconstruction (land assembly and parcel size) were changed

These components of a successful post-disaster rebuilding effort may not be universal, but on the other hand, neither were all present in either of our contemporary disaster-design debacles: the post–9-11 and post-Katrina efforts.

16 The phrase "design intelligence" refers to the work of Michael Speaks as well as the idea of a profession's intelligentsia. See Michael Speaks, "Theory was interesting...but now we have work," *arq: Architectural Research Quarterly* 6, no. 3 (2002): 209–12; and Eliot Freidson, *Professional Powers* (Chicago, IL: University of Chicago Press, 1986).

Reconstructing the Inner City

These five conditions for design's post-disaster relevance can be further interrogated by examining a disaster of an entirely different sort: the mid-century American housing crisis. As World War II and the effects of the Depression were coming to an end, housing advocates and civic reformers amped up the rhetorical volume on the nation's housing problems. Housing shortages and substandard living conditions were characterized as a crisis by spokespersons ranging from housing activist Catherine Bauer Wurster to President Herbert Hoover to developer William Levitt. Surveys of center-city conditions yielded field data on blight—substandard conditions that included overcrowding, poor construction, plumbing inadequacies, health-related problems, inappropriate mixtures of land uses, and illegal dwelling units. Blight was, in one sense, *created* through the process of surveying older, poorer sections of cities inhabited by people of color. Different constituencies came together around urban renewal—housing activists, real estate interests, politicians, civic boosters, health and social welfare advocates—at local, state, and federal levels.

Ready to respond to the widespread interest in ridding cities of slums were planners and architects who had traveled abroad in the interwar period to see the modern housing developments built in Europe, particularly in Germany and England. Affordable housing that was safe, decent, and sanitary—terms that became the watchwords of our public housing apparatus—seemed possible in the United States, and legions of architects hoped to design such projects. Modernism found little purchase in the United States except in state projects like schools and subsidized, large-scale housing. That modernist architecture would be the right answer to the housing crisis is the result of all these conditions, and at least one more: the fact that the housing would have to solve what were previously intractable problems. This led to the agreement that the solution—that is, the architecture—would need to be new.

While many critical assessments of urban renewal's flaws exist, there are too few thoughtful evaluations of the first wave of public housing.[17] The predominant garden housing was a model for its time, from the late 1930s to the early 1950s, with site planning that separated vehicular and pedestrian circulation, ventilation on two sides of each dwelling unit, easy access to the outdoors, and community facilities that included splash pools and laundry. Heavy criticism of the high-rise public housing built largely in the 1950s and 1960s unjustifiably tainted evaluation of the low-rise alternative. Low-rise experiments in public housing were quite livable, representing real advances in affordable residential building.

Among design forces in response to disaster, there is one component present but not clearly visible in the Chicago fire analysis, yet apparent in the postwar housing crisis: a group of civic leaders is needed to define the problem and its solution in terms that are specifically relevant to architectural innovation. This leadership involves an intelligentsia of architects and planners who are ready with a new direction. A loose agreement exists that constitutes the next wave of architectural

17   See Gail Radford, *Modern Housing for America* (Chicago, IL: University of Chicago Press, 1996); Lawrence J. Vale, *From the Puritans to the Projects* (Cambridge, MA: Harvard University Press, 2000); Dana Cuff, *The Provisional City* (Cambridge, MA: MIT Press, 2000).

thinking, and that school of thought can be unleashed on the next comprehensive problem.

This notion links back to Scott's idea that states solve problems by thinking in abstractions, reducing complexities to the detriment of all those involved. Such pure utopian thinking is constructively perverted by disaster: it is highly site specific, and requires a level of pragmatic urgency. It is intrinsically grounded, and thus resists homogenizing approaches to reconstruction. This has negative consequences as well as positive: in New Orleans, for example, rehousing priorities overshadowed broad infrastructural reconsideration of the levees.

Chicago and the postwar housing crisis each began the work of reconstruction on a tabula rasa, and although their sites were not perfectly empty, they were generally considered as such. The "site" was open to the new not only in physical terms, but in political, economic, and symbolic terms as well. The new beginnings fed a utopian hubris that accompanied rebuilding in inner cities as well as in turn-of-the-century Chicago. The utopian urge faded into urban reality in Chicago with the continual evolution of the city's architecture and infrastructure. But the public housing developments that replaced American slums were plagued by their own totalizing solutions. Within four decades the new, idealized housing had become the next slums, in spite of the original optimism of the architecture. In the context of urban renewal's overall problems, modern public housing, planned as garden apartments, was a design success undermined by poor management and operations.[18]

If Chicago's substantial resurgence was insured by its *not* being comprehensive, public housing was damned by the fact that it overtook so much of the prior downtown landscape and isolated itself from its surroundings. By remaking all of the blight it displaced, the modern housing could itself be undone in a single wipe of the slate. In fact, keeping the slate intact is a central issue in an emergency. From these two historical cases, components of design-productive disaster can be discerned, but so can certain problematics—simultaneity and overreaching, to be specific. Though grounded and specific, the treatment of

18　See Roger Montgomery, "High Density, Low-Rise Housing and the Changes in the American Housing Economy," in *The Form of Housing*, ed. Sam Davis (New York: Van Nostrand Reinhold, 1977), 83–111.

the disaster zone as a single entity can create enclaves that are subsequently vulnerable.

Accidents and Increments

How, then, to avoid the abstract, imposed order that real crises elicit from the large-scale institutions that respond to them? The answer considered here is to examine the radical increment. A break in normative behavior, like a surprise, sits at the opposite end of the continuum from the cataclysm, and may hold insight for environmental designers. The radical increment is firstly a scalar shift away from comprehensive solutions. Rather than catastrophes, architects and urbanists might begin working from accidents—emergencies that sweep clean small slates. Compared to disasters, accidents are less likely to invoke memorials, less comprehensive in their political implications, and yet, more likely to serve as prototypes for other urban interventions. In other words, more so than large-scale catastrophes, accidents comprise the generative components of architectural innovation, without some of the more complicated problematics.

Theorist Paul Virilio sets up the opportunity that accidents present for design. He begins with the observation that the inherent, overwhelming speed of contemporary life breeds a preponderance for accidents, which we see occurring with greater frequency.[19] He argues that every invention contains its "accidental" demise, converting the accident from an unpredictable uncertainty to the accident waiting to happen. The train's invention was, therefore, the simultaneous invention of derailment. Extending to the city, a master plan contains its variance, an architectural spectacle creates its degraded copy, a plant prefigures its closure, a new technology embodies its displacement by a newer technology. Carrying Virilio's observations of invention and accident one step further, the accident presents, at least in the city, the opportunity for another invention. In theory, then, the accident holds the kernel of reinvention. The relatively minor disasters that are present within existing urban contexts where architects work (abandoned

19   Paul Virilio, *The Original Accident*, trans. Julie Rose (Cambridge, UK: Polity, 2007). See also the exhibition The Museum of Accidents, from the Cartier Foundation, Paris, http://www.onoci.net/virilio/pages_uk/accidents/liste.php?th=1&rub=1_3 (accessed 28 July 2009).

buildings, sites with obstructions, places deteriorating under adverse conditions) can actually offer unexpected opportunity for invention. Drawing again from Bourdieu, it could be said that the minor crisis offers a slate contaminated by a habit to be broken, given its incidental failure. For architects, that habit would be architectural convention. And the unconventional response, the radical increment, is as much a prototype as a project. Lastly, the radical increment embodies the future perfect: it now appears that it will have become something in the not-too-distant future.

Before offering examples that prove the contaminated site is indeed fertile breeding ground for a break with convention, it is worth conceptualizing the breaks (post-accidental reinventions) a bit more fully. Architecture's reinventions are never purely formal, but involve local communities, clients, and occupants—the small sociopolitical communities surrounding any building. Like a minor literature, a minor architecture promises the possibility to enunciate political and collective values not part of dominant practices.[20] Also similar to minor literatures, the architectures of accidents can be subversive, if they can avoid co-optation by long-standing dominant practices or by those that waited impatiently to gain a foothold. When the Los Angeles area ran out of sprawling, multi-acre school sites for its teeming population of students, schools were required to consider nonstandard sites that were smaller, in industrial areas, and in repurposed buildings. A stream of architectural experiments occurred, in private and public schools alike. Along with Morphosis's Science Center School in a museum's parkland and Coop Himmelb(l)au's High School for the Visual and Performing Arts at the freeway's edge, there are the Camino Nuevo schools by Daly Genik Architects (see pp. 110–13), located in an abandoned mini-mall and a rehabbed industrial space.

While the architecture of each school in the Camino Nuevo system is itself a radical increment, their sum converts an entire block into a micro–school district and, to some extent, they are the heart of a neighborhood.[21] Sited on one block of Burlington Avenue, the street is now lined with a series of architecturally innovative

20   Gilles Deleuze and Félix Guattari, *Kafka: Toward a Minor Literature*, trans. Dana Polan (Minneapolis: University of Minnesota Press, 1986).

21   The same client subsequently built a high school, but not in this block.

projects that are populated by a lively group of children and the adults who bring them to school each day. The site was previously riddled with problems—backing up to a drug-ridden alley, an abandoned building housed guard dogs and discarded mattresses. As a result, the micropolitics of the site—including nearby residents, the neighboring fire station, and the city councilman—were primed for change. Behind the particular situation is one principle of accidental architectures: experimentation is more possible in adverse conditions, particularly where circumstances appear to create a worsening trend. Other radical increments to arise from deterioration come to mind, such as Andrew Zago's conversion of an auto dealership into the Museum of Contemporary Art in Detroit (MOCAD), or Eric Owen Moss's recreation of the Culver City industrial landscape, the Hayden Tract.

Deterioration is an impetus for the radical increment because such urban sites sit within relatively built-up landscapes. But consider Pruitt-Igoe's ghostly site in St. Louis, whose vast expanse seems to promise the opposite—it is so barren and immense that a collective belief in its potential can hardly be sustained. The nascent logic of architecture in disasters and accidents raises the question: How does the scale of a site implicate design after disaster? After hurricanes Katrina and Rita, the 150-mile devastation along the Gulf Coast was such a daunting reconstruction project that it inevitably produced prescriptive, utopian misfires (see, for example, the long list of reports from the Mississippi Renewal Forum charrette) and their ad-hoc counterattacks (e.g., homeowners rebuilding in spite of preventative city ordinances).[22] The question is productively reframed in light of Nozick: How much nothing and how much something does the architect need? From small school sites to miles of infrastructure, the accident is distinct from a disaster by virtue of its local definition. Its potential somethingness is not the vision of the public many, but the project-related few.

The issue of scale has less to do with size or quantity than with balance. Instead of emptiness, it is a matter of the gap. The gap, obviously, implies an emptiness defined by its surroundings.

22 Besides the eleven individual towns that were provided form-based codes, there are broader sets of guidelines that were developed during the charrette, including an architectural pattern book, a model code, and so on. There have been many appeals since the issuance of the report that towns should hold fast to the form-based code. http://mississippirenewal.com/info/plansReports.html (accessed 14 July 2009).

When, in 1999, Georgia Tech graduate student Ryan Gravel saw the potential in an abandoned rail loop encircling downtown Atlanta, the twenty-two-mile BeltLine parkway was born. Its momentum came not only from the strong conceptual hold the BeltLine had on public imagination, but on the practical advantages for the forty-five separate neighborhoods that would be linked together with green space and transit, and the opportunity to add twelve hundred acres of park land.[23] The tabula rasa was woven through the existing fabric of Atlanta, a balance of opportunity and context. The rail line contained its own abandonment, and this spatial accident in Atlanta's fabric sparked a new way of seeing the city. Such accidents, or ruptures of the norm, exist in the residual spaces where a river meets the grid or in a coherent development that receives infill at some later date. Diller Scofidio + Renfro's Lincoln Center transformation is a good example of the latter. Lincoln Center in its first incarnation was the product of a collaboration among illustrious architects—including Eero Saarinen, Philip Johnson, and Gordon Bunshaft, among others—that never quite added up to the sum of the parts. While some sections were neglected over the years and others were renovated in a haphazard manner, Diller Scofidio + Renfro created a series of varied, smaller projects that refashion the programmatic and public spaces not only of Lincoln Center, but also of the surrounding Upper West Side. The urban collage, composed of existing fragments and new interventions, has a legacy in architectural discourse starting with Colin Rowe. ›› fig. 4

23   This represents a 40 percent increase in green space for the city. Whether the project will also incorporate innovative landscape or architectural design remains to be seen. See http://www.beltline.org/Home/tabid/1672/Default.aspx.

fig. 4 ››   Aliso Village public housing in Los Angeles, designed by a team of architects led by Lloyd Wright and Ralph Flewelling and completed in 1942

Finally, along with deterioration and gaps, there are collisions. These occur where obstructions become productive of a radical incre-ment. Rem Koolhaas (OMA)'s IIT McCormick Tribune Campus Center is such a collision: the Chicago Green Line elevated train passes through its site, wedging the student-services building into a creative new landscape under and around the train. The collision created an unconventional site, which in turn set up the project to break architec-tural conventions, with its landscape of inclined planes and circulation, punctuated by student program. Another collision occurs at the High Line, in New York City, where a 1930s-era elevated railway was converted into a floating, linear promenade by the landscape/urban firm of James Corner Field Operations and architects Diller Scofidio + Renfro. The new parkland created on the High Line is also a new ground plane, one story above grade, that collides with its surrounding building envelopes. This datum converts abandoned industrial waste into infrastructural landscape. Opening its first sections in 2009, the High Line catalyzed not just additional development, but a new building type that addresses not only the original streetscape, but also the above-grade parkway. New residential towers by Neil Denari, Lindy Roy, Renzo Piano, and James Polshek capitalize on the rejuvenated, hip open space.[24]

24   See Nicolai Ouroussoff, "On the High Line, Solitude is Pretty Crowded," the *New York Times*, 24 Dec. 2006, http://www.nytimes.com/2006/12/24/arts/design/24ouro.html?fta=y.

Each of the projects mentioned here are contemporary examples of what could be called post-utopian or accidental architectures—interventions where some kind of extranorma-tive condition predominates. Projects like these recognize some absence or emptiness in the city, a minor tabula rasa, as well as some abnormality, a break in the habitus. Together, these two qualities open up the possibility of architectural invention and offer insight about the scale of productive disaster. Architectural experimen-tation depends less on size or quantity than on the balance between nothing and something.

This range of projects, from Los Angeles to New York, are in keeping with the fast-forward notion of an emergent urbanism rather than a prescriptive master plan. Camino Nuevo, the High Line, IIT, and Lincoln Center are sparked by an accident of geography that provokes transformation subsequent to the opening gambit. The projects are ambitious, but do not feign comprehensiveness. Rather than being a map that organizes space in temporal simultaneity, the tabula futura imperfecta unfolds step-by-step. Like a card game, there are rules (accommodate political realities/generate political support, create financial opportunities, work within the given site boundaries, be prepared for domino effects, and so on), but the play that ensues remains dependent upon a range of particular conditions, as well as the sequence of events. Indeed, the projects described in this essay raise the architectural bar for the urban actions that follow them.

Conclusion

None of these contemporary projects resulted from disaster per se. Instead, they arose from the accidents of colliding urban systems; from abandoned, neglected, and underutilized sites; and from the decay that sets in around them. These accidents represent holes in the urban fabric, and the design projects operate as catalysts within them. The IIT campus center took an underpopulated no-man's-land, in a part of the campus crisscrossed by train tracks and footpaths, and redefined it as a hub that dignified that circulation. The High Line, an unconventional site cutting across Manhattan's grid, required solutions that had no precedent. Each project represents a radical break from some norm; each project started with a site that contained the void of an accident—a form of nothing that presupposes something will occur; and each project was imagined as the start (or continuation) of something larger that expanded beyond the time and site of the original intervention.

The origins of many architectural projects can be framed as accidents, as a void, a break in habitus, a collision, or an abandonment. In part, such framing is the work of narrative—a minor fiction that gains currency as the project proceeds. Disasters by contrast imply a shared understanding. In the case of Chicago after the fire, the booster-recovery narrative reflected a certain coherence not only among the powerful elite rebuilding the city, but the population as a whole.[25] The postwar housing crisis in the United States required more creative

25 Rozario, "Making Progress," see especially 35–41.

narrative construction: propagandistic photographs, journalistic flourish, and a building industry that was chafing at the bit to get busy again after the Depression. The comprehensive recovery narratives of disaster bind architectural responses to a comprehensive, and thus utopian, approach. Condemned to the failure of such grandiosity, architecture is emasculated by disasters at the scale of Katrina and 9-11, where the nothingness is so loaded that it perverts the subsequent somethingness that will replace it. But what I have called accidents carry more promising opportunities. The five disaster preconditions (future perfect site, public will, new means, design intelligence, and restructuring) are localized, and so are shielded from the predominance of prevailing norms. To establish a motive for design-after-accident means building a minor architecture, with some group of interested parties to push the narrative through implementation.

The examples here lead to the conclusion that it is better to build from something rather than nothing. Moreover, radical increments can produce minor architectures, the outcome of accidents. Rather than an apology for architects in post-disaster operations, this work suggests that comprehensive solutions are to be avoided, replaced by more opportunistic, localized, conditional responses. The creation of an emergent urbanism—one generated not by following some master plan, but by responding with agility to specific conditions—is more possible in accidents than catastrophes.

This work opens a way for designers to look at the disasters, large and small, all around us. Our own professions might be justifiably accused of adding to the catastrophes in the Gulf Coast and in New York City. But the projects described above offer an alternative— examples where design rejects the modernist tabula futura perfecta for the imperfect future. That is, the architectural and urban future cannot be perfectly foreseen. Rather than imagining that spatial innovation is bred out of nothing, the argument here upholds that something is likely to come from something. The unclean slate is easiest to see in uneven disasters and in minor crises—each of which produce accidental architectures that construct a city ripe for design experimentation.

Among Suburban Abecedaria

Lars Lerup

Aimlessly roaming the Suburban City has been my habit for several years. Inevitably the roving photographic eye—not focused on anything in particular—hesitates over the repeated, then makes the mechanical wink that paparazzi do as a profession. In time, an arsenal of images begins to form clusters and eventually arrays of similarities. These tropes—churches, gas stations, coffeehouses, feeder road DNA—are all apparently autonomous agents in the agency that we know as the Suburban City.

Assembling these agents into an abecedarium—a suburban alphabet—has been, for some time, central to my work on Houston. In the beginning, I probably thought in the lazy corner of my reptilian brain that this would be easy—that I would find an endless flat field where everything was repeated over and over. Well, I was wrong. Many years later I am still at it, now employing the upper parts of the cerebral domain. Once one acquires a certain familiarity with a number of agents, they begin to stir in complex ways, questioning their own figurative autonomy to construct an eerie blurring of human activity and suburban form.

In this short, seven-entry trailer of a more exhaustive abecedarium, something much larger than the alphabetic figure suggests itself. For example, as we lift our sight above the atomic level in the case of the Bayou—the first entry included here—a Mega Landscape emerges. Snaking and carving its way through the flat Houston Field, the Bayou (with the additional help of a prevalent canopy of trees—the Zoohemic Canopy) occupies a complex setting that I refer to as the field room. Thus, three entries in the abecaderium—Bayou, Zoohemic Canopy, and Houston Field—make up the most characteristic life space of Houston's dwellers, a near-mythic construct that now holds in place and time both the artifice and the denizens that the artifice generously accommodates.

Once this making of conceptual assemblies begins, it is hard to know when to stop. In the case of the Downtown entry, the dilemma of resolving the uniqueness and figurative clarity of its many parts—suggesting another assembly of alphabetic figures (gridiron, high-rise buildings, parking, and so on)—is answered by what I have come to refer to as a Megashape (the shape of the built environment perceived while driving past or through it). Other alphabetic "states," such as Homeless and Storm, are affective qualities that add occasional character to the Megashapes and Mega Landscapes. Oil Refinery and Faith-Based Community are miniature universes whose side effects are (in the case of oil) all-encompassing and (in terms of religion) suggestive of immense extraterritorial domains, like the Bible Belt. Finally, the Planned Unit Development—functioning as a miniature internal Jeffersonian grid—has evolved into a planning figure that dominates, in some form, the entire suburban domain.

Suddenly the alphabet finds itself in the throes of a speculative and analytic grammar, undoing the cool discreteness of the individual letter to form sticky clusters of significance. The abecedarium becomes a tool with a complexity far beyond its first appearance as a mere assembly of separate figures.

Bayou

›› fig. 1 Winding its way across the moist prairie, the bayou is the arterial system of the prairie's various waters, from the mere condensate of settling humidity to tropical downpours. Slowly, the bayou carves its serpentlike body into the gumbo soil. When its curvatures meet and are filled in, oxbows form—banana-shaped pools of stagnant water filled with rich, primitive pond life. Before the Army Corps of

fig. 1 ›› Bayou

Engineers petrified the bayou, its ecology was an astonishing compression of flora and fauna. Thick greenery along the banks quenched its thirst and sheltered a rich compendium of prairie life. When left intact, bayous are the most beguiling and graphic expressions of the moist prairie. The sources of the bayous are the watersheds hidden in the grounds of the delta. The management of the vast complex of prairie, bayous, and delta watersheds, now peppered by suburbanization, is as complex as the management of life itself.

figs. 2 + 3 ›› Downtown

Downtown

›› figs. 2 + 3 Lit up twice a day by the rising and setting sun, downtown Houston glows like a giant candelabra. Boldly jutting out of the seemingly endless suburban field set perpendicular to it, the towers of downtown—despite their individual design, size, and location—form a jagged but confident whole. The grid on which the towers sit is square and neutral, a perfectly "democratic" playing field. In plan, section, and profile, however, the assembled towers confidently radiate corporate power, successful speculation, aspiration, and progress—all thoroughly undemocratic. Bypassing the street, elevators in Houston's downtown carry the corporate denizens down to connect with an underground network of air-conditioned tunnels that lead to garages with direct access to the freeway system and the subdivisions beyond. Banished to the street are the service people: delivering goods, waiting to clean the offices, or taking the bus. Class is literally inscribed in the towers, the street, and the tunnels below: vertical integration with lateral separation.

But these striated conditions are changing radically in Houston, as they are in almost every downtown along the southern littoral, particularly in New Orleans and Los Angeles. The Houston Downtown Coalition, a nonprofit organization with planning and implementation capabilities, is slowly but surely removing the impediments to openness by reinventing the street as a common ground for everyone. Eventually, what is now an office park for the energy industry will become a real downtown, and, as has happened before, the geography of openness will change.[1] The coalition understands that the neglected street surface is the true battleground of a great city: here is where the public, by tradition and instinct, will gather, linger, and commune. Although downtown may still occupy the graphic center of the city, it will never again be the center of the Suburban City—the atomization of the city's activities is complete.

1 Earlier change was driven by Central Houston, Inc., under the able leadership of President Robert Eury and his former partner, Guy Hagstette, in close cooperation with the city and the many companies that took hold in downtown Houston.

Homeless

At the lower end of the housing spectrum (many steps below the middle-class housing types common to suburbia) lies virtual housing, points where the poor have briefly staked out a place to huddle in a park or under a bridge. Bizarre as it may sound, in Houston such ephemeral loci reflect a suburban humanity too.

Here the homeless are barely visible. When seen, as in the case of a solitary man who occupies a bench (rain or shine, night or day) on "my" street, the homeless are oddities, mere blips to the roving eye. When my "neighbor" leaves his bench (to shop? to eat? to go to the bathroom?), he leaves behind a grocery cart with "stuff," a folded umbrella and a blanket, the most rudimentary marks of habitation. With his back always turned to the street, he lives without the usual accoutrements of the American dream. When he walks by, however, he looks relaxed, well fed. Out on a stroll, free as a bird, the new Diogenes, the last pedestrian, Walter Benjamin's flaneur, and—in his isolation and utter solitude—the ultimate suburbanite. This concept of the homeless makes even more sense when we turn to another huge Suburban City.

Until recently, 40 percent of America's homeless lived just south of downtown Los Angeles. They flocked around social service outlets, stores, and made-up piazzas. According to interviews, many lived there by choice, an extreme version of a DCI (Development of Common Interest). Their housing was a tent city lined up on the sidewalks, the diverse shelters separated by tiny but equal side yards. The entire settlement looked hauntingly like a subdivision, the Tudors and the Georgians replaced by various types of tents, from upscale North Face models to homemade tarp shelters. The "house lot" was the sidewalk, ironic given that this public margin is now almost extinct in suburbia, eradicated by paranoia and porch phobia versus TV-room security. Although the tent city inhabitants did not behave like their suburban counterparts, the setting was conceptually identical to that of a gated community, here surrounded by a police presence, which provided the traditional cordon sanitaire. A human tragedy thus comes uncomfortably close to a conceptual farce. But the new downtown scene in Los Angeles could not afford such a blemish, so the "lite" subdivision was closed and its denizens sent packing. Still, the poverty of form in the suburban design imagination is startling. Rich and poor alike occupy the same solitaires, held in place by the same militaristic striations.

Faith-Based Community

It is pure speculation to claim that millions of inhabitants miss the traditional city's public domain, especially since it was never there. Yet it is also clear that many compensatory systems now provide communion for those seeking it. A basic need for civic community apparently cannot be entirely killed off, even in Houston. Tongue-in-cheek, I call these compensatory urban forms "replacement therapies." Some are so effective that they may forever obscure the actual need for a public domain. Lakewood Church in Houston is a case in point. Its early website proclaimed the following after the church purchased a onetime arena for its new home:

Jesus brought the gospel into the market place, the village square—everywhere people gathered, and The Lakewood International Center will become the "village square" of Houston. With more than 2 million people currently attending events each year, there is hardly a more visible or familiar landmark in the city. Its location alone will allow us to present a message of hope to more people than any outreach in the history of Houston.

Today, it is a sports and concert arena. At the Compaq Center, millions of people have watched the most gifted sports figures and entertainers in America. Its history has been one of excellence, crowning champions in the world of sports.

And continuing in that great and awesome tradition, The Lakewood International Center will become a place that will crown "Champions of Life."[2]

2   The Lakewood Church, previously located outside Houston's inner loop, has at the time of this writing joined the general flight back to the city. The former Compaq Center, an inner-loop site for sports and entertainment, has been transformed into the Lakewood International Center. www.lakewood.cc.

Lakewood Church inaugurated its sixteen-thousand-seat auditorium on July 16, 2005. Several million people visit each year, which makes Lakewood the largest church in the country. Through direct reference to the ancient "village squares" of the Holy Land, Lakewood equates the traditional community life of the public domain shared by all citizens (including Jesus) with the village square inside its own church, although here only the messenger (Pastor Joel Osteen) and his flock have entry. Gone are the Romans, the moneylenders, the hawkers, the kibitzers—in short, the citizens. All have been replaced by the flock (or the tribe, in nomadic terms), which includes, along with worshipers, a staff of psychiatric counselors, childcare workers, disaster assistants, and the spiritual leader.

This subtle sleight of hand has transformed the public into the semiprivate, here populating the communal space with "Champions of Life." As in the Suburban City, the city cops of the village square have been replaced by "security," and public land has become private space. A faith-based spiritual domain has seamlessly joined with the sociopsychological domain and, only distantly, the old city square. The ubiquitous nongovernmental organization (NGO) has taken over for the city, and both city and society have been erased. Beyond Lakewood's spiritual square and an assortment of other pseudosquares lies only the system: the streets, the parking lots, the runoff technologies, and the endless freeways. We have clearly arrived in the Suburban City.

Oil Refinery

On my horizon to the east lies Texas City, a "city" of refineries. A 2005 accident at the BP refinery sent a plume of smoke, with a shape somewhere between a mushroom cloud and a smoke signal, thousands of feet into the air. A restart process went haywire, fifteen people died, and one hundred people were injured. The breaking up of the crude oil chain using boilers—in which a heated column of various products allows cracking, unification, and alternation to produce further derivatives—is a complex and delicate process. The 2005 accident happened when faulty gauges allowed the undissolved oil to be heated to a much higher temperature than it should have been. Attempts to drain the oil caused it instead to geyser out of the tower into a pool, which then ignited. Like a microcosmic parallel (both poetic and sinister), the explosion in the refinery seems to prefigure the superheating of the entire region—just waiting to blow.

fig. 4 ›› Planned Unit Development (PUD)

Planned Unit Development (PUD)

›› fig. 4 The extraterritorial jurisdiction (ETJ) attached to Houston's arsenal of expansionary agencies has allowed an extraordinary land grab, expanding Houston far beyond its own borders. Couple this with the city's municipal utility district (MUD)—which allows developers to plan buildings on lots both big and small without approval or input from city planning and zoning, financed by floating bonds, all of which the city complacently applauds—and you have a formidable real estate machine. Once the MUD is established, the developer finds builders with the necessary technical and economic ability to build planned unit developments (PUDs) as portions of the MUD. The result is what is commonly known as sprawl. This is an unfortunate misnomer, since both PUDs and MUDs are highly organized, but faced with a PUD horizon that is both given and most often highly irregular, analysts stumble and refuse to see the planning behind it.

Storm

Each city has its own hidden disaster scenario, its own version of "the storm"—some worse than others. All are characterized by a collusion of natural and artificial events. Los Angeles and the San Francisco Bay Area have their earthquakes, brush fires, and mud slides; Phoenix has its heat and drought; the Gulf Coast from Texas to Florida has its hurricanes; the Midwest has its tornados; Mexico City has its thermal inversions; and Randstad, Holland, has its inundations, now from the rivers rather than the ocean. Because of its size and complexity, the Suburban City is now shaping its own environment—constructing its own artificial ecology—one tainted by certain levels of inherent toxicity. In Houston, when a storm rides in from the southwest to inundate the moist prairie, vast natural systems have to fend for themselves, compensating for our technological intrusions as they try to handle the natural onslaught. The result is recurring natural storms that have characterized this part of the Gulf Coast for longer than we can remember.

White-Collar Prison

For developers faced with rising land prices and the chance to assemble large parcels of land, the four-story apartment complex surrounding a multistory parking garage has become the building type of choice. Ironically, these apartment blocks derive their form from the perimeter block of the traditional city. By surrounding each complex with a fence that allows only one entry and exit via the garage, though, their capacity to construct a city is dramatically arrested. Instead, the buildings and their garages embedded in the atriums just constitute very large pavilions, isolated from their context. Strangely similar to prisons, with their fences and guards at their entry, these apartment blocks typically house the rapidly expanding white-collar workforce. By rejecting all forms of democratic collectivity in favor of socioeconomic tribalism, a sequestered suburban thinking permeates all aspects of the attenuated Suburban City.

Field Operations

The true abecedarium of Houston is, of course, endless (my last version has some fifty entries), clustered around Prairie, Subdivision, Speedzone, and Streamers, and in turn suggesting other formations, such as the Megashapes and Mega Landscapes—all motivated by the prevailing car culture. All of the tropes under these various headings are agents in the continued remaking of the Suburban City. Here, every day is a new day—the traditional Texas ice house is displaced by the refrigerator, but then is rejuvenated as a modern roadhouse. In the end, assembling an abecedarium is the easy part. Finding out how all of the tropes more or less inadvertently make up the Suburban City is another issue.

Each trope, such as White-Collar Prison, is in fact an entire "society of agents" (to loosely use the vocabulary of Marvin Minsky's 1985 book *The Society of Mind*), ranging in this case from the numerous actions of its builders to its tenants to, finally, its service personnel. Each "society" is preoccupied by building and/or performing its particular form of agency. All of these actions are time- and energy-consuming, leaving to other forces the integration of these numerous autonomous preoccupations into the larger agency of the Suburban City. Since in Houston's case no one agency is in charge, I am assuming that some form of self-organization is taking place—aside from the construction of the centrally orchestrated principal infrastructure.

So, inside the autonomous agent of a PUD, the main preoccupation would be the organization and delivery to market of an agglomeration of single-family houses laid out along modestly curving streets. The MUD's preoccupation would be to see that enough service and (importantly) space exists for the PUD so it does not interfere with surrounding MUDs or prohibit access to the freeway system and all the accoutrements of the modern Suburban City. The endless Houston

Field has generously seen to this. But this generosity comes with an enormous expenditure of land (resulting in a Holey Plane), with parcels that may sit and wait for development for years. Once activated, these totally unregulated, leapfrogged lacunae allow for the real cowboy developers to live out their dreams. The result of this mosaic of the organized and the unplanned is a frazzled field characterized by a remarkable internal similarity, suggesting that a "collective mind" shared by all the players must govern these sprawling grounds.

Indeed, this initial collectivity prefigures and inscribes the outlines of life in the Suburban City. The built residue—the shadows of the collective action of the builders—in turn forms the fields, receptacles, and avenues of the city's denizens. Is suburban life, then, a mere facsimile of its construction? Clearly a strange and haunting formalism emerges as the planners, real estate agents, and PUD directors—but maybe even more so the carpenters, drywallers, plumbers, and landscapers in their highly stylized dance—construct the blueprint of suburban life. Might there be a formal linkage between the incessant cleaning performed by suburban dwellers and the overwriting of the previous work of its builders?

What will happen to the dwellers when builders begin to slowly convert their construction processes from the most "rational" to the greenest? Will they then change their lifestyle and turn from consumption to husbandry? Will Jefferson and Thoreau return to walk among us again? Will the shapes and 'scapes become one? (Of course they already are, even if we refuse to see this and act accordingly.) This insistent demand for integration will force each alphabetic trope in the abecedarium to abandon its introversion—its autonomy—and to radically lose its own horizon so as to act collectively, and thereby undo my entire project.

If my hint of self-organizing determinism has any bearing, then new builders have an opportunity—even a mission—to produce Massive Change and thereby help us begin anew.[3] The New Suburbia will no longer consist of fields of confetti with each morsel on its own errand, but will be a vast organism pulsating, however awkwardly, with what may be a kind of life.

3   Bruce Mau, Jennifer Leonard, and the Institute Without Boundaries, *Massive Change* (London: Phaidon Press, 2004).

Recycling Ecologies
Projects

Sharp Centre, Ontario College of Art and Design (OCAD)

Toronto, Canada, 2004
Will Alsop

The "tabletop" superstructure of the Sharp Centre takes the form of a paral-lelepiped 9 meters (30 feet) high, 31 meters (102 feet) wide, and 84 meters (275 feet) long, with striking black-and-white pixelated skin. It hovers 26 meters (85 feet) above the ground on 12 multicolored legs, creating a link-age between OCAD, the street, and Grange Park to the west. The radicality of the design solution was in truth the result of input from the community—students, staff, and locals—who made it clear, through a series of workshops, that they adamantly opposed a building that would occupy the designated site, cutting off both their visual and physical access to the nearby park. The solution for where to put the Sharp Centre was as pragmatic as it was unlikely: the building was levitated to such a height that it would not obscure the views of the park from the adjacent nine-story condominium tower. This in turn allowed the ground site to become an outdoor venue for additional arts-related events, at the same time directly linking neighbors to McCaul Street, as was their desire.

The new building provides two stories of studio and teaching space. It is connected to an existing facility below by an elevator-and-stair core that forms the central focus of a new four-story entrance hall, which unites the existing college buildings. The OCAD reminds us that we live in an archi-tectural free-for-all—a moment at which there is an ever-growing diversity of approach and style and no single design methodology. In such a context, the project represents one answer to the question of what might result if the architect invites a wider group of stakeholders to influence his/her work—what could be called *making noise*. In its unexpectedness, the Sharp Centre argues for a design process that is characterized less by solipsism, and more by a voyage of discovery, shared with the broad band of users who constitute today's public body.

Sketch done after a public design workshop revealed that the neighborhood did not want a building on the ground site

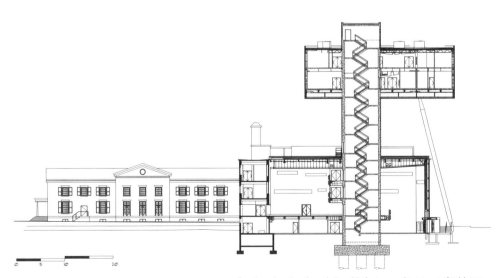

Section showing the relationship between the new roof tabletop and the existing building

The finished Sharp Centre: The tabletop evolved into a two-story box.

Looking south down McCaul Street

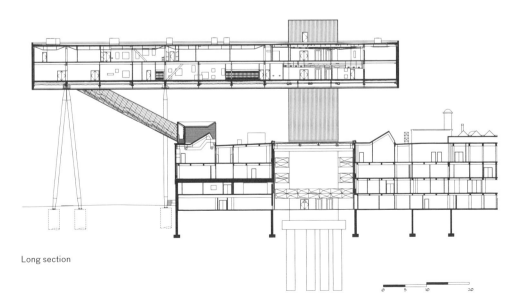

Long section

Camino Nuevo Charter Academy

Los Angeles, California, 2003–8
Daly Genik Architects

Created in response to substandard conditions and overcrowding in the local schools, the Camino Nuevo Charter Academy is an ongoing redevelopment project and experiment in public education in MacArthur Park, one of the most impoverished and densely populated neighborhoods in Los Angeles. The campus is the result of serial modifications to a group of low-rise wood-frame and masonry structures—the type of background buildings that make up much of Los Angeles and are used interchangeably as offices, warehouses, and commercial buildings. This group of buildings, constructed over a fifty-year time frame and largely derelict, were acquired over a period of five years and renovated in a "just in time" manner to accommodate the increasing enrollment and additional grade levels of Camino Nuevo.

Urban renewal strategies usually rely on an increase in density as part of their formula for success, as if density and urbanity were identical concepts. The Camino Nuevo neighborhood was already one of the most densely populated districts in Los Angeles, so an increase in density was not an issue. We felt a key factor in the reclamation of the neighborhood was to demonstrate to the community that the street could be successfully and safely reinhabited. We also had to acknowledge that the urban fabric that made up the Camino Nuevo sites was a bit tattered, and that the task of restoring it completely was well beyond the level of investment possible in these projects. We opted for a strategy of creating voids and transparencies in the existing building fabric in a manner that would allow views from the street to extend to the middle of the block, without compromising the secure perimeter of the buildings.

The first phase of the project reuses an existing mini-mall and parking deck, transforming this familiar commercial building type into a twelve-classroom elementary school. The school is organized around a courtyard used as a multipurpose outdoor assembly and play area. Curved lattices of Nexwood, a recycled wood product, shade the building and offer limited views of play activity from the street.

The second project, Camino Nuevo's middle school, was constructed in two stages: first, classrooms were built in a bowstring-trussed warehouse along an interior "street" that is open to the sky and provides natural light to each teaching space. This street is shared with the second part of the project, a renovated office building, which holds classrooms, labs, and a community health center. The facade of the complex facing Wilshire Boulevard was modified to allow natural daylight control through a scrim of perforated panels.

Adjacent to the middle school, in a third phase of work, a preschool and shared nonprofit dance studio were created by removing portions of another warehouse to create a mid-block garden and complete the process of adding to the neighborhood through subtraction. The area to be removed from the warehouse was established by state guidelines for outdoor play area per student. The newly created garden is visible through screened views from the street, bounded by the reconstructed-classroom perimeter of the playground.

Mini-mall as originally constructed

Second modification: Addition of
a classroom and utility building to
enclose the courtyard

First modification: Addition of
stage and access areas

Third modification: Addition of main exit stair
and lattice handrails at second-floor walkways

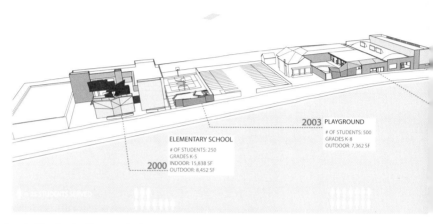

2003 PLAYGROUND
OF STUDENTS: 500
GRADES K-8
OUTDOOR: 7,362 SF

ELEMENTARY SCHOOL
OF STUDENTS: 250
GRADES K-5
2000 INDOOR: 15,838 SF
OUTDOOR: 8,452 SF

Chronology and enrollment of the Camino Nuevo project

View of the finished Camino Nuevo Elementary School

Burlington Avenue elevation prior to renovation

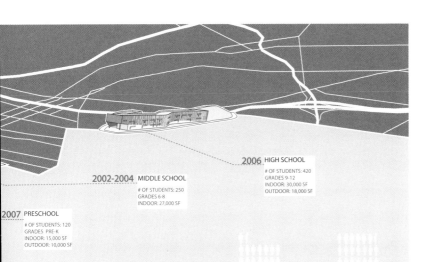

2006 HIGH SCHOOL
OF STUDENTS: 420
GRADES 9-12
INDOOR: 30,000 SF
OUTDOOR: 18,000 SF

2002-2004 MIDDLE SCHOOL
OF STUDENTS: 250
GRADES 6-8
INDOOR: 27,000 SF

2007 PRESCHOOL
OF STUDENTS: 120
GRADES PRE-K
INDOOR: 15,000 SF
OUTDOOR: 10,000 SF

Camino Nuevo High School from Silver Lake Boulevard

Burlington Avenue elevation following completion (from left) of Camino Nuevo Preschool and Middle School

Chia Mesa

Phoenix, Arizona

cityLAB / Roger Sherman Architecture and Urban Design

The repurposing of the strip center becomes the rebranding of Phoenix—from land of malls to land of mesas. Wrapped with a hydroponic farm, Chia Mesa represents both a prototype for transforming failing urban commercial centers and a recovery strategy for cities like Phoenix, where unbridled horizontal expansion into the outlying landscape has destroyed both its self-sufficiency (food supply) and identity. With Chia Mesa, a new image-ability emerges for the city as a whole—one whose morphology ironically recollects that of the landscape it is rapidly consuming. The Mesas will be the new landmarks of Phoenix's urban future, as the indistinct identity of that city develops an iconicity as unique and recognizable to the world as Dubai's palm islands or, closer to home, Las Vegas's neon glow.

Makeover

Chia Mesa brings life to a defunct strip mall, literally and figuratively. This 3.5-surface-acre hydroponic farm instantaneously gives the existing structure both an exterior identity and interior ambience, making it over into a bona fide urban destination. Occupying a zone varying between 3 and 9 feet in thickness, the farm is made up of water-fed plant trays and attendant service walkways covered by operable polycarbonate louvers. Three stories of additional rentable space and a new parking structure are accessed by means of bridges that span across a pedestrian "gorge" from one Mesa to the other. Those businesses advertise themselves to passersby on the north and west faces of the project, where the farm's polycarbonate screen is indented with "cliff-sellings," or signage that identifies the tenants behind. A drive-through biodiesel station, in a repurposed existing building, offers a direct link between the farm and consumer.

Chia Mesa = Chia Pet + Black Mesa (AZ) + strip center

Growing Green

Chia Mesa offers a strategy for land-constrained cities where farmland is no longer available. It offers residents fresh, locally grown produce, sparing the embodied economic and environmental costs of importing from California and beyond. Capitalizing upon the extreme productivity and profitability of hydroponic farming, it provides a financial robustness that pays for the cost of transforming the existing mall by gaining leverage from an industry whose long-term prospects are more secure than most retail and commercial tenants. But more than that, the color-striated lettuces, vegetables, flowers, and algae that wrap the shops and offices literally demonstrate a new desert ecology of cars, consumers, and productivity: climatically and socially "cool hotspots" in an arid field. The farm's interface with the commercial spaces and attendant parking is synergistic, offering an oasislike ambience and microclimate that redefines the shopping experience and public spaces associated with it. Chia Mesa will attract tenants ranging from natural food stores to juice bars, gyms, and urban spas—even a weekly farmers' market selling produce harvested on-site. The farm also brings collateral benefits to its microecology, as the hydroponic system naturally oxygenates the building's microclimate, generates moisture and precipitates that clean the high amounts of particulate matter in an arid climate, and, through evaporation, naturally cools the space.

Project team: Miguel Alvarez, Sergio Figuereido, Mira Henry, Quyen Luong, Brendan Muha, Travis Russett, Magdalena Stolarczyk, Jennifer Gilman (graphics), Mike Amaya (renderings), Tom Bonner (photography), and Jessica Campion (model)

View from Scottsdale Boulevard

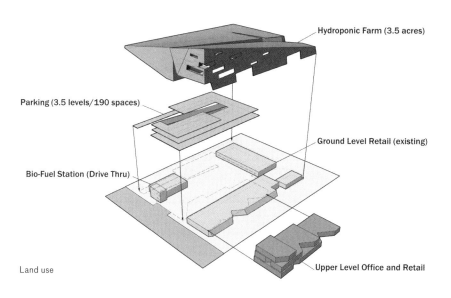

Hydroponic Farm (3.5 acres)

Parking (3.5 levels/190 spaces)

Ground Level Retail (existing)

Bio-Fuel Station (Drive Thru)

Upper Level Office and Retail

Land use

Chia Mesa from adjacent neighborhood (facing west)

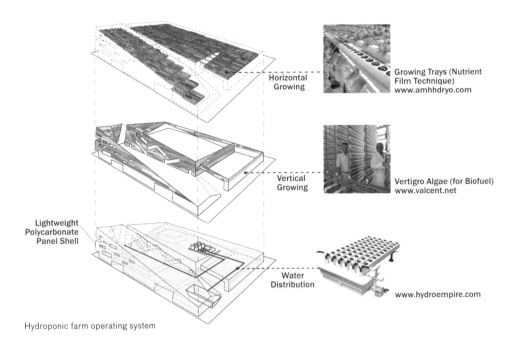

Horizontal Growing

Growing Trays (Nutrient Film Technique)
www.amhhdryo.com

Vertical Growing

Vertigro Algae (for Biofuel)
www.valcent.net

Lightweight Polycarbonate Panel Shell

Water Distribution

www.hydroempire.com

Hydroponic farm operating system

Model overview (from southeast)

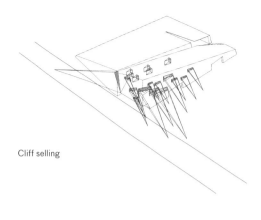

Cliff selling

View through gorge looking east

Bird's-eye view of the cumulative effect of Chia Mesa's proliferation on Phoenix's urban landscape

Chia Mesa from adjacent neighborhood (facing west)

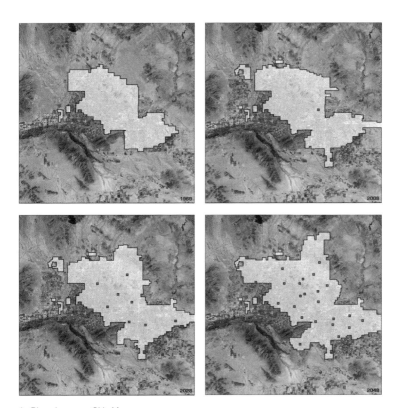

As Phoenix grows, Chia Mesas are sown.

Rerouting Infrastructure
Essays

Slow Infrastructure

Mario Gandelsonas

The infrastructure built in the United States in the first half of the twentieth century is crumbling. We are at a point in history where the problems caused by deferred maintenance have produced a number of major disasters. The August 2007 rush-hour collapse of a six-hundred-foot bridge along highway I-35W in Minneapolis that killed thirty people is only one in a long list. In May of 2003, the Silver Lake Dam in Michigan failed, causing one hundred million dollars in damages. Two years later, the inadequacies of the levees in New Orleans became horrifyingly clear in the aftermath of Hurricane Katrina in August of 2005. Only a month before the Minneapolis bridge collapse, a hundred-year-old steam pipe had erupted in midtown Manhattan, causing millions of dollars in lost business. These events have brought up questioning of the inaction that led to their occurrence, and increased calls for the repair and expansion of existing infrastructure.[1]

However, the problem goes beyond maintenance. The tendency to associate the term "infrastructure" with public works from the twentieth century prevents us from addressing the urgent need to rethink the very idea of infrastructure itself. Radical changes in telecommunications and "telemediatization," following the development of new technologies of media, communication, and information processing, have begun to challenge our understanding of our infrastructures—in particular those related to transportation—and the cultures associated with them.[2]

America's crumbling infrastructure is the manifestation of the early-twentieth-century European architectural avant-garde's notion of urbanism. Modern urbanists, most notably Le Corbusier, fantasized about replacing the dark, tortuous streets of the old cities with a new city that would welcome the sudden appearance of the machine, and, more specifically, the car. The

1   Bob Herbert, "Our Crumbling Foundation," *New York Times*, 5 Apr. 2007.

2   Telemediatization is defined as modes of electronic communication and media that together have fundamentally transformed global connectivity, time-space relations, and cultural experience. Telemediated practices include internet surfing, instant messaging, tweeting, Google-based research, television, texting, mobile phone photo-sharing, web-based social networking, and so on. See John Tomlinson, "Globalization and Cultural Analysis," in *Globalization Theory: Approaches and Controversy*, ed. David Held and Anthony McGrew (New York: Polity, 2007), 148–68.

modernist city was organized on the basis of the oppositional separation of drivers and pedestrians to facilitate the fluid movement of the automobile. The old city streets were seen as obstacles to movement that should be surgically removed.

The very same European cities that were seen as impediments to progress by the modernists also shaped our notion of an urban culture, which is embodied in an infrastructure of urban rooms, streets, and alleys.[3]

3   This text does not consider the less visible infrastructure (e.g., water, sewer, utilities, and so on) in order to focus on mobility in its relationship to accessibility and urbanity.

The role of this urban infrastructure had always been to allow for the movement of people, goods, and information, and therefore to provide accessibility and contact. It took centuries to restructure the existing labyrinth of urban streets and alleys into a network of wide avenues and boulevards to allow for more fluid movement. This began with Pope Sixtus V's restructuring of Rome at the end of the sixteenth century, with new avenues linking churches to allow for the flow of religious processions, and culminated in the late nineteenth century, with major European capitals being reworked into networks of avenues that slashed through the old medieval fabric, providing more direct access to cultural and political institutions. Train terminals occupied an important space in this network, marking the symbolic presence of the mechanical revolution in the form of the railroad.

Modernist urbanism, based in the hard technologies of the late-nineteenth- to early-twentieth-century mechanical revolution, promoted new urban concepts such as the grid, the highway, and the superblock. These concepts would completely replace the fabric of the old European city and allow the uninterrupted movement and high speed of the car to replace the slow speed of the pedestrian. On both sides of the Atlantic, changes in infrastructure, most notably the highway system and suburbanization, affected both the physical city and urban culture. In particular, the U.S. freeway system is one of the most important infrastructural works of the twentieth century, and constitutes the best example of the change in urban form as the result of changes in infrastructure. Overdetermined by the Cold War and the possibility of nuclear warfare, the National System of Interstate and Defense Highways was built to implement the strategy of dispersal called for by the National Industrial Dispersion Program, which planned for survival after an atomic attack. Laid out by highway designers in consultation with federal civil defense agencies, the highway system was inspired by the German Autobahn, built in the thirties.[4] The American highway system is still completely embedded in our urban life and consciousness as the infrastructural backbone of mid-century suburbanization.

However, for the last fifteen years we have entered a different situation characterized by a new condition of accessibility. Twentieth-century infrastructure allowed physical mobility based on the hard technologies of the mechanical revolution that dominated the previous century. In contrast, today's softer technologies—of electronic information processing and of media and communication systems—are generating new possibilities of interaction and contact for the production, reception, and distribution of information.[5] The processing of information had always been a unique role offered by cities, but the accelerated growth of telemediated activities has generated a radical change in the way we understand and practice accessibility. New values, experiences, and emerging fantasies are producing what has been called a new culture of immediacy. "Watching television, typing, scrolling, clicking, and browsing at the computer screen, talking, texting, or sending and receiving pictures on a mobile phone; tapping in PIN codes and conducting transactions on the keypad [of an ATM] although so much a routine and taken for granted should be seen as cultural practices."[6]

With the introduction of the latest information and communication devices, new couplings are produced between the new media, old media, hard infrastructure, the physical city, and the body. In fact, the vast spaces of train terminals represent the physical relationship between the railroad—the nineteenth-century hard infrastructure of transportation—and the city. While the coupling between the train and the city accelerates the latter's growth and density without modifying its structure in a substantial way, the

4   Peter Galison, "War Against the Center," *Grey Room* 4 (Summer 2001): 25.

5   John Tomlinson, *The Culture of Speed: The Coming of Immediacy* (Los Angeles: Sage Publications, 2007); see also Paul Virilio, *Open Sky*, trans. Julie Rose (New York: Verso, 1997). There have been two successive technological revolutions in mobility: the late-nineteenth- and early-twentieth-century transportation revolution and the late-twentieth- and early-twenty-first-century communications and media technologies revolution.

6   Tomlinson, *The Culture of Speed*, 94.

articulation of the city and the car, which takes place through the coupling of the house and the car, radically breaks away from the known city, creating a completely new urbanity.

This new urbanity, promoted by the dominance of the cars that rapidly replaced public transportation, also involves a third territory: the old media. The articulation between physical spaces and media started in the early twentieth century with the joining of the house, the telephone, and the radio—a grouping that had been dominant prior to World War II.[7] The growing dominance of the automobile in the mid-twentieth century established a new paradigm: the car as a mobile private space entwined with the fixed spaces of the city, and in particular with the house as well as contemporary media.

The coupling of the house and the radio was transformed by the introduction of the car and the television: the TV occupied the place of the radio within the house and displaced the radio to the car. A profound symbolic restructuring took place, where the logic of the supplement eventually supplanted what it was supposed to augment.[8] In the suburban context, the TV began to take the place of the central city and the car started to supplant the house.

Neither the mid-twentieth-century media nor the couplings mentioned above presupposed the obsolescence of the old media; the newer media altered the relationships established by the old media and at the same time, produced new ones. The physical/spatial city was also altered: old downtowns were radically transformed by the flight to the rapidly expanding suburbs, which soon surpassed the downtowns in size. Over the last fifteen years, new media technologies, like the personal computer, and associated practices have undermined the mid-twentieth-century paradigm and are now starting to produce the first new couplings of an emerging, early-twenty-first-century paradigm. The rituals of television culture and the collective reception of the 1950s (where the TV set was the focus of the family) are being replaced by rituals of a new culture of immediacy that is composed of structures of social networking and forms of producing, consuming, exchanging, and archiving information.[9]

7   Mario Gandelsonas, *X-Urbanism* (New York: Princeton Architectural Press, 1999).

8   Jacques Derrida, *De la Grammatologie* (Paris, Éditions de Minuit, 1967); see also Jacques Derrida, *Of Grammatology*, trans. Gayatri Chakravorty Spivak (Baltimore, MD: Johns Hopkins University Press, 1976).

9   Particularly for teenagers, telemediated activities and the related management of information are occupying an increasing amount of time, while the time devoted to the car and television are rapidly decreasing. The number of

teenagers using the internet grew 24 percent between 2001 and 2005 and is only continuing to climb, while the national rate of licensed sixteen-year-olds dropped to 29.8 percent in 2006 from 43.8 percent in 1998 according to the Federal Highway Administration. Mary M. Chapman and Micheline Maynard, "Fewer Youths Jump Behind the Wheel at 16," *New York Times*, 25 Feb. 2008.

10   Melvin Webber, "Urban Place and Nonplace Urban Realm," in *Explorations into Urban Structure* (Philadelphia: University of Pennsylvania Press, 1964).

11   See Diana Agrest, "The Misfortunes of Theory," in *Architecture from Without: Theoretical Framings for a Critical Practice* (Cambridge, MA: MIT Press, 1991).

12   The dangers of driving while using cell phones for calls or texting is increasingly leading states to prohibit cell phone use by drivers. Similarly, some teenagers prefer to be driven by parents so they can keep texting their friends, or even text friends in the car with

How are the media technologies integrating with patterns of physical mobility and space in the fluid, light modernity in which we live? Telemediatization is not promoting a sedentary life, as urban theorist Melvin Webber predicted in the 1960s and as urbanist Paul Virilio has argued more recently.[10] Rather, telemediatization has dynamically integrated an increasingly mobile population into a fluid modernity. It is fluid because contemporary culture is unfolding in the movement of the restless streets of the busy metropolis rather than in the isolated, controlled, and serviced environment of a wired dwelling. Beginning in the early twentieth century, the house functioned as a center for information management, first through radio and telephone and then through television. The increased mobility provided by the coupling of the latest technologies and the body has caused a shift in the role of the house, which has become the fixed personal center of telemediated activities where the "heavier" infrastructure is located, such as servers, large-screen televisions, and high-speed, wired connections to the internet.[11] How does the new media technology change the imagined relationship to the places we inhabit? The constant switching—from radio to TV to music player, to email and to internet browsing, to computer and to phone—is an activity not just associated with the stable, fixed place of the office or home but now commonly projected onto the public or semipublic spaces of the city.

While the introduction of the car produced radical changes in urban structure, the rise of new technologies is causing a similar shift in the role of the car as the dominant means of transportation in the United States. In fact, the car is incompatible with the perceptual demands of telemediatization. On the other hand, public transportation, such as the train and the airplane, are rapidly adapting to these new demands. The incompatibility of driving and telemediatization presupposes the need for forms of transportation that allow the mobile twenty-first-century individual to maintain contact.[12] The transportation needs of the mobile, telemediated individual will certainly promote in

them to avoid being overheard. See Laura M. Holson, "Text Generation Gap: UR 2 Old (JK)," *New York Times*, 9 Mar. 2008.

13 "As metropolitan regions continued to expand throughout the second half of the 20th century their boundaries began to blur, creating a new scale of geography now known as the megaregion." America 2050, "Megaregions," http://www. america2050.org/megaregions. html (accessed 30 Aug. 2009).

14 I am paraphrasing Virilio, *Open Sky*, 9–25.

15 Ibid.

16 Saskia Sassen, *The Global City: New York, London, Tokyo* (Princeton, NJ: Princeton University Press, 1991).

the middle and long term a fundamental restructuring of cities themselves.[13]

In the twenty-first century, it is the notion of mobility itself that is changing. For example, Virilio argues that there has been a shift in emphasis from the physical mobility of people and objects through physical space to the virtual mobility of signal input and output, and from departure to arrival within electronic space. As opposed to the coupling between infrastructure and the city represented by the monumental train terminals of the mechanical revolution, a new relationship exists between the new soft technologies and the body. The new terminals cease to be fixed points in physical space organizing our patterns of mobility. We carry them with, and perhaps soon within, ourselves.[14] Each of us is a potential terminal. This transformation is made possible as the easy communication of the mobile phone morphs into a mini handheld computer, social networking device, and tiny, individual movie screen. The new effortless and ever-present technology appears to close the gap—preserved by the mechanical revolution—between here and elsewhere, now and later, desire and fulfillment.[15]

The coupling between new technology and the body also has major implications at the social level, and in particular at the economic level, where cities behave as economic engines. For example, the new global economy contains electronically based communities of individuals and organizations that interact in the nonphysical, nonspatial, electronic realm. The internet enables these economic actors to relate to each other in real time, seemingly disregarding the fixed spaces of the physical cities around them.

Despite its pervasiveness, this new economic geography is only one fragmented moment in a vast chain of events that remain embedded in nonelectronic spaces that are never fully dematerialized.[16] Digitization has not eliminated the need for spaces and infrastructure, but has fostered a dispersal of activities that can be developed independent of any fixed physical location. In most instances this dynamic has contributed to the most negative aspects of exurban growth: the internet exchanges and the groups of scaleless distribution centers, built in places such as Woodbridge and other New Jersey towns, but also all over exurban America. The counterpart of the dispersal promoted by the digital is a new logic for the aggregation of activities. An example of this are the forms of articulation of people and territory revealed by the patterns of spatial centralization in the dense new suburban subcenters, correlated to the continuing growth of the exurban city. [17]

17   The 2004 U.S. Census describes the new suburban "centers" developed by Latino communities in Atlanta, Georgia.

Perhaps the most profound implication of this paradigmatic change takes place in the restructuring of the experience of urban contact. The accidental physical encounter—the quintessential attribute of the urban realm—had been greatly reduced in twentieth-century American cities because of the dominance of the car as a mode of transportation and the type of urbanization it promoted. Instead, we saw an increase in various forms of attenuated contact, such as visual interaction between drivers and the violent contact of the car accident, which has been described as an accidental, physical encounter fostered by the suburban and the contemporary exurban city.[18] In fact, since the mid-twentieth century the possibilities for this kind of interaction, opened by twentieth-century infrastructure, have increased exponentially, while the possibilities for face-to-face contact have been greatly reduced, first with the development of the suburban city and then in the last twenty-five years by the new diffuse, scattered, and ever-expanding exurban city.

18   Mario Gandelsonas, introduction to *In Search of the Public*, a forthcoming publication from the Center for Architecture, Urbanism, and Infrastructure at Princeton University; see also Jon Garvie, "Who lives by the road, dies by the road," in *Times Online*, 3 Dec. 2008, http://entertainment.timesonline.co.uk/tol/arts_and_entertainment/the_tls/article5278712.ece.

Another type of attenuated contact that has increased exponentially is the digital encounter promoted by the internet. Some of the constraints of human embodiment have been overcome by the coupling of the new teletechnologies and the body/subject: first, because of the portability of new media and the perception that the world moves along with the individual at its center, and second, because of the phenomenon of telepresence and the resulting condition of immediacy that has created an apparent closure of the gap between people. However, the immediacy of contact limited to the modality of electronic communication is not supplanting face-to-face contacts, but seems to complement them.[19] Although the recent development of internet-based social networking (on sites like Facebook and MySpace) would first seem to work against the survival, persistence, and growth of face-to-face interactions, the opposite seems to be true, as seen, for example, in the increased popularity of libraries in the last few years, a situation that has accelerated with the current financial crisis.[20]

Contact is precisely what provides social enjoyment and the high returns that make urban life truly rich. For this reason, the desire for a coupling between new technology and spaces that offer opportunities for and facilitate contact—both the accidental physical encounter and the digital encounter allowed by teletechnologies—will continue to grow as well. The accelerating increase in the use of libraries, the exponential growth of cafes in the last few years (both independent and owned by corporations), and the proliferation of indoor and outdoor places for physical activity illustrate different forms of this new desire for contact. And mobility is increasing as well: the new connectedness is increasing both internet traffic and real traffic, in particular because the new social networks include people who do not live nearby and therefore travel to connect. The constraints of the physical world, of the embodied human condition, and ultimately of the exurban city are contributing to the continuous growth of the vast contemporary economy of transportation in America, with a growing emphasis on trains and light-rail.[21]

What will the infrastructure that serves the new culture of immediacy be? What would be the twenty-first-century equivalent of the mid-twentieth-century Interstate and Defense Highway system? Current trends point to the creation of a new slow infrastructure: public transportation that can perform as a "mobile base" for the millions of body-terminals that are constantly plugged into the new soft electronic infrastructure. The new slow, or soft, infrastructure that traverses every one of the eleven megaregions proposed by the Regional Plan Association will be connected to a restructured, augmented, and expanded twenty-first-century

19 Jeffrey Boase, John Horrigan, Barry Wellman, and Lee Rainie, "The Strength of Internet Ties," *Pew Internet & American Life Project*, 25 Jan. 2006, http://www.pewinternet.org/Reports/2006/The-Strength-of-Internet-Ties.aspx?r=1.

20 Contrary to fears that email would reduce other forms of contact, there is "media multiplexity": the more contact by email, the more in-person and phone contact. As a result, Americans are probably more in contact with members of their communities and social networks than before the advent of the internet. Ibid.

21 "With $8 billion in federal stimulus money allocated for passenger rail projects, the States for Passenger Rail Coalition foresees the beginning of a new era of expanded intercity passenger rail service throughout America. The projects will expand and enhance passenger rail service in multiple ways, while creating thousands of new, good-paying jobs across the nation. In addition, President Obama has indicated that another $5 billion can be expected over the next five years, from the administration's proposed transportation budget." Trains for America, "States Expect

Rail Growth," 18 Mar. 2009. http://trains4america.wordpress.com/2009/03/18/states-expect-rail-growth/. These projects could be considered the first step in the consolidations of the megaregions (see note 13).

22   "Most of the nation's rapid population growth, and an even larger share of its economic expansion, is expected to occur in 10 or more emerging megaregions: large networks of metropolitan regions, each megaregion covering thousands of square miles and located in every part of the country....The recognition of the megaregion as an emerging geographical unit also presents an opportunity to reshape large federal systems of infrastructure and funding....Just as the Interstate Highway System enabled the growth of metropolitan regions during the second half of the 20th century, emerging megaregions will require new transportation modes that work for places 200–500 miles across." America 2050, "Megaregions."

23   Donna Jeanne Haraway, "A Cyborg Manifesto: Science, Technology, and Socialist-Feminism in the Late Twentieth Century," in Simians, Cyborgs, and Women: The Reinvention of Nature (New York: Routledge, 1991), 149–81.

fast, and hard, infrastructure.[22] While the restructured, hard infrastructure will consolidate the megaregions and link them together at a national level using high-speed trains, buses, and airlines, a new slow infrastructure will organize the multiple scales within the different megaregions (from microscale to macroscale, i.e., from the neighborhood to the town, city, metropolis, and megaregion). This slow infrastructure will also restructure the green and open spaces, provide alternative energy, manage the waters, and allow for a multiplicity of movement systems that will support the millions of body-terminals. Architects and urban designers should be assigned the urgent task of finding public moments and spaces where interaction and contact with others are possible and developing the strategies and tactics needed to inhabit these emerging public spaces.

The new slow infrastructure proposes a displacement from the spatial to the temporal, from strict functionality to a multiplicity of overlapping activities and spaces of enjoyment. This displacement opens up new possibilities with respect to the object and the subject of infrastructure. This is particularly true for the new twenty-first-century body: a body that has been restructured in the last twenty years with prosthetic extensions and connecting fields that have constantly and continuously reinvented it.[23] Rethinking the object of infrastructure will displace the exclusive focus on the kind of accessibility that is provided by physical mobility, and replace that focus with an awareness of the new telemediated accessibility that constitutes the culture of immediacy. Rethinking infrastructure will also promote the

study of possibilities for articulating new twenty-first-century infrastructure inside, on top of, beneath, and beside hard twentieth-century infrastructure. It will also create new sites for architectural intervention, for the design and implementation of new types of sustainable, slow infrastructure from the local level to the national level of the megaregions.

Infrastructure of Urban Enjoyment: The South Amboy Greenway

The construction of the railroad in the nineteenth century produced one of the most important changes in the spatial and social organization of the United States: the generation of a new urbanity. For instance, every stop of the New Jersey Transit Rail encouraged urban growth. However, the demise of a number of routes and services in the mid-twentieth century produced a no-man's-land that cuts through towns and cities, fragmenting them and separating neighborhoods. Service cuts also produced a reserve of undeveloped land, and an opportunity uncovered in the South Amboy Greenway project, developed by Agrest and Gandelsonas Architects.

24   The South Amboy Greenway (SAG) is an example of slow infrastructure at the microscale of a town. SAG will have to be developed down to the scale of the neighborhood and up to the scale of the entire town. It is a close-up of a town that needs to be articulated within a necklace of greenways, forming a green spine at the mesoscale of the state of New Jersey, the densest state in the United States and the geographic center of the northeastern megaregion.

The South Amboy Greenway recuperates 340 acres of undeveloped land adjacent to the railroad in the city of South Amboy, one of the stops of the New Jersey Transit Rail. The project proposes a transformation of the old, semifast infrastructure of the railroad into a new type of slow infrastructure: a green zone for walking, jogging, biking, rollerblading, skateboarding, and horseback riding articulated by public spaces and sports and cultural facilities, all powered by solar panels and clusters of wind turbines.[24]

At the physical level, the greenway sutures the cut inflicted by the railroad, stitching together the neighborhoods that have been split from the downtown. At the social level, the transformation of the urban object—the undeveloped land adjacent to the railroad—produces a transformation of the subject—the twenty-first-century urban actor and viewer—providing new "activity nodes," articulating continuously flowing green vectors, and linking new viewing positions that completely change the perception of the city.

Stitches and Insertions

Linda C. Samuels

The city can no longer be understood holistically, if indeed it ever was. Comprehensive urban visions, with their bureaucratically determined hierarchies and rigid order, not only lean toward the exclusionary and elitist—in both process and product—but their stiffness denies the real fluctuations of occupation at ground level. Even the semipredictable development waves of expansion and gentrification have slowed and veered off course in an environment no longer suited to limitless consumption. Though the majority of the world's population now lives in urbanized areas, our current definition of "urbanized" is simultaneously more inclusive and more amorphous.[1] The new city (from void center to densifying exurb) is no longer one to be abandoned (for a more idyllic suburbia) or hidden (through gentrification), but one to be reconfigured (with stitches) and refilled (with insertions). The city must cease to expand, and must instead be treated and retrained. This urban strategy goes beyond traditional reuse and recycling and calls for reinvention through the reconsideration of architecture as a form of urban surgery.

This new city requires flexibility, where regulations and limitations bend to accommodate new uses, people, and ideas. Because the categories of urban and suburban, center and periphery are no longer valid geographic descriptors, some reconfigurations intentionally juxtapose these once-oppositional attributes. Urban historian Dolores Hayden first proposed bringing urban ideals to the suburban setting in her 1980 article, "What Would a Non-Sexist City Be Like?" By taking thirteen typical (and typically inefficient) single-family suburban lots and combining their private backyards and select service spaces—kitchens, laundry rooms, and garages—into shared utilities, the collective gained public amenities, reduced redundancy, and created work opportunities

1   According to the Census 2000 Geographic Definitions (which can be accessed online at http://www.census.gov/geo/www/geo_defn.html), the "urban" designation includes all "territory, population, and housing units located within an urbanized area (UA) or an urban cluster (UC)," which are defined as "block groups or blocks that have a population density of at least 1,000 people per square mile at the time and surrounding census blocks that have an overall density of at least 500 people per square mile at the time."

2 Dial-a-ride is an on-demand car service that, in addition to providing a new suburban job type, also would reduce or eliminate the need for individual car ownership and car storage.

in the newly introduced grocery store, day care center, and "dial-a-ride."[2] This reconfiguration also allowed a distribution of home-based tasks and new social opportunities to help combat suburbia's domestic segregation. In Hayden's scenario, the single-family house could alternatively be subdivided into a denser triple unit—consisting of a two bedroom, a one bedroom, and an efficiency apartment—with private gardens and shared amenities. These reconfigured houses could be liberally scattered among their more conventional single-family neighbors, allowing for a hybrid compactness that maintains the usefulness of existing housing stock and open space.[3] Though Hayden's collective living strategies have rarely been implemented by architects, in places such as Gulfton, Texas—where fast-growing immigrant populations have filled the same garden apartments once populated by young singles—suburbia's density overall is beginning to exceed that of some still-sparse urban cores. Once a sprawling neighborhood of ranch houses and two-roommate units, Gulfton is now the densest neighborhood in Houston, with a population estimated to be as high as twenty thousand people per square mile.[4]

3 Dolores Hayden, "What Would a Non-Sexist City Be Like?, Speculations on Housing, Urban Design, and Human Work," Signs 5, no. 3, supplement: "Women and the American City" (Spring 1980): 170–87; available online at http://www.jstor.org/stable/3173814.

4 Susan Rogers, "Superneighborhood 27: A Brief History of Change," Places 17, no. 2 (Apr. 2005): 36–41. Comparatively, Houston in general has an average citywide density of roughly thirty-five-hundred people per square mile according to the 2000 U.S. Census.

This reconfiguration strategy is also being tested in the commercial markets of suburbia. Excessive numbers of strip malls and big-box stores constructed during boom times have resulted in millions of vacant square feet of abandoned large-span retail. In Charlotte, North Carolina, an old Kmart has become the Sugar Creek Charter School, housing kindergarten through eighth grade with a plethora of parking and vast spaces for indoor athletics. Rather than a typical fast-food franchise or retail chain, the adjacent outparcel building is the Sugar Creek Neighborhood Services Center—a library, JobLink center, and police headquarters. Journalist Joel Garreau speculates on big-box recycling in his "Edgier Cities" essay, published in *Wired* magazine. In one scenario, the abandoned big-box stores are rediscovered by hippies and bohemians seeking large amounts of cheap square footage for artists' studios. The new inhabitants cut holes in the expansive roofs for skylights, fill potholes in the parking lot with greenery, and use the open dock spaces for welding massive metal sculptures. In another scenario, the old Macy's and Nordstrom in the high-end mall are turned into the lecture halls of great universities, vacant hotels become dormitories, and abandoned office parks morph into a clustered fraternity row. Ultimately, the most elaborate of the malls are again reinvented, exploited for their granite opulence as giant temples to house growing populations of devout Muslims and Mormons.[5]

5   Joel Garreau, "Edgier Cities," *Wired* (Dec. 1995): 158–63, 232–34.

Architecture firm Lewis.Tsurumaki.Lewis (LTL) picks up where Garreau's speculation leaves off, pushing the strategy from stitch to insertion. Their New Suburbanism proposals eliminate redundancy in the vein of Hayden (hers programmatic and spatial, theirs structural and spatial) while capitalizing on the underutilized opportunities of the massiveness of our suburban prototypes. Unlike the programmatic replacement of Garreau, LTL's hybrid projects seek to urbanize suburbia, transferring the square footage and luxury of the McMansion onto the currently unused roofscapes of big-box stores. ›› fig. 1

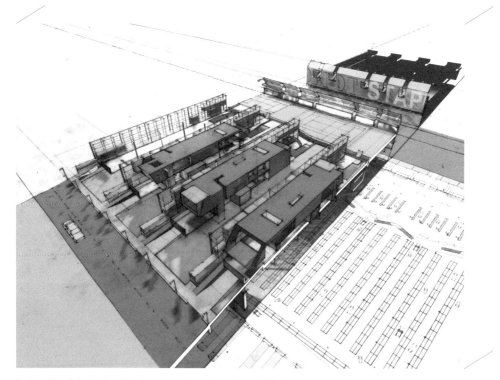

fig. 1 ›› New Suburbanism: Housing, recreation, and big-box retail hybrid

The structural grid below provides support, lot lines, and formal order for the housing above. Fire sprinklers double as lawn irrigation; excess heat production from the retailers contributes to the landscape ecosystem of the housing.[6] » fig. 2

6   Paul Lewis, Marc Tsurumaki, and David J. Lewis, "New Suburbanism" in *Lewis. Tsurumaki.Lewis: Opportunistic Architecture* (New York: Princeton Architectural Press, 2007), 100–9.

A dense suburbia seemed nearly impossible when Hayden dreamed of it in 1980, but today it is not so inconceivable to imagine taking new advantage of the vast physical attributes that once defined suburbia: parking, column-free square footage, green space, and linear road surface, all in abundance. These traits were initially part of a more spacious and healthy lifestyle and could again be reimagined as amenities rather than

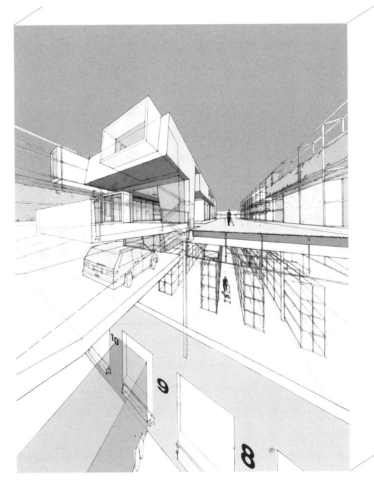

fig. 2 » New Suburbanism: Separate housing is above and commercial space below, with multipurpose utilities. Fire sprinklers from the big-box stores double as lawn sprinklers for the residential yards, and houses tap into the commercial-scale heat and air-conditioning systems to reduce redundancy.

detriments—particularly as their social and political roles demand reconsideration in the public/private negotiations of this new hybrid (sub) urbanity. As architect Michael Sorkin's book *Variations on a Theme Park* envisaged, the city of the 1990s and early 2000s would be one coping with the neoliberal results of privatization and paranoia, resorting to a publicness found primarily in the commercial outlets of shopping, the media outlets of first television and now the internet, and the collective, mesmerizing space of the freeway.[7]

7 Michael Sorkin, ed., *Variations on a Theme Park: Scenes from the New American City and the end of Public Space* (New York: Hill and Wang, 1992).

The Dead Malls Competition, run by the LA Forum in 2002, was a proactive attempt to focus attention on the opportunities made available through the architectural reinvention of suburbia. In this competition, the mall was revealed as a location requiring often drastic reconsideration of its current anti-civic, profit-oriented isolationism. Like the Sugar Creek Charter School, the cross-platform strategies propose programming that capitalizes on the spatial similarities of the mall prototype, either in scale or typology, with displaced or unmet needs. The adaptation of Big Town Mall in Mesquite, Texas, by Jeremy Hahn, Beau Smith, and Tate Selby matched a glut of large retail space against a shortage of high school athletic facilities, placing a sporting goods store and a hockey rink in the anchor positions while removing the roof and select stores along the central spine to reconfigure the space for other sports programming. Most common in the competition entries were strategies reimagining the privatized mall as a self-sustaining community, particularly by densifying the existing open site with the complex functions necessary to sustain a real city: markets, office space, schools, parks, religious institutions, and housing. Ecologically sensitive solutions opened up the segregated environments of interior versus exterior and paved versus plantable to create a more balanced relationship between controlled and uncontrolled environments. Capitalizing on the sheer scale of the abandoned mall, several proposals included alternative energy capture as a new ambition for empty parking lots and untapped roof surfaces. Many solutions sought reengagement with the local community either by providing civic resources or by more directly connecting the retail function to regional suppliers rather than distant conglomerate chains. Regardless of the precise design direction, nearly all the solutions required that the quasi-public space of the current mall be reconsidered as a real public space, meaning that its economic model be based on more than a traditional, single market to succeed in the flexible, socio-spatial economy implied by insertion urbanism.[8]

No American city is more in need of repair and reinvention than Detroit. A city that in the last fifty years has lost 50 percent of its population, Detroit has become an infamous symbol of slow urban decline.[9] Several projects of note apply stitching or implantation strategies in an attempt to rethink the city's next phase. Interboro's Improve Your Lot! project formalizes a preexisting trend, where homeowners surrounded by vacant lots purchase or "borrow" the empty land next door for their own use. These "blots" (block + lot) begin to stitch small urban lots into two, four, six, or more lot combinations that, fenced together, create inner-city suburban estates, while at the same time saving the city millions of dollars per year in property upkeep costs. These new lot combinations also alter the rigid thirty-foot-by-one-hundred-foot lot grid and provide a variety of scales and configurations to meet the self-determined needs of the remaining city inhabitants. In the words of Interboro, the blots are "a gradual rewiring of the City's genetic code: a large-scale, unplanned re-platting of the City that will happen through the bottom-up actions of thousands of individual homeowners." The flexibility of the blots and of the city to legally accommodate alternative means of property appropriation begins to distribute control from the typical top-down scenario to one that is grassroots inspired.[10]

Stalking Detroit, a 2001 volume of essays, design projects, and photographs, documents a kind of obsessive-compulsive affair with Detroit's dereliction just prior to the turn of the millennium.[11] Through a multidisciplinary collection of observers, the loved but rotting body of the city is exposed as both a vestige of the historical lineage of Ford's invention and a thick palimpsest ripe

8 Warren Techentin, ed., *Dead Malls* (Los Angeles: Los Angeles Forum for Architecture and Urban Design, 2004).

9 These figures are a comparison of the 1950 Census and the 2000 Census as referred to in Charles Waldheim and Marili Santos-Munne's essay, "Decamping Detroit," in *Stalking Detroit*, ed. Georgia Daskalakis, Charles Waldheim, and Jason Young (Barcelona: Actar, 2001), 105.

10 Tobias Armborst, Daniel D'Oca, and Georgeen Theodore (Interboro), "Improve Your Lot!" accessible at Cities Growing Smaller Downloads, http://www.cudc.kent.edu/shrink/CGS/cgsdownload.html.

11 Daskalakis, Waldheim, and Young, eds., *Stalking Detroit*.

for new insertions. The essay "Decamping Detroit," written by Charles Waldheim and Marili Santos-Munne, begins with a recap of the shocking 1990 *Detroit Vacant Land Survey*, which quantitatively formalized the drastic decline in inner-city population and recommended the decommissioning of the most blighted areas of the city. "The empty houses would be demolished and empty areas fenced off. They would either be landscaped, or allowed to return to 'nature.'"[12] These recommendations were met with hostility even though they actually reflected the ongoing demographic reality. Rather than disregarding this complicated truth, "Decamping Detroit" takes the prevalence of "unbuilding" as a design generator. The essay proposes decamping seven areas of Detroit with greater than 70 percent vacant land, beginning with the process of dislocation: relocating remaining inhabitants, cutting services, and encouraging the natural entropic processes. Dislocation is followed by erasure, absorption, and infiltration, each of which further clears the land of remaining development detritus (even encouraging the role of the arsonists) while introducing a zone-specific, rapid-growth ecology. Post-decommissioning, these spaces are available for new insertions (the team's design suggestions include a suburban campground, migrant worker mobile-homesteads, and an exurban survival training course).[13] As James Corner responds, the city is not simply 'scaped, but *scraped*, newly rid of "its various residues: symbolic, political, and material," leaving it ready for reinvention and rebirth.[14]

The *Detroit Vacant Land Survey* can't help but bring to mind a similar suggestion made in the "Bring New Orleans Back" plan for evacuation of the Lower Ninth Ward and other flood-prone areas destroyed by Hurricanes Katrina and Rita. In the case of New Orleans, the suggestion to abandon these areas of the city (which include the homes of the city's poorest and most disenfranchised) was also politically volatile. Like politicians in Detroit twenty years prior, New Orleans Mayor Ray Nagin rescinded his support of the shrinking city initiative in favor of a plan that trumpeted every citizen's right to return and rebuild, regardless of geographical

12 "Day of the Bulldozer," *The Economist*, 8 May 1993; as quoted in Waldheim and Santos-Munne, "Decamping Detroit," 105.

13 Waldheim and Santos-Munne's team also included Tom Reid as project assistant and Barbara Ackermann, Jaydeep Baghat, Daniela Konrad, Henrik Lunden, Silke Lux, Igor Marjanovic, and Andrew Young as production assistants.

14 Waldheim and Santos-Munne, "Decamping Detroit," 105–25.

fragility. In both cities, though, there are architects and planners who recognize that traditional reconstruction is a retrospective, if politically safe, response. In New Orleans the more radical and visionary solution may be drastic dissections and transplants that return low-lying areas to more natural, flood-protective wetlands, and increased density on higher ground; water must be reimagined as a volatile yet long-term resource rather than an uncontrollable enemy. Where Detroit's decline is just becoming old enough for some emotional objectivity, the freshness of the Gulf Coast wounds make the personal tragedy still too inseparable from the urban tragedy to entertain such controversial visions.

Lastly, the space of the road is an untapped site for both stitches and insertions. The long stretches of highway between the old core and its outer sprawl remain underutilized, though several small-scale projects hint at ways we might reconsider the road space. Mark Oberholzer's entry in the *Metropolis* Next Generation design competition for 2006 incorporates wind turbines in New Jersey barriers to capture the currently wasted energy generated by multidirectional car traffic.[15] In the same competition a year later, fieldoffice's runner-up entry superABSORBER consisted of a barrier wall with a chemical additive that helps oxidize airborne pollutants. This roadside experiment is currently being tested in Los Angeles, where a 2003 restriction on school building near highways and a shortage of affordable and accessible sites are in direct conflict.[16]

These types of technologically forward details, combined with large-scale stitches like the High Line reinvention in New York City, are initial steps in the greater effort to reimagine our vast infrastructure as new sites for social, spatial, or ecological insertions. Forward-thinking infrastructure competitions like WPA 2.0, run out of UCLA's cityLAB, encouraged the reimagining of once-monofunctional, pragmatic services into public and productive urban contributors.[17] The winning scheme, Carbon T.A.P. // Tunnel Algae Park by PORT: Architecture + Urbanism, is a new infrastructural prototype, an insertion between Manhattan and Brooklyn that, by operating on the Brooklyn-Battery Tunnel,

15 Rebecca Cavanaugh, "The *New* Jersey Barrier," *Metropolis*, posted 10 Jan. 2007, http://www.metropolis-mag.com/story/20070110/the-new-i-jersey-barrier.

16 Suzanne LaBarre, "School Haze," *Metropolis*, posted 19 Mar. 2008, http://www.metropolismag.com/story/20080319/school-haze.

17 In the spirit of full disclosure, the author is a senior research associate at cityLAB under the leadership of Dana Cuff (cityLAB director), Roger Sherman (cityLAB codirector), and Tim Higgins (cityLAB associate director).

transforms polluting carbon emissions into alternative fuel generators, housed on a pivoting armature that also functions as public park space, bike paths, and a wildlife preserve. ›› fig. 3 Many of the more-than-three-hundred submissions explored stitch and insertion strategies, turning banal water, energy, and mobility infrastructures into eco-sensitive, multifunctional, design-savvy public amenities.

fig. 3 ›› The pivoting Tunnel Algae Park armature between Governors Island toward Lower Manhattan captures carbon dioxide from the Brooklyn-Battery Tunnel below to supply a large-scale algae farm that doubles as a dynamic urban park, replete with structured wetlands, aquatic and avian habitats, recreation amenities, high-speed bike lanes, and public promenades.

There is no shortage of opportunities to reconfigure and refill the existing city. One spreading example is the urban agriculture movement, a prolific, visible, and fairly inexpensive yet highly effective stitch.

According to Richard Reynolds's book *On Guerrilla Gardening*, a group known as the Green Guerrillas began cultivating abandoned lots on New York's Lower East side in the 1970s.[18] Now guerrilla gardening is an international phenomena, where those interested in the health and aesthetics of their neighborhoods—in addition to alternative ways to form community—have begun to maintain "orphan lots." Reynolds's objective, like many other guerrilla gardeners, is not sustenance-related per se, but encourages active participation in the quality and appearance of the city, and in the action of citizenship itself. By taking back responsibility for our physical environment—by stitching and inserting from the ground up rather than from the top down—we break "out of the unconstructive role we've cast ourselves in as citizens," and instead of just being passive nondestructors, we become active contributors and producers.[19] Along the same lines, Fritz Haeg's Edible Estates project inserts the urban garden into the suburban front lawn, taking cues from Hayden and LTL to maximize suburban spatial infrastructure, disrupt the expectations of public and private, and dispel the artificial purity of suburban prototypes and symbols. ›› figs. 4 + 5

18 Jon Mooallem, "Guerrilla Gardening," the *New York Times Magazine*, 8 June 2008, 78.

19 Ibid.

figs. 4 + 5 ›› Edible Estate Regional Prototype Garden #2: Lakewood, California

From the micro to the macro, these strategies of stitching and insertion demand structural flexibility to break the limitations that have helped maintain the trailing vestiges of a hegemonic urban cosmology. To save the city, we must first let it go. This brief survey of projects lays out a precedent set of alternative models for architecture that deserve deeper attention and more widespread application. With the near global shrinking of spending and increased attention to natural resources, design incisions must operate more strategically to challenge the status quo of urban repair. Gained flexibility encourages design visions that cross disciplines—architecture, planning, landscape, transportation—and stereotypes—suburban, urban, yard, road, big box, mall. The intentional dematerialization of these boundaries allows the cracks in the city to be progressively reconfigured and refilled rather than more predictably recycled and reused.

From Form to Space

Albert Pope

Consider for a moment that old, gridded cities like Los Angeles and New York are today as quaint and outmoded as the medieval hill town. They are outdated because the cores of these cities are regulated by an ancient urban meter—a regular, structured order of city blocks that establishes the baseline of traditional urban experience. This structured order exists in almost every city today, and I will argue that it constitutes the very definition of a city. Like the gridded cities that preceded it, the primary characteristics of the American gridiron are derived from a direct experience of these structured block forms. It is in this regard that we can describe the urban cores of Los Angeles and New York as preeminent examples of cities that are dominated by form.

That the city of form still commands our urban imagination does not change the fact that the structured order of city blocks vanished as the dominant motif of urban production in the years following the Second World War. At that time, the city that had heretofore been dominated by structured form was replaced by a city that was dominated by an unstructured type of urban space. Over the past half-century, this new type of unstructured space has come into existence as an apparent by-product of sprawling, megalopolitan development. At the word itself implies, sprawl has no cognitive structure that is equivalent to the traditional, metric order of blocks and streets. Sprawl is routinely characterized as a horizontal expanse of isolated and indifferent objects arbitrarily set within large fields of amorphous space. It is the experience of this space, not the forms within it, that determines the principal characteristic of the megalopolis. The importance of this shift from a city dominated by form to a city dominated by space cannot be underestimated. It is the precipitating cause underlying the dramatic transformations that have occurred in cities built over the past half-century.

Despite the ubiquity of megalopolitan sprawl (and the fact that the majority of the world's population lives in buildings built in the past fifty years), the extinction of gridiron urbanism still fails to command our attention. This is not only because so much gridiron infrastructure still exists, but also because the city that is dominated by structured form continues to claim our urban imagination. The continued equation of urbanism with structured form accounts for the central predicament facing our attempts to construct urban theory today: *our understanding or imagination of the city runs counter to the urbanism that is currently being produced.* In other words, how we think of the city does not coincide with how we build it. Despite the fact that it is obsolete, the city of structured form continues to dominate our conception of the city. This inability to keep up with what is actually happening on the ground is perhaps not surprising, but it has thrown the logic of the actual city into a conceptual shadow, leaving our understanding of contemporary urbanism drastically limited. Useless, pejorative terms—sprawl, slum, blight—are the tacit indicators of a subspecies of urbanism that has failed to claim our imagination.

This essay attempts to elucidate the logic of a city that is dominated by unstructured space, and to formulate an architectural specification based on that logic. I will argue that the megalopolis is anything but sprawl, but has a manifest order that, when properly recognized, can be effectively engaged in the process of design. While the urbanism of an unstructured space is new, its mode of organization is not. This mode of organization is called urban aggregation, and while it is establishes the underlying order of just about every form of urbanism practiced by humanity, it is seldom associated with contemporary development.

What distinguishes aggregation from, for example, a master plan is that the object of design is not a comprehensive plan but the single aggregate unit, from which an overall plan emerges. This is as true for the megalopolis as it was for the cities of antiquity. To say the obvious, the megalopolis is built piece-by-piece. It is the repetitive aggregation of these similar pieces that constructs a tentative whole that makes the megalopolis something more than a random sprawl. In a nutshell, aggregation is the structuring logic of so-called sprawl. When understood as units of urban aggregation, the architecture of the megalopolis takes on a specific urban meaning. Insomuch as the structure of the unit impacts the urban whole, it is through this urban architecture that the megalopolis is ultimately affected. This leads to two interesting questions. The first: If we know the city block functions as the unit of aggregation in a traditional city of form, what functions as the unit of aggregation in a city of space? And the second: Are there structural similarities that exist between each of these megalopolitan units? What follows is an extended answer to these questions.

1. The City and the Anti-City

In order to pursue the logic underlying the *megalopolitan* city of space, it is useful to contrast it with its immediate predecessor, the *metropolitan* city of form. The metropolis is historically defined as the type of large, industrial city that emerged at the beginning of the twentieth century, reached its zenith in the 1920s, and was wholly superseded following the Second World War. The metropolis is an urbanism with three specific qualities: metric form, continuity, and a dominant center.

With regards to metric form, I would argue that the most consequential feature of the metropolis is its gridiron infrastructure. Gridiron urbanism is best represented in theory by Idelfonso Cerdà's 1867 Teoría General de la Urbanización (General Theory of Urbanization) and best represented in practice by the 1811 Commissioners' Plan for Manhattan. These two paradigms established the gridiron metropolis as an urbanism of mechanically structured form, where identical blocks facilitate new urban expansion that is not designed per se, but extends automatically, block-by-block, at whatever pace the market can bear. Out of this substrate, the gridiron city evolved over a century and a half to become, in its final stages, what we refer to as the metropolis. Being the last of a long line of cities dominated by the metric deployment of urban form, the metropolis continues to represent the city in our imagination, despite the fact that it no longer constitutes the dominant mode of urban production.

Following the dominance of the gridiron's structured form, the second quality of the metropolis is its open continuity. In contrast to the traditional gridded city, the gridiron city was both open and infinitely extensible. The gridiron street was, by definition, interminable: it would not yield to a city wall, an agricultural allotment, or even significant topographic features. The gridiron street was understood to reproduce itself mechanically—block after block—creating hundreds and thousands of numbered streets. Together, these streets establish a coherent urban field that is the ground and prerequisite of metropolitan urbanism. This expanded infrastructure is meant to be limitless because it was built to accommodate a modern political, economic, and cultural dynamic that was also believed to have no limit.

These two paradigms established the gridiron metropolis as an urbanism dominated by structured forms that are organized upon a continuous, infinitely expandable field of open-ended streets. At this point, the third quality of the metropolis comes into play. The open and endless continuities of the structured field are anchored by a single, emphatic, hierarchical center, typically defined by maximum densities. Whether expressed as an intense aggregation of buildings (Midtown) or as a dominant urban district (Manhattan), the metropolis always culminates in a dominant center. In this regard, the metropolis is capable of being defined as a single thing; it is perhaps the last in a long history of structurally coherent urban entities.

While the preeminent example of a city dominated by structured form is the metropolis, the corresponding example of a city dominated by unstructured space is the megalopolis. Megalopolis is a term coined by the Scottish geographer Patrick Geddes in the 1920s and redefined in the 1950s by the French geographer Jean Gottmann. Gottmann intended megalopolis to be a place-name for a new type of urban development that was emerging along the northeastern seaboard of the United States. As it turned out, the term has come to represent an entirely different mode of urban production that characterizes the urbanism produced in the second half of the twentieth century. Gottmann believed the megalopolis to be an unprecedented urban phenomenon that was characterized by the merging of preexisting urban centers to create a dispersed, polycentric network, or "conurbation."

With the coming of the megalopolis, the structured logic of the gridiron metropolis was inundated by a new, unstructured type of urban space. This transformation was signaled by a spatial explosion of the urban periphery that pushed outward into the hinterland with a powerful wave of so-called urban sprawl and backward into the existing city with an equally powerful wave of so-called urban blight. Moving both forward and backward, space was interjected into a process of urbanization in an unprecedented manner. Growth that would once have produced a cityscape dominated by form instead produced one dominated by an unfamiliar and unexpected variant of urban space. In the megalopolis, urban space translated, not into collective space, but into a world of neglect, very nearly dropped from the consciousness of its inhabitants. This space was perceived then, as it is today, as being without qualities—unstructured and inert. As a result, space was not regarded according to the freedoms it afforded, but merely as the benign host of fractured forms—chaotic, uncontrolled, and ultimately sub-urban. These fractured forms produced an enormous residuum of space that we are still loathe to call urban.

What links the polycentric conurbations identified by Gottmann to an urbanism that is dominated by space is the expanded field born of unstructured urban space. If the metropolis is structured by continuous, metric forms and dominated by a single, hierarchical center, the emergence of the megalopolis is marked by an inversion of this logic. With the megalopolis, infinite streets were truncated in the cul-de-sac. With these truncations, spatial discontinuities emerged, constituting a new field condition that is defined negatively, if at all, by space. Unlike the continuous extension of the gridiron that theoretically met the horizon, the megalopolis created "exterior" spaces tethered to loose aggregations of polynuclear forms. The "residual" nature of these exterior spaces is defined by an urban tradition that has left us unequipped to grasp the dominance of space over form. This tradition has created an obstacle to our best design intentions.

It should be noted that the absence of a continuous, metric field condition in a megalopolis might not be an absence at all, but a redefinition of the urban field itself. While the block structure of a megalopolis is not standardized, repetitive, or threaded by an open matrix of corridor streets, we should not discount the potential of a field condition that is unique to the city of space. The many and great differences between metropolitan and megalopolitan fields are due entirely to the latter being constituted not by form, but by space. Until such time as we can switch our mental poles to privilege space over form, the megalopolis will remain a conundrum for those who wish to define it as a design problem.

Outmoded Logic

For a half century, we have constructed and inhabited a megalopolitan complex that is hardly recognized by either the professionals who design and build it or the many millions who now live and work in it. This lack of awareness may be an entirely understandable reaction to an urbanism that is only in its formative stage. The relative novelty of a city of space pales in comparison to the long-lived history of the city dominated by structured form. The result is that we are not yet prepared to see its inherent qualities. We instead regard the megalopolis as a proto- or subordinate urbanism, or as a "yet-to-developed" part of a city that will eventually mature into a city of form. It can be argued that every time we use the word *suburban*, the understanding of an underdeveloped urbanism is passed on. It is absurd, however, to consider the megalopolitan city of space as a preliminary or transitional step toward a city structured by form. Habits of speech, however, continue to betray habits of mind.

We continue to work according to the logic of form, when what is really driving urban production—what we do not know how to address and what functionally matters—is the logic of space. The question then becomes: How do you build an understanding of space equal to and surpassing our understanding of the outmoded urbanism of form? The inversion of form, continuity, and centrality are perhaps obvious, but it is difficult to see if a simple inversion can lead to an effective strategy. It is perhaps more fruitful to focus, not on the differences between the city and the anti-city, but on their similarities. I propose that, despite so much evidence to the contrary, what is similar between the two forms of urbanism is a mode of organization called aggregation. Heretofore, aggregation has been defined by the aggregation of form, but another type of aggregation is suggested—one that is defined by space. We must, however, come at space indirectly.

2. Urban Aggregation

The importance of urban aggregation can best be grasped by contrasting it with its opposite: comprehensive planning. Comprehensive or master planning exists when a single conception orders all parts of the city into one fully prescribed whole. In other words, the purpose of each part of a comprehensive plan is to serve a preconceived whole. By contrast, the whole of aggregate planning is not preconceived. In aggregate urbanism, the whole is guided by the part alone. That part is multiplied to create one out of many possible wholes, none more likely than the next. While some parts of the metropolis and the megalopolis are comprehensively planned—large institutional buildings, for example—their overall configurations are achieved through an aggregate logic that is contained in each constituent part. In gridiron cities, for example, the specification for the urban block directs the outcome of the city. It goes without saying that a city determined by the design of the whole is entirely different from the city determined by the design of the part. An entire city that is imaged by a totalizing form—an island in the shape of a palm, for example—is of a different order than a city that is imaged by an aggregated form, such as a skyline.

The megalopolis's lack of any sort of comprehensive plan is often used to support the claim that it is entirely without structure—that it is merely sprawl. This claim invariably precedes the call for the draconian measures of comprehensive planning, as if the willfulness of top-down organization is the only remedy for the chaos of the contemporary environment. (The political problems attending comprehensive planning need not be spelled out here. It is only necessary to say that there are always alternatives to it.) Comprehensive planning is not, however, inevitable. The megalopolis is not urban chaos seeking a comprehensive order: it is, instead, a specific demonstration of aggregate urbanism.

A Compact Specification

The aggregation of traditional urban form is tied to the specification of the city block. To employ an overused analogy, the city block constitutes the DNA of aggregate urbanism. The block contains within it the technical, social, economic, and experiential logic of an entire urban agglomeration. More than a legal instrument, it is built information that contains the logic of the city's production. Deceptively simple, this information determines the block's relative proportion (from a compact square to an elongated rectangle), its absolute width and depth, its orientation, and its parcelization logic, including the presence or absence of an alleyway, the presence or absence of an interior courtyard, height restrictions—the list could go on.

Examples of this compact specification abound, and their importance is not diminished by their apparent banality, as can be seen in a comparison of Manhattan and Barcelona. The 1811 Commissioners' Plan for Manhattan specified long, 200-by-800-foot blocks, oriented east-west without fixed height restrictions or alleyways. This block specification gives a coded understanding of Manhattan in its entirety. The quick succession of short blocks syncopates north-south movement, speeding up the urban dynamic. Likewise, the stretching of the east-west blocks subdues almost every street, where movement in and out of buildings becomes slower and more deliberate. This is the great and subtle effect of the aggregate unit as it engages the inhabitant at an existential level.

While encoding similar values, the block specification of Idelfonso Cerdà's 1859 plan for Barcelona could not be more different from that of Manhattan. Cerdà's unit employs similar (gridiron) parameters, but a very different kind of unit encoding. The Barcelona plan specifies 131-meter-square blocks with no preferred orientation, but a strict height limitation, the same for each block. The plan also specified a large number of variations based on a single slab, the length of which was fixed by the side of the block. Anything from a perimeter block to a block with one, two, or three open sides was made possible by the unit specification. Also, a parallel arrangement of slabs within the block, or a single slab on its own could be accommodated. Given that they were both constructed on an open, infinitely extensible gridiron infrastructure, the profound differences between Manhattan as a whole and Barcelona as a whole are due almost entirely to unit encoding. The argument could be expanded to include variations, based on Chicago's massively deep 300-by-600-foot blocks or Houston's very modest 250-foot squares. In all cases, the cast for each city was set into place by the aggregate unit, whose ostensibly subtle variations are magnified a thousandfold by the processes of aggregation.

Five Qualities of Aggregation

Insomuch as our comprehension of the city is dependent on an understanding of its structural logic, it is important to recall exactly how aggregation creates urban qualities. The first quality of unit aggregation is that urbanization is not restricted to a single time: building campaigns can occur at various times, with long periods of dormancy in between. Cycles of boom and bust, for example, result in a rich fabric of buildings from different periods of urban growth. Only the most restrictive measures could schedule the untold industry that goes into producing the aggregate effects of a city. The second advantage of unit aggregation is that urbanization is not restricted to a single place. Unbuilt parcels are skipped over, leaving gaps to be filled in at a later date. There is thus no need for seamless development when various infill options are available. The third advantage of unit aggregation is that urban construction is not restricted to a single scale. Projects can range from the development of single buildings on small parcels to the construction of larger, multiple units or superblocks that spread multiple buildings across the block structure. A fourth, and perhaps the most important, advantage of aggregation is that incremental growth is not restricted to a single outcome. This eliminates the folly that invariably attends the prediction of future events. It also removes the need for any kind of ultimate authority to mandate a fixed or final form. On the contrary, an aggregate city has no final form that is fully anticipated.

At any stage in its development, an aggregate city presents a cumulative form that is no more significant or desirable than the cumulative form at any other stage. This alters the meaning of the city considerably, as it comes to be understood not as an object that is evolving toward an ultimate configuration, but as an active site of continuous, never-ending construction. The modern city is nothing if not a work in progress, with each generation adding to its accrued value.

It is difficult to summarize the obvious but usually ignored benefits derived from the mechanics of urban aggregation, other than to say that they allow the work of wildly diverse interests not to fall into a debilitating formlessness, but instead coalesce into an urban whole, however fragile and tentative that whole may be. The creation of this whole is the fifth advantage of bottom-up unit aggregation. Urban aggregation maintains the integrity of the part, yet adds up to a whole that is greater than the simple sum of its parts. As this list summarizes the five qualities of aggregation, it is important to note that the megalopolis, though an aggregation, shares almost none of them.

The Legibility of Aggregation

Surprisingly enough, the most obvious benefits that come from urban aggregation do not apply to the megalopolis. Despite the fact that the megalopolis aggregates piece by piece, it does not seem to be built at various times (it all seems to be built in one day: yesterday), nor does it seem to accommodate a great variety of scales (it indiscriminately reproduces generic shopping malls, office buildings, and tract houses). Finally, with its many large subdivisions, commercial centers, and office parks, the megalopolis often seems to be the very example of master planning. Most of all, the megalopolis does not meet the fifth noted advantage of aggregate urbanism: it refuses to add up to anything coherent or legible, remaining instead a seemingly random collection of nondescript buildings that do not achieve an urban whole. I believe that the paradox presented here—an aggregate urbanism that does not enjoy the benefits of aggregation—explains much of our present urban predicament.

There are many reasons that an aggregate urbanism does not have the benefits of traditional aggregation—several will be discussed here—but I believe each reason can be traced back to a single problem: in a system of urban organization that is built up from parts, *the parts must be legible*. There must be a cognitive grasp of the relationship of the parts to the parts and the parts to the whole. The problem of legibility becomes immediately apparent if we extend the analogy between form and space. The aggregate unit in a city of space would not be a block of form but a *block of space*—a virtual city block. While this analogy seems unlikely, I believe it is worth pursuing aggregate logic in light of their potential benefits to the megalopolis. With a legible unit of aggregation, the megalopolis could be seen as something that is fundamentally structured and thus open to the potentials of design intervention at an urban scale.

The absence of a legible unit of aggregation in the megalopolitan city of space poses two difficult problems, both of which are cognitive. The first is, of course, that space is not legible in the way that form is. Given the ever-present reading of figure and ground, we are historically conditioned to read the figure as positive, never as residual. A second problem is that the scale of megalopolitan organization exceeds that of human cognition. Driven by contemporary economies of scale, the unit of aggregation has become so large that it has simply swallowed us up in a seemingly infinite interior.

3. Distribution, Deference, and the Megablock

Before describing the potential of a megalopolitan aggregation, it is necessary to describe how the megalopolis can be understood as an instance of aggregate ordering. The megalopolis's lack of a systematic, uniform aggregation does not mean an absence of aggregate order, but an absence of a systematic disposal of the forms. Dumping out a box of dominoes, for example, is not the same thing as dumping out the contents of a junk drawer. The resulting field of dominoes would have a structure that is altogether lacking in the field of junk. Imagine that a singular urban module, more or less uniform in its aspects, is spread randomly. The possibility exists that this module could create a coherent urban field despite the arbitrariness of its distribution. It is in the reproduction of a singular unit that the definition of aggregation resides, not in the logic of its distribution. This broader interpretation of aggregation is needed to reach beyond the limited understanding of aggregate form and consider the possibilities of aggregate space.

It must be noted that this "dumping" of equivalent modules (as of the contents of a drawer) may produce a kind of order, but leaves space unaddressed. In the dumping scenario, space functions as merely the random residue between a series of unrelated blocks. Form still distracts, even if it is not systematically deployed, and space is still indifferent and unrecognized, even if it dominates the urban scene. It is my intention to show that an aggregated field can be more than a series of arbitrary urban forms occupying a vast field of indifferent space. It is instead possible to imagine space as an active agent with the capacity of ordering a diffuse but related set of urban forms.

Form Brings Space into Existence

With regards to the relation between form and space, we might first assume that an easy symmetry exists that would allow for a direct transition from the world of form to the world of space. By easy symmetry I mean that the procedures of spatial aggregation can be defined by a simple inversion of the procedures of formal aggregation. While having an interesting history, such figure-ground reversals are far too simplistic in regards to defining a spatial paradigm.

The inadequacy of a symmetry between form and space becomes apparent in simply trying to define the spatial unit. In the traditional city, this definition was accomplished by subdividing the urban fabric down to its basic unit, the city block. Subdivision will not work for a city that is dominated by space. The dominant space of the megalopolis is amorphous and unstructured. Unlike form, space has no intrinsic subdivisions, no topographic ruptures or fissures, and no obvious breaking points. Only space that is dominated or neutralized by form can be measured out and subdivided. This leaves us with an interesting alternative: the block of space is built up rather than broken down, and it is built up out of a series of forms that are deferential to space.

The way forward with the problem of spatial aggregation lies in the simple recognition that space and form are a symbiotic pair. Space cannot exist without form and form cannot exist without space. This bond between space and form is true regardless of which side of the equation is dominant. What this suggests in regards to identifying a spatial unit of aggregation is that these virtual units must be tied to the forms that create them. In identifying this reciprocity between space and form, a specification of megalopolitan architecture begins to emerge, leading to a simple hypothesis: units of spatial aggregation are hybrid or binary units composed of an interrelation of space and form. This interrelation is imbalanced, insomuch as the built forms remain deferential to the spaces that they themselves construct. These indexed or deferential forms will be one of the most important design features of the architecture of the megalopolis. Megalopolitan architecture thus acquires a new specification: the creation of coherent increments of urban space. The thing that principally distinguishes the form of the megalopolis from traditional urban form is that architectural form is not its actual unit of aggregation, but functions as the deferential side of a form/space hybrid. The diminishment of architectural form is a precondition of spatial aggregation; the difficulties this precondition presents to architects and designers should not be underestimated.

It is apparent from the start that a unit of urban space cannot be subdivided in the way that a unit of urban form is subdivided. Despite the problem of spatial subdivision, however, it seems certain that the production of space will involve the use of architectural form. This claim may at first seem contradictory, yet the traditional use of urban *poche* and figure/ground diagrams teach us nothing if not of the ability of form to produce space without dominating it. In other words, form can remain secondary to the primary space that it creates. Exactly how deferential form produces space is key to a specification of the unit of spatial aggregation.

Superblock, Megastructure, Megablock

It is interesting to note that the existence of a unit of spatial aggregation is already implied in our casual terminology. I am referring to the term *superblock* that is frequently used in the context of the megalopolis. It is possible to argue that the very persistence of "block" terminology reveals the desire to create an aggregate logic in the context of contemporary urbanism. But the megalopolitan superblock as it is defined today does not function as a traditional city block, and the reason why is clear: the superblock, like the block it is based on, presumes the dominance of form. The environment in which the superblock sits, however, is based on the dominance of space.

Given the identification of key elements of a megalopolitan architecture, it is now possible to further refine some existing terminology: superblock, megablock, and megastructure. The megalopolitan unit of aggregation will be referred to as the megablock. It replaces the superblock, but inherits two important characteristics from it. The first is an attempt to make good on a promise implied by the word *block*. The superblock suggests the potential of urban aggregation in a megalopolitan context. The megablock is an attempt to exploit the superblock's potential as a unit of urban aggregation. The second characteristic the megablock inherits from the superblock is scale. The superblock achieved the all-important transformation of the block form from a metropolitan to a megalopolitan scale.

With the definitions of superblock and megablock in mind, I would like to add another familiar term into the mix: megastructure. If the megablock is one unit of larger aggregation, the megastructure is a world unto itself. It is, like the proverbial ocean liner, a complete cultural, political, and economic unit. While the megablock, like the megastructure, is scaled up to contemporary dimensions, it is also a unit of aggregation and is not complete within itself. Being distinguished from both the superblock and the megastructure, a more precise definition can be given for the megablock: it is a large-scale architecture that functions as a unit of contemporary spatial aggregation.

In contrast to the superblock, I suggest an alternative strategy: a unit of aggregation that is not a superform, but instead, superspace. In this regard, I propose a *spatial* unit of aggregation—a block of space. Like the superblock, the block of space is updated to the scope and scale of modern urban production, yet its purpose is to integrate this new scale into an urban field that is dominated by space rather than form.

4. The Displacement of the Cognitive Meter

The potential of a megalopolitan unit of aggregation has been described, along with an architectural specification for a hybrid, space/form megablock. It is now necessary to return to the problems posed by a unit of aggregation that is too large to be cognitively understood. I indicated above that cognitive legibility of the traditional city block was the decisive characteristic of urban aggregation that did not translate into the city of space. The lack of cognition can be dealt with by returning to the logic of traditional urban aggregation. In the preceding section, I discussed the quantifiable aspects of aggregation. Here I would like to note the experiential quality of aggregation, which I referred to earlier as the metric effect of structured form. This effect stems directly from the perception of the block structure. The cognitive organization of the city can be introduced as a sixth quality of urban aggregation.

The power of aggregate urbanism is found in the iteration of the unit. This iteration creates a measured urban field that not only describes a mode of urban production (aggregation) but also describes an important cognitive effect. The city block is both an abstract unit of organization and a vital part of lived experience. The regular structure creates the experiential baseline of a city of form, street by street, block by block, becoming the literal measure of daily urban existence. In this way, it can be said that the urban grid creates an existential logic—a metric that literally measures out the daily lives of those who inhabit it. The word *existence* is used here in its broadest sense, insomuch as metric cognition operates subliminally, inhabiting the deepest levels of our environmental perceptions. This regulating cadence of the public domain creates and sustains a world of immanent occupation that is central to our understanding of urban environments, if not our very definition of the city. We come to depend on this metric order, if only subconsciously, and it has a decisive effect upon our actions.

In addition to creating the underlying experience of block and street, the cognitive meter also preconditions every building built upon its rhythmic structure. A simple example tells the story. Urban infrastructure not only technically supports the various architectures built upon it, but it pervades them experientially. The experience of a building constructed on a gridiron infrastructure is profoundly different from the experience of an identical building built, for example, on the feeder road of a freeway, or on the fringes of an exurban office park. Each infrastructure—gridiron, freeway, cul-de-sac—imposes a predisposition on the architecture, and each suggests a unique architectural response. I will return to the interdependence between architecture and infrastructure later in this essay. For the moment, it is only necessary to establish that in the city dominated by structured form, the unit of aggregation establishes our cognitive grasp of urban existence, producing a reliable, cognitive map of the urban world. This sets an important specification for any aggregate unit, whether it is found in the gridiron block structure of the metropolis or in a presumed megablock structure of the megalopolis. This cognitive understanding lies at the heart of reproducing a legible system of aggregation.

The Persistence of Effect

I have argued that the cognitive grasp of a city of form is provided by its unit of aggregation. Using a kind of mirror logic, I have also argued that the city of space contains the equivalent of an urban block, a virtual block of space. There is, however, a flaw in this conclusion. The similarity between the city of form and the city of space ultimately break down because of the difference between metropolitan and megalopolitan scales. The superscale of contemporary infrastructure effectively preempts any cognitive effects. Being tied to the human sensorium, cognition does not scale up to megasize. In the gridiron city, the relation between the building block and the city it forms is experiential or cognitive. Because of the enormous scale increase of the megalopolis (and the supersizing of its block structure), the relationship between the megablock and the megalopolis is not cognitive, but abstract. Because of its size, megalopolitan infrastructure cannot reproduce the regular, metric order of blocks and streets that establishes the baseline of traditional urban experience. However obvious, it is important to emphasize that though the city of space possesses an aggregate logic, it is not experiential.

The megablock emerges at the moment the scale of urban infrastructure grows beyond our ability to cognitively grasp it. It is the moment that urban organization ceases to be experiential. In the absence of a cognitive urban metric, we simply become engulfed in the apparent formlessness of space. It is precisely this spatial engulfment that signals the arrival of the megalopolis.

Yet, despite all the evidence that the megalopolis provides, the cognitive meter lives on as a deep-rooted, existential reality based on millennia of urban experience. In our imaginations the cognitive meter remains the very definition of urbanism. This cognitive experience is what sends so many film crews, time and again, back into the derelict or gentrified city cores. It is why authors continue to plot urban narratives. It is why advertising and branding prefer outmoded streetscapes as a stage. It is why tourists shun the urban periphery and flock to the core, no matter what city they are in. It must be emphasized that the cognitive meter is not to be confused with a typological tradition. It is not the product of nostalgia, nor is it an *essential* experience. It is, instead, based on *existential* facts whose outmoded vestiges we relentlessly reproduce, consume, and sometimes (though decreasingly) inhabit. The continued importance of outmoded urban cores—Los Angeles and New York, for example—suggests that the cognitive meter has not lost its relevance to the present. Before succumbing to sentimentality, however, it is necessary to reject the outmoded forms of the past and, instead of inhibiting our understanding of the megalopolis, find a place for the cognitive meter within the realties of megalopolitan development. The modern megalopolis cannot cling to the obsolete cognitive order resident in a vestigial city of form. Instead, a radical displacement of the cognitive order is required. This displacement is a key component in the specification of the megablock.

Displacement of Effect: The Blind Box and the Cul-de-Sac

When gridiron urbanism ceased to be the dominant mode of urban production nearly fifty years ago, its legible unit of aggregation disappeared. Since that time, no new cognitive infrastructures have been created. This eclipse of the cognitive infrastructure coincides with the full emergence of a noncognitive city of space. The cognitive urban meter did not, however, go away with the disappearance of gridiron block structure. I argue that it continues to exist, displaced, in the architecture of the megalopolis, specifically in the forms of the blind box (at the architectural scale) and the cul-de-sac (at the urban scale).

With regards to the blind box, the displacement of cognitive form in the commercial mall—food courts as plazas, anchor stores as monuments, storefronts as display windows, filtered top-lighting as passing clouds, and a plethora of fountains, planting beds, and street furniture—is a largely thematic attempt to reproduce the city that has been preempted by a spatial dominant. This is an unabashed form of urban displacement, where a street scene gets reconstructed, like a stage set, in the confines of a blind box. Beyond thematic contrivances, however, displacement is characterized by interior modulation that marks the form of the megablock. This modulation may take the form of simple demising walls separating waiting areas, reservation desks, boarding gates, tiny undersized "shops," or large numbers of movie theaters. These cognitive inserts reproduce the parceling structure of traditional urban blocks that can no longer exist, but nonetheless endure as the very definition of urbanity.

At the opposite end of the scale, the displaced metric occurs in the cul-de-sac organization of mass housing. Axes of internal organization that happen to be made of asphalt and dimensioned for cars with curbs, street signs, and gutters are routinely referred to as public "streets," but they are not. They instead co-opt the vocabulary of civil engineering at the service of those that live, play, and sometimes work behind the subdivision gatehouse. In contrast with the blind box simulations, these displacements can be characterized as a nonthematic or non-self-conscious use of public language. Traditional urban streets are defined as public armatures, off of which private parcelization occurs. The cul-de-sac streets of a subdivision are not public, but private, armatures. The actual public armatures lie outside the subdivision, and the entire subdivision is but a single private parcel. What we call cul-de-sac streets function more like service drives within any private subdivision (such as an industrial park or a corporate campus). Like the subdivision of the blind box, they reproduce the cognitive meter that we continue to regard as an authentic urbanity.

In summary, the cognitive meter that is embedded at an existential level in gridded cities has a definite scale to it, a scale defined by the limits of human cognition. It goes without saying that the scale of megalopolitan organization has long exceeded this limit, yet the cognitive meter persists as a displaced form. It constitutes an autonomous logic that grows out of a diminishing existential reality, drawn from the deepest levels of environmental perception. This does not alter the fact that the cognitive meter of gridiron urbanism is anachronistic and, as the blind box and the subdivision show, is virtually impossible to reproduce in its essential or true form. It persists, nonetheless, as a device to produce the semblance of public order in an exclusive, private world.

The cognitive urban meter need not exist as a simulation, but can be translated as an existential experience that makes manifest an urban organization. I would like to suggest that this displacement of the cognitive order becomes one of the salient features not of the block of space, but of the form that creates it. In other words, the deferential form that defines the unit of spatial aggregation also absorbs the cognitive meter—the legible unit of aggregation—characteristic of traditional urbanism. This displacement of form is the beginning of a solution to the problems posed by the illegible unit of megalopolitan aggregation. At this point, it is possible to suggest the combination of this internal, formal modulation of the cognitive meter with the external, spatial modulation of the virtual block and put forward a tentative specification for the architecture of spatial aggregation. The architecture of the megalopolis is ultimately animated by a double modulation—internal/external, formal/spatial, cognitive/virtual—that is grounded in the logic of urban aggregation.

Against Cognition: Embracing Urban Space

The demise of the gridiron city's cognitive meter quickly gave rise to a nonmetric city of space. Apprehension over this new and unmeasurable type of urban organization has always run high, and has only intensified over the years. This anxiety is registered in the persistence of the pejorative meanings associated with contemporary urban space, meanings so deep-seated as to be embedded in language that remains largely unexamined. For example, the emergence of contemporary urban space in brownfield sites automatically produces what we call "slum" or "blight," while the emergence of contemporary urban space in greenfield sites automatically produces what we call "sprawl." The negative connotations of these terms are evidence enough that what is being referred to here as contemporary urban space is a widely misunderstood and undertheorized condition. I would argue that nothing can be accomplished urbanistically until these assumptions regarding the inherently negative qualities associated with contemporary urban space are challenged and overcome.

Such "entropies" of space—slum, blight, sprawl, and the suburban—emerge when the scale of urban infrastructure grows beyond our ability to cognitively grasp it. The negative qualities of contemporary urban space emerge at the point at which we lose our cognitive bearings. In other words, they emerge out of a moment of trepidation. In the absence of an urban meter, we simply become engulfed in the apparent formlessness of space. Space no longer accommodates us, and no longer functions as an anthropomorphic index; it is indifferent to us. In the words of architect Michael Bell, "Space replaces us." This produces apprehension, yet if we can temporarily suspend our fears, this increase in disorganization gives rise to a series of interesting questions. Is there a precise measure of spatial disorganization? How large does the urban metric need to be before it exceeds our cognitive capacities? How irregularly can its forms be arrayed before it ceases to register as an organized urban field? Key to understanding the quality of megalopolitan space is the recognition that it emerges at the threshold of the cognitive, the threshold of disorganization.

In light of our own negative judgment, contemporary urban space might better be defined as entropic, because entropy is nothing more or less than a quantitative measure of the disorganization of a given system. Such detachment allows us to see the judgment of slum and sprawl for what it is: an ideological position that must be resisted if conceptual work on the megalopolis is to advance. As we know, the space of modern architecture and urbanism was conceived as open, generous, and imbued with natural qualities. Can we not imagine that the qualities of space advanced by modern urbanism—space that is not hierarchical, not monumental, not perspectival, and not subjugated by form—could be rehabilitated and bent to progressive ends? The very same space could then be invested with ideal qualities rather than shunned and ineffectively "remedied." The answer to this question will of course depend on whether one's urban perspective is dominated by form or by space.

If there is widely felt apprehension in the disorganization of urban space, is the only responsible action to reproduce the block structure that we cling to in our urban cores? Such a widespread reform is neither possible nor desirable. The megablock will always be a house divided between cognitive form and noncognitive space. And it must be defined in such a way that the two can never be reduced back down into a hegemony of form. While cognitive form has its place in the megalopolis, it is important to acknowledge that this place is limited, a pale reflection of the ubiquitous presence that cognitive form possessed a scant fifty years ago in the metropolis. The space that matters most, the space to which we must acclimate, is the noncognitive space that is native to the megalopolis. It must be emphasized that it is neither possible nor desirable to render megalopolitan space cognitive in order for it to possess real urban value. In other words, the displacement of cognitive form into the architecture of the megalopolis should not lead to a revival of the city of form. Here, the entropic space of the megalopolis trumps a regressive humanist perspective whose only path of retreat is ineffectual sentimentality.

5. Module and Field: Aggregate Reform

One of the greatest limitations of megalopolitan architecture is that each building is perceived to be complete in itself, unrelated from all that surrounds it. The shopping mall, the industrial park, and the airport all seem to exist as isolated worlds, slumbering behind an enormous *cordon sanitaire* and turning inward against everything beyond their self-imposed boundaries. This perceived isolation of megalopolitan form has made any kind of urban intervention seem gratuitous simply because urbanism is defined as that which exceeds the sum of the parts. If parts exist only in isolation, there simply is no recognition of a legitimate urbanity and thus no basis for design at an urban scale. In order for urbanism to come into play in the megalopolis, a direct attack on the isolation of built form is required. I have suggested that the megablock is responsive to the vast scale of megalopolitan space, but this does not mean that it is irreconcilable to the cognitive scale of its internal organization. Alternately, I have suggested that the internal organization of the megablock is cognitively modulated, but this does not mean that it must be isolated from its external environment. Given such simple alternatives, it is not difficult to imagine a megalopolitan architecture that exists at the intersection of these internal and external forces. A binary or bivalent logic of the megablock raises the possibility of an architecture that is anything but isolated in space. If it is possible to establish the megablock as a unit of spatial aggregation, the reciprocity between block and field will not only overcome the isolation of megalopolitan architecture but also reform the wider field itself. Such reciprocity between part and whole constitutes a specific program for megalopolitan architecture.

The Binary Field of the Megalopolis

The megalopolis today is characterized by an absolute division between architectural form and urban space. Any reconciliation between the two is obstructed by the closed nature of megalopolitan development. This closure exists in both the blind box of megalopolitan architecture and in the cul-de-sac street of megalopolitan urbanism. Through their implacable boundary conditions, the subdivision and the blind box literally produce the vacuum of space that surrounds them. An appreciation of this nearly absolute division between megalopolitan form and space can only be understood in relation to the integration of form and space that preceded them in the metropolitan city of form.

The gridiron infrastructure of the city of form created a ubiquitous network of open and continuous streets. Because each street extended infinitely, gridiron infrastructure created a nonstop network that had no boundary. Like no urbanism before or since, it created a totalizing urban environment that enveloped its inhabitant in a comprehensive matrix of solids and voids. Insomuch as this comprehensive field linked every part of the city—every building, street, intersection, and block—to the far horizon, there was no exterior to its potential expansion. In this way, gridiron urbanism produced a type of urban space that truly warranted the often-evoked aspiration of the universal.

The emergence of megalopolitan conurbation was world-shattering precisely because it fractured the open and extensible gridiron system into a myriad of closed figures (cul-de-sac enclaves and big boxes). In other words, the closed interior condition creates an exterior condition that is unknown to gridiron urbanism. This exterior possesses no formal, cognitive, or metric effect. It exists, instead, as amorphous space. This sudden emergence of an exterior dominated by an amorphous spatial field not only established a spatial dominant, but threw the very definition of urban space into crisis. The megalopolis replaces a continuous, univalent, spatial field with a discontinuous, bivalent, spatial field.

While a potential interaction always remains, this binary field is presently locked into a polarity that seems impossible to reconcile.

Interior forms become isolated and arbitrary, while exterior space becomes alienating and non-accommodating, with any dialogue between them preempted from the start. It can of course be argued that this division between urban form and space produces interesting qualities, but it would be equally shortsighted to ignore its extreme limitations. These limitations can be summed up as the inability to produce an urban whole. This whole requires an architecture that is commensurate to the urbanism in which it exists.

Block Specification

The unit of megalopolitan aggregation—the megablock—has two major influences that are played out on its binary structure. These pull the megablock in opposite directions, bringing to the table an extraordinary pair of architectural demands. The first demand is that of spatial dominance, which requires the deployment of deferential forms to respond to a primacy of space. The second demand is that of the displaced cognitive meter, which internalizes a cognitive urban structure. Each of these demands suggests a different aspect of the binary organization of the megablock.

The first influence is that of spatial modulation. The megablock could be conceived as a hybrid form/space entity in response to the spatial dominant of the megalopolis. In other words, the binary relationship that structures the megablock cannot be "balanced," but must be intentionally, perhaps awkwardly, skewed toward space. Despite the fact that this relationship implies a certain effacement of form (something that does not come easily to designers), this effacement is the first specification by which the megablock emerges as a unit of spatial aggregation.

This requirement for deferential form is joined to another, equally important requirement for cognitive organization. The metric structure of gridiron urbanism exists at the deepest level of environmental awareness. From an existential perspective, cognitive structure constitutes the urban. Since the cognitive structure of the gridiron city was no longer reproduced in the infrastructure of the megalopolis, the megablock must establish its own internalized, cognitive meter.

Polarity to Duality

The ultimate rationale for the unit of aggregation lies in the field it creates by replication. However, instead of starting with the unit and speculating on the field it produces, I would like to reverse the order and start with the existing, polarized, spatial field of the contemporary megalopolis. This polarized field was constructed by a closed unit of architecture (the blind box), and a closed unit of urban infrastructure (the cul-de-sac street). With this understanding of the spatial field, and the units that construct it, we are now able to speculate on a new unit of aggregation that might potentially transform the spatial field of the megalopolis. The intent of the transformation would be to break down the exclusive polarity of the field and construct in its place an interactive duality that would establish a give and take between the form and space of the megalopolis.

Now an agent of reform, the aggregate unit would both act as deferential form (responding to the primacy of space) and incorporate a cognitive meter. Given significant architectural interaction between the deferential form and the cognitive displacement, a working relationship or functioning duality would emerge within the megablock. If this functioning duality were then placed into a binary field and replicated through the existing channels of urban production, the polarization would begin to slowly thaw, and a functioning urban field dominated by space would begin to emerge.

It is at this point that the prospect of megalopolitan aggregation comes within sight. Sprawl can finally be seen to possess a structure specifically calibrated to its spatial biases. The megablock is intended to provide the megalopolis with an aggregate unit capable of defining a more coherent spatial field. Yet, it is a spatial field that is far more dispersed, amorphous, and frankly entropic than the history of urban form has prepared us for.

6. Megalopolis Grows to No Cumulative Effect

How far we have to go toward understanding megalopolitan architecture is indicated in how different it is from the architecture that preceded it.

A structured urban grid conditions the vast majority of the history of architecture. This history also includes the most prominent buildings of the past fifty years. For example, over the first decade of the twenty-first century, most notable museums, libraries, and concert halls have been realized in traditional urban environments that are metered by a cognitive grid. What distinguishes such works is that they are carried out following a logic of urban production that is historically outmoded. Being entirely dependent on a preexisting infrastructure, these projects endorse an architecture that conforms to the logic of a city of form. In other words, they serve to decorate the interstices of yesterday's urbanism, indicating a dramatic rupture between modern architecture and the modern city to which it is inextricably bound.

To trace this rupture back to its postwar origin is not difficult, for there are so many examples that emerged in the late 1960s and early 1970s that a list would encompass a history of the period. Perhaps the most poignant and most celebrated example is the Centre Pompidou, which was designed to be wholly dependent on the *arrondissement* in which it is sited. The dependence of the building on metered urban form drastically limited the project's relevance to the urbanism of its day, as it does to our own. That the grand ethos of the megastructure would ultimately be played out as the foci of an ancient urban district is an irony of postmodern urbanism that has yet to be fully absorbed. The real impact of the Pompidou was not in establishing a new urban paradigm, but instead in elevating the Beaubourg district to be a global touristic network. In this capacity it became the template of urban ornamentation that carries us to Gehry's Bilbao and OMA's Porto and beyond.

I would like to argue here, as it was done in the 1920s and again in the 1950s, that an architecture that fails to offer us an urban future is extremely limited in its capacity to inspire. While the ongoing renovations to the city of form certainly have their place, they have far more to do with urban obsolescence that with urban regeneration.

While the postmodern rejection of modern urbanism certainly liberated our ingenuity from the often-severe restrictions of an urban project, it is fair to ask: What is modernism without an urban project? How should we consider Le Corbusier without the Radiant City, Frank Lloyd Wright without Broadacre, Mies van der Rohe without Lafayette Park, or Team X without a project at all? Indeed, how should we consider the new world order of the megastructure being played out as a cultural bauble? It is not difficult to argue that modern architecture without an urban project is not modern at all: it may be more accurately labeled *modernistic*, equivalent to German Expressionism or Art Deco, both of which lacked the scope of a greater urban project. Overcoming, once and for all, limitations of academic architecture, modernism rejected disciplinary boundaries that would reduce it to petite-bourgeoisie monument-making and the conservative patronage that those monuments would support. This reversion to the premodern priorities of a city of form is directly related to an inability or unwillingness to grasp the spatial dominant of contemporary urbanism.

The Aggregate

In closing, I would like to ask why this unity of modern architecture and urbanism should not simply be set aside. To put the question more directly: Why shouldn't the architecture of the megalopolis be free from contemporary urban constraints? At this point I hope that the answer to this question is clear. If there is a crisis regarding the megalopolis, it stems from the existence of thousands or millions of buildings that simply do not matter because megalopolitan construction adds up to nothing more than a quantity. In other words, *the megalopolis grows to no cumulative effect*. It hosts instead an entropic growth, random but virulent, like weeds. By contrast, the very definition of the city is based on a cumulative sum that exceeds the addition of its parts. The absence of such a sum throws the definition of a city into question. Is it possible to reproduce this cumulative effect in the megalopolitan aggregation? The key to these synergies is latent in the specification of the individual part: the block itself. The intention here has been to construct a specification of an aggregate unit for the megalopolis, in order that it may stimulate these synergistic effects.

The most important characteristics of megalopolitan form—the internalization of the cognitive meter and the integration of that meter with an unstructured space that surrounds it—establishes the logic of an aggregate city of space. This new spatial block may combine with others, but not in the manner of the O, L, and U shaped lofts of our recent past. Insomuch as an aggregate whole constitutes the very possibility of the city, what we are ultimately gauging here is architecture's "will" to a greater whole. But to return to the question: Why should anyone wish to commit architectural form to the displacement of the cognitive meter or the structuring of space into virtual blocks?

The answer is that our ambitions for an urban environment remain constant; or, to say it another way, the idea of the city is simply indelible. Cities are so central to our understanding of the world that, if they no longer existed, we would have to invent them. The idea of the city will always persist, even when the actual experience of it has long disappeared. We would continue with our habits of naming built-up areas, even if they exhibit the least of urban qualities. We would continue to produce street maps and guide books, and boast qualities of place that do not exist, even if they are no more than a loose aggregation of inconsequential, unrelated forms. In other words, even if all the buildings made over the past fifty years together added up to nothing resembling our urban expectations, we would still insist on calling them "city."

The ambition, finally stated, is to construct out of the megalopolis something that can rightly be called a city, turning its greatest deficit into a cause. Not knowing what a megalopolitan aggregate might actually look like, it is perhaps best to simply refer to this project as the "Aggregate." The Aggregate is, after all, part fact, part wishful thinking, and part manifesto. The way to the Aggregate is through its unit of aggregation, the block of space—the megablock—that is the architecture of a city of space.

The accompanying illustrations serve as preliminary templates or projections for a unit of spatial aggregation—a tentative step toward designing an urban architecture that is unique to the megalopolis. As such, the drawings are to be understood not as diagrams, but as the outline of an aggregate urbanism of space. Their projected geometries are concerned with instating a two-part dialectic of interior form and exterior space. This complex modulation of form to space can be better understood with reference to the closed forms that presently exist in the megalopolis, the blind box, and the cul-de-sac. Against the singularity of these existing forms, two opposing typologies are deployed at an architectural scale: the concourse and the platform. The concourse offers a way to animate a hermetic interior and the platform responds to an amorphous spatial exterior. The mediation of these two typical forms through a syncopated modulation creates reciprocity between the internal and the external, the formal and the spatial, the cognitive and the virtual, the architectural and the urban. This reciprocity attempts to transform the existing forms of the megalopolis into a fully fledged aggregate urbanism, unique to its extraordinary situation. These drawings suggest the synergistic evolution of megalopolitan form in the direction of sustaining some sort of cumulative urban whole. It should be noted that, like diagrams, these templates intentionally avoid a naturalistic perspective. Naturalistic one- and two-point perspectives, including those generated by computer modeling, are likely indicators of a privileging of form. Such perspectival techniques can be used to generate space, but they generate an outmoded type of space that is dominated by form. In contrast, the accompanying illustrations attempt to relearn an old lesson: one cannot represent modern space by employing the devices of Renaissance perspective regardless of the sophistication of projection technology. In other words, an environment where space is privileged over form cannot be produced through the projection of illusionistic space. A more studied and sophisticated layering is required, between the flattened, two-dimensional space of plans, sections, and axonometrics and a projected, three-dimensional object.

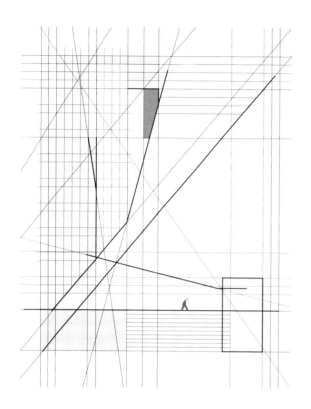

Megablock Template: This drawing combines the plan, elevation, and axonometric of a generic megablock. Visible in the left margin is a glazed tower that ties directly into a podium structure. The podium has a large, open platform covering its roof that is sliced through by diagonal circulation. The perimeter of the podium is modulated into repetitive cells, while the tower contains generic loft space.

Platform Excavations: This drawing combines elevations and an axonometric of a large commercial podium covered by a public platform. The view shows a series of separate courtyards carved one level into the depth of the podium. These courtyards are modulated to an interior concourse that runs asymmetrically along the length of the podium. The embedded blocks and the tower contain generic loft space.

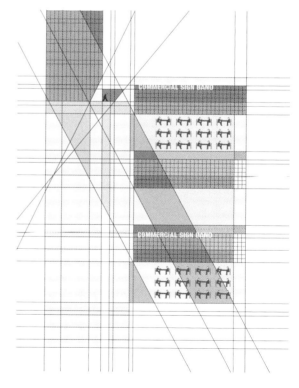

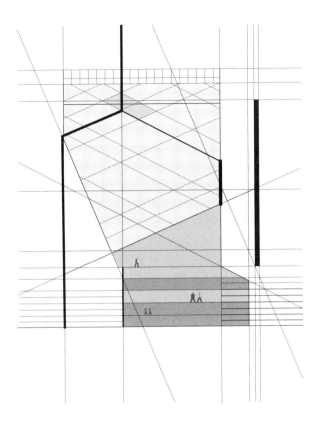

Platform Extension with Steps: This axonometric projection shows the platform addition of an interior concourse that extends beyond the elevation of a blind box in order to define a portion of adjacent space. The platform is surfaced in concrete, which transitions into sod. A large canopy extends across the concrete portion of the platform.

Viaduct Interior at Firewall: This section cuts through the intersection of a podium concourse and a pedestrian bridge. The embedded column of a residential tower appears in the left-hand side of the image. A clerestory allows natural light between the outer podium wall and the setback tower.

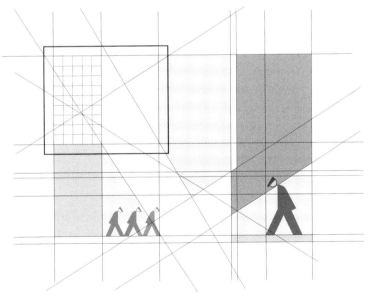

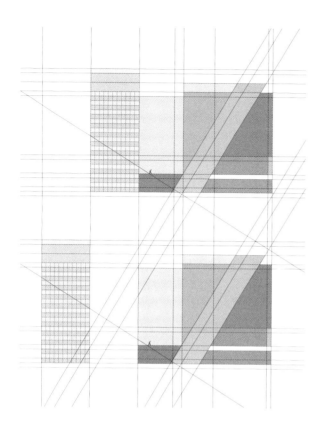

Adjacent/Against/Upon: These two drawings show alternative relationships between a podium and a tower in axonometric projection. The top drawing shows the tower placed directly against the podium. This relationship is typical of renovated gridiron structures. The bottom drawing shows an adjacent podium and tower that allows for circulation between the two structures. A strategy first invented by Frank Lloyd Wright, adjacent blocks compensate for the absence of infrastructure. A final, unillustrated disposition puts the tower directly upon the podium, completing the didactic structure: adjacent/against/upon.

Building Board with Shed and Platform: This oblique projection shows an axonometric and elevation of a generic strip development. The key components are a tall, one-story shed with a ramp leading to a large public platform that covers the entire roof. A large billboard facing vehicular access is opposite the open platform.

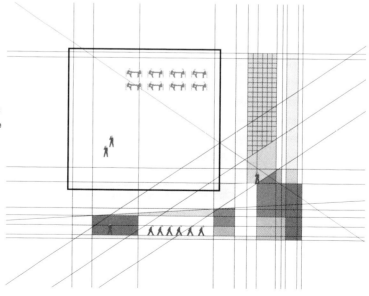

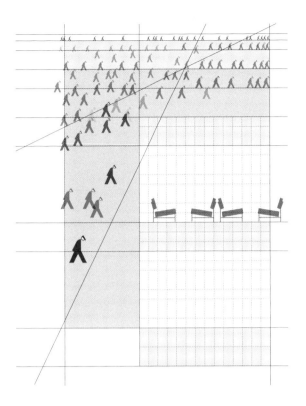

Transit Authority Tower: This drawing shows the elevation of an office block looking across to a podium platform beyond. The platform covers a mixed-use space that contains a transit station. Boarding gates are banked along the right edge of the platform.

Concourse Terminus with Large Window and Observation Deck: This projection shows the end elevations of two parallel concourses. A large window opens each of the concourses to the surrounding runways. These openings are complemented by landscaped observation platforms that are accessed at multiple points along the length of the concourse.

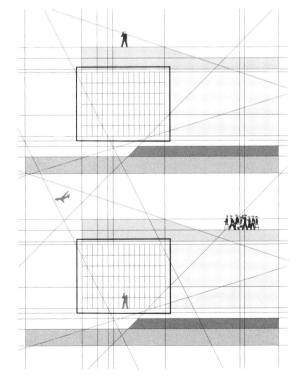

Rerouting Infrastructure
Projects

Stripscape

Phoenix, Arizona, 2000–present

Darren Petrucci

Stripscape is the first public/private partnership to develop prototypes for both city public spaces and private development. The project is located along Seventh Avenue, a one-mile commercial corridor in Phoenix, Arizona, chosen for reasons both physical and economic. In 1968, Seventh Avenue was widened by the Arizona Department of Transportation to create a high-volume north/south transportation corridor that handles an excess of sixty thousand cars per day. Landscape improvements, typically located between the street and sidewalk, were absorbed by the increased width of the street, and the city was unable to make conventional infrastructure "beautification" improvements.

These conditions, combined with the strip's decay due to competition with regional malls, power centers, and strip malls, led the Seventh Avenue Merchants Association—a coalition formed in 1997 of more than sixty merchants along the street—to call for a design strategy that would increase the value of their properties and businesses. Their objectives were threefold: first, to establish a character for the strip that would be identifiable in the greater metropolitan area; second, to increase business by promoting renovations of existing stores and new development; and third, to reduce discursive and undesirable conditions by forming a stronger pedestrian connection with the surrounding neighborhoods. Given the area's diverse clientele, the project required a process of tactical analysis based upon individual merchant improvements, with a strategic plan that the city could deploy at the end of the research. Stripscape utilizes an inclusive methodology that critiques both the totalizing view of conventional master planning and the smaller tactical interventions illustrated in contemporary urban theories such everyday urbanism.

Stripscape features Amenity Infrastructures (a term coined by Darren Petrucci to describe urban infrastructures that are also amenities to the sites for which they are designed) that combine shade, lighting, ground surfaces, landscape, and signage to transform conventional pedestrian and automobile infrastructures (such as sidewalks, street lighting, and parking spaces) into amenities such as shaded parking, display areas, outdoor seating, and recreation areas. Unlike conventional street infrastructures focused only on life safety, these new amenities are designed with the merchants and neighborhoods in mind. The prototypes were installed by the city in public right-of-ways and are available for purchase by merchants for their private properties, creating a seamless transition between the public and private realm. This public/private integration extends boundaries and encourages "ownership," appropriation, and activation of public space. As a revitalization tactic, Stripscape is a flexible and "emergent" urban infrastructure that develops with the city, establishing a new identifiable district for each neighborhood it connects to, while accommodating the specific existing conditions of each site.

Amenity Infrastructures

The main architectural element in Stripscape is the Lampshade. This amenity infrastructure combines shade, lighting, and signage (or graphic art) into one flexible unit. The Lampshade does in one move what is typically done in three, thereby cleaning up the visual and physical litter along the commercial corridor. These elements have been optimized for cost and maintenance, and are durable and affordable for a private business owner to purchase. The Lampshade has been approved by the City of Phoenix as a standard urban detail and is available for both public use and private installation as a new signage opportunity for merchants.

Public art is an integral part of the Stripscape infrastructure. A new program was established with the Phoenix Public Art Department for the project. Art Panels—vertical wall elements that function as both shading devices for the lower afternoon sun and as lightboxes for graphic art—were created for the avenue. Reproductions of artists' works are printed on translucent panels and illuminated at night. Every six to twelve months, the panels are replaced with a new artist's work. Therefore, in keeping with the dynamism of the site, Stripscape functions as an urban gallery, and is now a popular remote location for Phoenix's First Fridays ArtWalk.

One-mile stretch of Seventh Avenue, with
proposed interventions at quarter-mile
intersections and along corridor: The
demonstration site is outlined in the box.

Demonstration site detail

The Project Continues

Stripscape is an evolving and growing urban revitalization initiative.
After the initial success of the first-phase demonstration site, the City
of Phoenix deployed three more Lampshades along the one-mile section of the Seventh Avenue corridor. We are working with the City of
Phoenix and the Merchants' Association to continue enrichment of
the project and expand the Amenity Infrastructure program to include
a Community Garden/Art Park in an empty lot along the strip. This
will be ready for planting fruits and vegetables and "growing" art by
early 2011.

Night view of Stripscape along Seventh Avenue

Daytime view looking northeast

Signage along Seventh Avenue

Consumption of billboard transformed into production of shade

Covered parking, pedestrian lighting, and business signs are integrated into one system, thereby reducing the amount of clutter along the strip.

A vertical sun screen combines with monument signage and a new public art program to create the public art shading panel.

Existing Seventh Avenue streetscape

Appropriated Space: Space that is programmed for one use, but is used for another

Scrimscape: Landscape used like a theatrical scrim or curtain that is not part of a building

Retail Garage Sale: The advertisement tactic of turning the retail store inside-out by placing merchandise in the front parking lot (similar to a residential garage sale) in hopes of attracting the attention of passing motorists

Yan-Ping Waterfront

Taipei, Taiwan, 2008

Stan Allen Architect

The task at Yan-Ping Waterfront was to create a new public park near major existing commercial and transportation centers in Taipei, Taiwan. The project's site lies on the Tamsui River—at the base of a newly planned urban corridor anchored by Taipei's central rail station—and is characterized by the presence of large-scale infrastructures: a bridge, an elevated highway, and a flood wall. The site is currently disconnected from the city and configured as leftover space. An existing eight-meter-high flood-control wall limits access and blocks views, while the ecology of the open space is an undifferentiated monoculture of non-native grasses. The scope of the project also included an intervention on the site of an existing parking garage, which allows for the presence of an iconic building to complement the park.

    The Taipei project operates at the level of urban infrastructure: its two major components—the reconfigured flood wall and the Eco-Net building proposed for the site of the parking garage—are functioning infrastructural elements that create new forms of public space within the city. The design of the project began by rethinking the architecture of the flood-control system. In place of the single wall at the edge of the city, a system of elevated levee structures—organized around a serpentine-crest landform—opens up unimpeded access to the site, and at the same time creates a variety of spaces and programs at the waterfront's edge. The architectural interventions reinforce the connectivity between park and city. The serpentine crest—which is strategically linked back to the city to foster increased access—creates an urban park with a wide range of uses that is nonetheless readily identifiable as a figure. Elevated viewing points are established across the length of the park, and the ecological potential of the site is improved, with diverse areas for natural plant regeneration. The new design cultivates social ecologies as well, allowing a greater diversity of activities to take place on the site by creating new programmatic and development opportunities.

Complementing the iconic shape of the new park—which unfolds in the "thick 2-D" of the horizontal dimension—is a new insertion in the skyline: a mixed-use Eco-Net building that connects the park to the city. The base of this building accommodates parking and transportation, creating an elevated urban garden at the same level as the park crest. Above this, spiral shopping concourses wrap around an aquarium, and, above that, an aviary. The program avoids the default options for configuring urban fabric today: shopping and commercial office space. Instead, it places a premium on public spaces and functions that have an ecological and educational dimension. The commercial aspect is not denied; instead, these institutional spaces are placed close to commercial space, creating opportunities for intersection and overlap. The result is a promiscuous mixture of natural and artificial, creating a hybrid identity for the twenty-first-century city.

Perspective view from artificial wetland

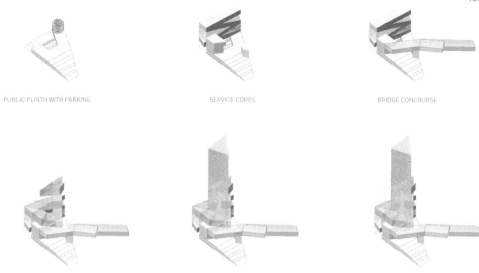

PUBLIC PLINTH WITH PARKING

SERVICE CORES

BRIDGE CONCOURSE

PUBLIC SPIRAL

TOWER

AVIARY & STRUCTURE

Eco-Net program diagrams

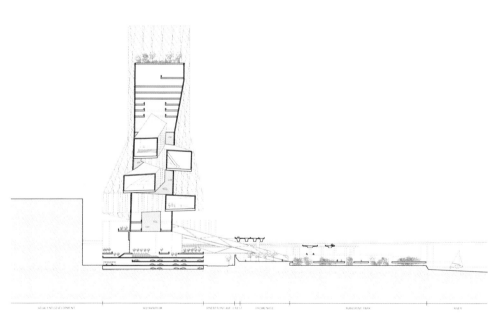

Section of Eco-Net building

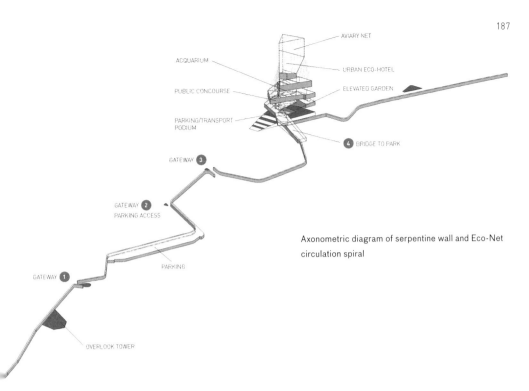

AVIARY NET

ACQUARIUM

URBAN ECO-HOTEL

PUBLIC CONCOURSE

ELEVATED GARDEN

PARKING/TRANSPORT
PODIUM

4 BRIDGE TO PARK

GATEWAY **3**

GATEWAY **2**
PARKING ACCESS

PARKING

GATEWAY **1**

OVERLOOK TOWER

Axonometric diagram of serpentine wall and Eco-Net
circulation spiral

Aerial perspective from north lookout tower

NeoPolitan Plan

Hell's Kitchen, New York, 2002

Richard Sommer and Laura Miller, borfax/BLU

"Underdeveloped" according to powerful real estate interests, Hell's Kitchen should logically accommodate the expansion of Midtown Manhattan's density. Yet bridges, ramps, and major access points associated with the Lincoln Tunnel, as well as the Port Authority Bus Terminal, the Jacob K. Javits Convention Center, and Hudson Yards form a barricade of "obnoxious" infrastructure, making the neighborhood resistant to laissez-faire development. NeoPolitan Plan was first developed on behalf of the Hell's Kitchen Neighborhood Association, to give them a plan with which to negotiate with the city of New York and various development interests. Against this background, the NeoPolitan Plan projects an admixture of use, height, and bulk zoning, literally figuring the overlapping political and socioeconomic interests vying for Hell's Kitchen, one of the most contested urban sites in a major American metropolis.

Going beyond project-based scenarios that respond primarily to one—or appease all—interests, agencies, and constituencies, the project's design procedures leverage one party's interests against the holdings or interests of others. The transferring of air rights and as-of-right densities creates a distinct physical profile and helps finance new infrastructure. A proscenium of high-rise development defines the district, allowing business and corporate entities to expand employment bases. Existing infrastructure is hybridized and domesticated with other programs; former impediments become networked amenities. A new convention center stacked above Hudson Yards replaces the existing Javits Center, doubling its area. The former Javits megasite is reparceled—forming a new NeoPolitan neighborhood, where housing, commercial uses, community programs, and open spaces hopscotch across the site strategically, serving the interests of local constituencies. Ultimately, the NeoPolitan Plan is less a plan than a design-based vehicle for private interest to become the subject of public debate and negotiation.

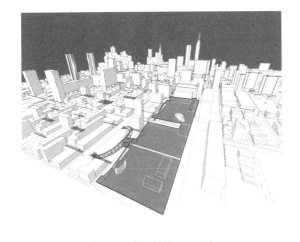

Stacking the Yards

1. Transfer obsolete Jacob K. Javits Center to the railyards.

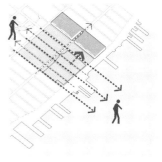

2. Liberate five jumbo-blocks for a new West-side neighborhood.

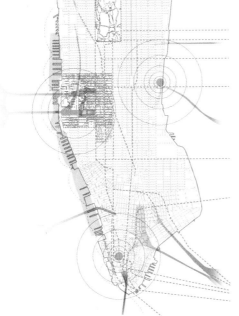

The purple shading shows existing major infrastructure, while the blue indicates proposed infrastructure to be added.

Garden

Convention Center

Car Park

Train Station

42nd Street

3. Network the site to local and regional infrastructure (from the High Line to the New Jersey ferries).

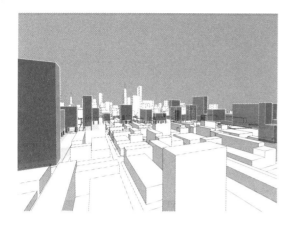

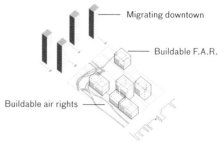

Migrating downtown

Buildable F.A.R.

Buildable air rights

Migrating Midtown

1. Accommodate flow of density westward.

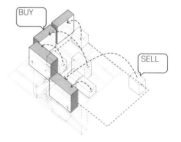

BUY

SELL

2. Transfer projected FAR from surrounding district to quasi-public transit air rights.

Commercial Flows of the existing Midtown business district are shown in pale green, while proposed "Midtown-West" commercial flows are indicated with darker green.

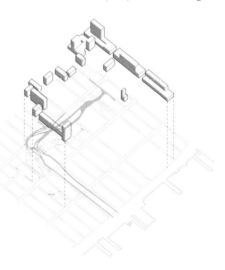

3. Create a porous development proscenium to Midtown.

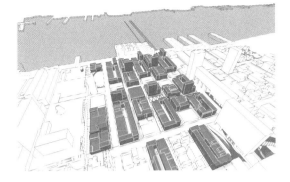

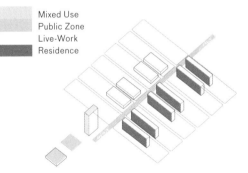

Mega

Fragmented

Playing Hopscotch

1. Disaggregate megablocks and reorder fragmented blocks.

Mixed Use
Public Zone
Live-Work
Residence

2. Sample Manhattan: It's in the mix.

Existing residential development is shown in light orange, while proposed residential development is indicated with dark orange.

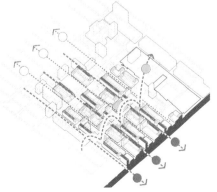

⟨○⟩···· 24-hour inbound live-work street
⟨◐⟩-- Public zone with park and plaza
⟨●⟩-- Outbound residential street

3. Create a district-wide NeoPolitan metablock.

Klip House

Houston, Texas, 1997–2000

Interloop—Architecture

Klip House is a consumer-based delivery platform that provides a physical and operational infrastructure for trade corporations to participate in the production of market housing. It was originally produced for the "Sixteen Houses: Designing the Public's Private House" exhibit, which was organized to generate concepts for affordable house designs based upon subsidies provided by government-funded voucher programs.[1] The design created by Interloop seeks to forward greater ambitions for architecture in the market housing milieu, and in the process return the performance criteria for residential architecture, which drives much of industry, to the consumer.

Federal and state initiatives provide financial assistance to qualified families and individuals by awarding housing vouchers to serve as the down payment on a private, single-family house. In its current format, the voucher system distributes financial support one voucher at a time. One voucher equals public assistance for one house. In spite of its innovative approach to giving financial support to deserving participants, the voucher system reinforces the current status of the housing industry. Architecture has little presence in the production of single-family residences outside of the design of custom houses, which are the exclusive territory of wealth and economic access. For the rest of the suburban landscape, housing is shaped by the interests of insurance companies, home mortgage corporations, code enforcement agencies, material distributorships, and builders' associations, which all constrict creativity in the system, and worse, deliver a generally inferior product.

Klip House explores the overall economic impact these vouchers might have if they are bundled rather than distributed. Instead of designing a single house that is constrained by the circumstances of the housing context, and has very little impact on the protocols of the current housing industry, Klip House works with the idea of consolidating the vouchers to underwrite development of a housing platform or infrastructure, allowing the opportunities and trajectories of the market to operate outside of the current model. Klip House proposes a fully serviceable, upgradeable, shrink- and expand-able, economically scalable, and technically advanced house.

The principal element enabling the Klip House platform to work is its adjustable footing, or "binder." The binder connects a series of functional components to each other, and to the ground. It accommodates a range of grade and soil conditions via leveling features and subgrade attachments. The binder is a mass-produced element that is purchased or leased and central to the functionality of the system. Components are created in a collaborative arrangement with corporations currently not associated with the housing industry whose products are synonymous with daily domestic life. These corporations, in conjunction with Klip House, advance a line of component features ranging from simple sleeping, bathing, cooking, and storing functions to a line of more advanced infrastructural components that allow for off-line living and specialized activities. Licensing agreements between Klip and appropriate corporate partners determine the index of possibilities for the platform. Individual memberships, each managed through ongoing Klip House accounts, curate the content and character of each project.

1 Interloop—Architecture was one of sixteen architects from across the country invited to submit designs for the Sixteen Houses exhibition. The exhibition opened on November 6, 1998, was curated by Michael Bell, and was sponsored by DiverseWorks Artspace and the Fifth Ward Community Redevelopment Corporation, both of Houston, Texas.

In winter sports, the correct fit of a binder—the primary piece of equipment that attaches the body to the ski or board— derives from experimentation, conditions on the ground, and the cumulative nature of component parts. For the Klip House footing, binders are deployed between an open array of housing components that can be added to, exchanged, reconfigured, and upgraded.

Klip House components are based upon a generic metric of three- and six-foot widths and are available with a variety of options, based on the sponsoring manufacturer and the activity associated with the component. Financial obligations match each consumer's level of economic comfort and stability.

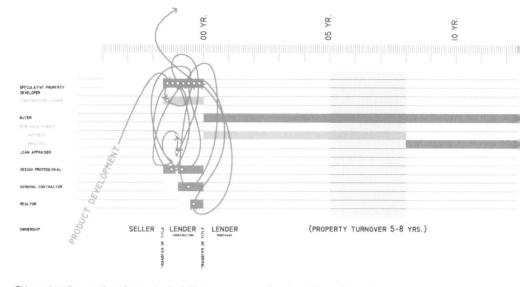

This product diagram shows how a standard thirty-year mortgage functions. All creativity and invention is front-loaded, and consumers or end users rarely participate in the process.

This service diagram describes how a situation-based housing platform like Klip House might work. Assets are built up along the way rather than in one large financial commitment, reflecting systems of financing that exist in the automotive and home appliance industries. New product lines are always "in the mill," financed against cumulative activity in Klip user accounts and aftermarket sales, the profits of which go back to the platform's bottom line.

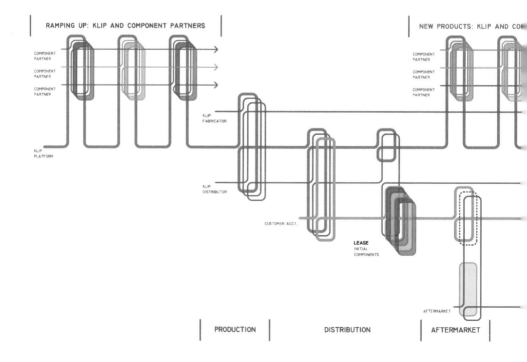

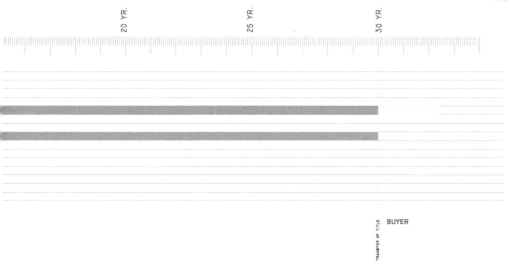

20 YR. 25 YR. 30 YR.

TRANSFER OF TITLE   **BUYER**

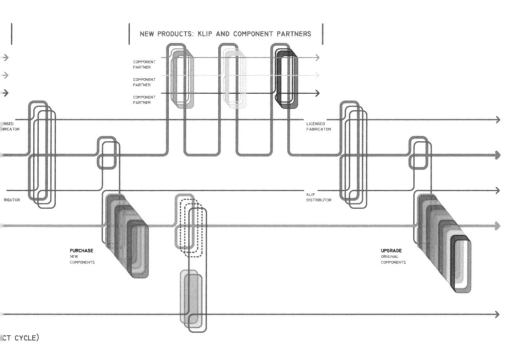

NEW PRODUCTS: KLIP AND COMPONENT PARTNERS

COMPONENT PARTNER

COMPONENT PARTNER

COMPONENT PARTNER

LICENSED FABRICATOR

KLIP DISTRIBUTOR

PURCHASE NEW COMPONENTS

UPGRADE ORIGINAL COMPONENTS

(CT CYCLE)

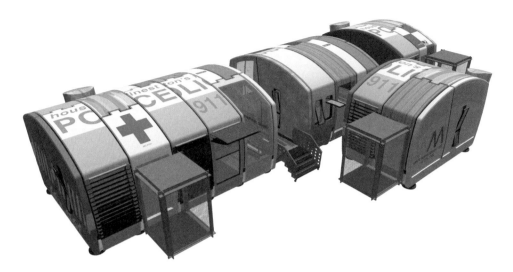

Images like this are perhaps the purest expression of the Klip House system, which anticipates the need for material disassembly, redistribution, and reuse of parts. Here, secondhand components are cobbled together to form a functional domestic universe, the significations of which seem invariably heterotopic.

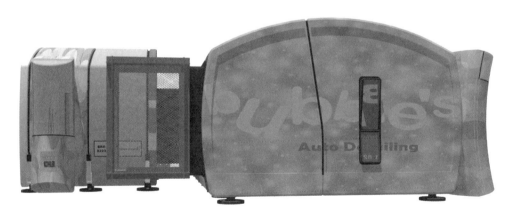

A secondhand facade component containing the plumbing infrastructure from an auto-detailing service makes for a nice, if slightly unconventional, master bathroom.

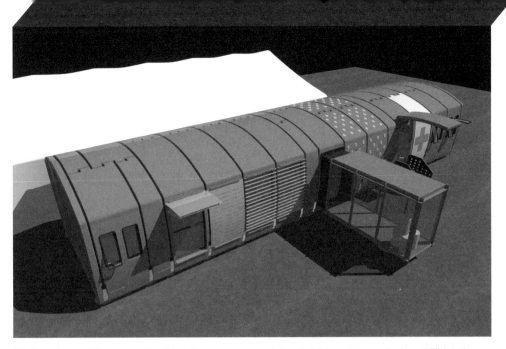

Klip House is an ambitious proposition. Given the enormous amount of capital that would be required to establish such a system, scenarios for how government-subsidized industry and government agencies might become involved prove useful. Here, Klip House components are used to create a remote surgery station for FEMA.

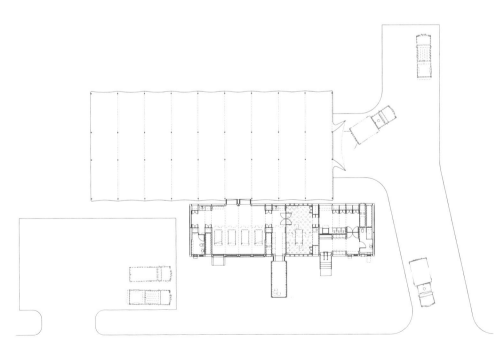

Site plan of the FEMA remote surgery station

The Critical Path

Columbus, Ohio, 2007

Interboro

Public transportation is good at two things: shuttling suburbanites to and from a center city, and moving people around a traditional, dense, mixed-use downtown. This is so because for many years, trips to, from, and around the center city accounted for most of the movement around a metropolitan region. However, this is no longer the case. As many urbanists have noted, the old, monocentric city is being overwritten by a newer, more polycentric one. In this new city—which resembles Michael Dear's conceptualization of the fragmented landscape of postmodernism more than Ernest Burgess's celebrated Concentric Rings diagram—growth happens in residential, commercial, and industrial nodes sprinkled around the urbanized region. Movement around this new city looks less like a hub and spoke than a network.

The Critical Path tries to address this problem by bringing public transportation to what Mark Robbins has called "the area between downtown and the small town." It takes as its laboratory an average, three-mile commercial corridor at the edge of Columbus, Ohio—a typical midwestern city where the automobile is used for close to 90 percent of trips to and from the home, office, and mall. A medium-trafficked, east-west corridor anchored on each side by busy beltway exits, the four-lane road services a familiar hodgepodge of light industry, regionally oriented retail, one- and two-story low-rent office buildings, and postwar-era single-family subdivisions.

At the heart of the scheme is a right-of-way, a bold new "suburban connector" that leverages transit investments to create exciting new public spaces. This new right-of-way—which can best be thought of as a hybridization of the parkway, main street, and the strip—is a two-way arterial that connects nodes along the many everyday commercial corridors of the city. Other recommendations include mixed-use, high-density growth in undeveloped land within the half-mile walking radius of the suburban connector's bus stops, as well as strategies for expanding transit options for "the last mile" (for example, by providing easements through backyards).

Right-Of-Way →

parkway detention water retention
sound berm
nature path
jogging neighborhood retail coffee shop
community garden bookstore
butterfly garden church **main** big boxes
fitness station **street**
village green drive-throughs **the**
town services **strip**
day care flagpole car sales auto services

← The Suburban Connector →

The rail and road systems in most American cities are hub-and-spoke systems, which are the most efficient for delivering people in and out of a central location.

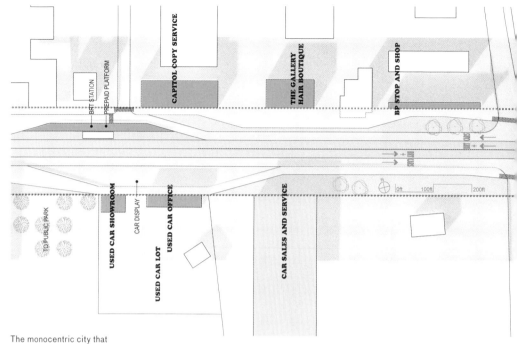

The monocentric city that characterized the early twentieth century is being overwritten by a new, polycentric, postmodern city.

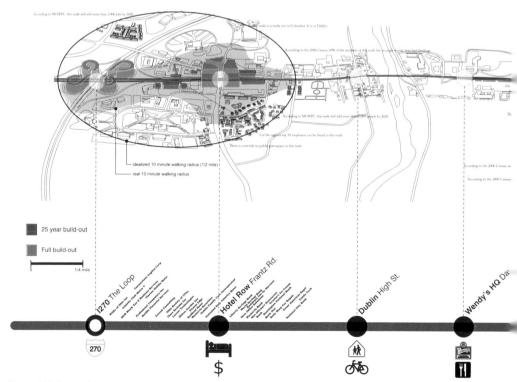

Plan and bird's-eye view

This new city illustrates Michael Dear's conceptualization of the fragmented landscape of postmodernism more than Ernest Burgess's celebrated concentric rings diagram.

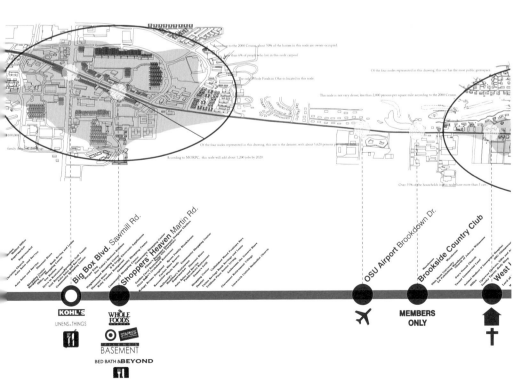

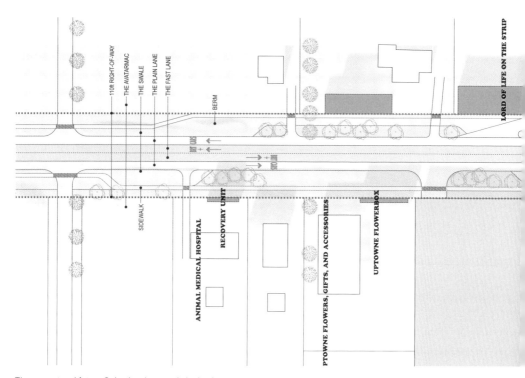

The present and future Columbus is not only in the downtown and in some mega-node in the suburbs, but in dozens of different nodes.

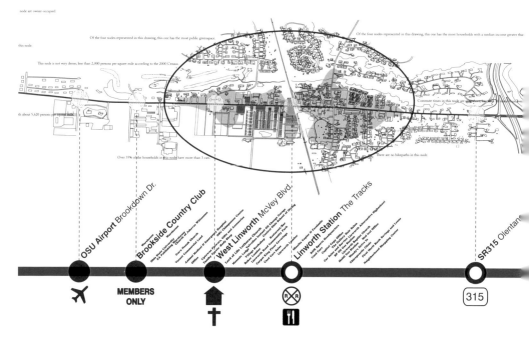

An ideal public transportation system would look less like a hub with spokes and more like a network.

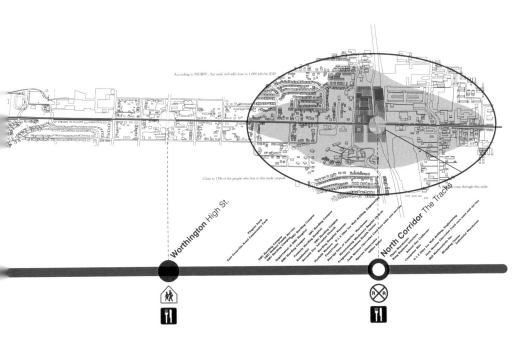

According to MORPC, this node will add close to 1,000 jobs by 2020.

Close to 15% of the people who live in this node carpool.

Worthington High St.

North Corridor The Tracks

Loops and Lilies

Toronto, Canada, 2006
WW with SAA

2.5-D

Toronto's waterfront catapults the city's density and Lake Ontario's emptiness toward one another. Its contours are neither entirely 2-D (flat) nor fully 3-D (volumetric). Program, ecology, legibility, economy, traffic, and structure thrive here in a 2.5-D bas-relief, a compressed urban system whose significance—performative and sensate—necessarily lies outside itself. In short, the promise of 2.5-D resides in its ability to catalyze the city-water alchemy. The waterfront's potential and 2.5-D's ambition exist not in self-expression but in their ability to foster legibility and exchanges across a compact yet aerated urbanism, a city composed of density and emptiness, work and leisure, commerce and public space, evening and daytime, dark and light. Loops and Lilies create an entirely new identity for the waterfront—an identity that announces "This is where you're going" rather than "This is where you are."

Island Life

Loops—both paved and green—enable island-hopping. Right-of-ways include bike lanes, sidewalks, and a ten-meter-wide "flexscape" along the southern side of the Queens Quay right-of-way. The flexscape's lighting, seating, landscaping, and events create continuous strands of waterfront life. At strategic intervals, the arbors and walkways of these east-west strands unfurl north and south, connecting the quay to both the water and the city. The loops' eddies and tethers have two aims: to create intensified urban pockets and to connect those pockets to one another, as well as to the existing city fabric.

Lilies—consisting of snack shacks, newsstands, art spaces, information booths, people-watching spots, reading rooms, bike rentals, ecostations, meeting rooms, catnap zones, wi-fi spots, and water exhibits—animate the islands, clustering near the culture buoys, the water's edge, and other destinations. They seed the waterfront's activities, catalyzing its dynamic cultural life.

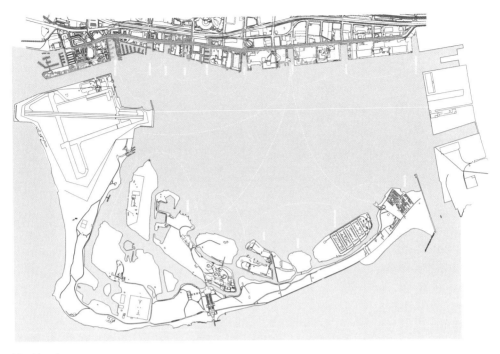

Island hopping

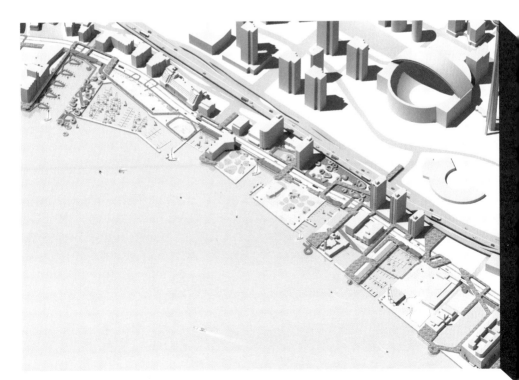

Aerial view

Island Culture

Each slip head is marked by a culture buoy—overlaps of loops and lilies that tie the islands back to the city and collectively offer both a programmatic and iconic identity to the waterfront. These culture buoys provide branch venues for city cultural and educational centers. They can also be rented as flexspaces by independent cultural groups or for special events, such as concerts, exhibitions, lectures, or wedding banquets.

Island Formation

Islands form over time, and Toronto's waterfront islands will develop in two phases. Phase one creates island incubators at the slip heads, which will in turn generate the full build-out of the project. This phase includes construction of all eight culture buoys, 15 percent of the lilies, and a continuous hardscape right-of-way along the length of Queens Quay, including landscaping in the immediate vicinity of the culture buoys. The full build-out of the waterfront project will complement phase one with the completion of the flexscape along the entirety of the quay, the extension of loops both to the water and toward downtown, and the full lily build-out, which will activate the overall waterfront and reveal Toronto's entire urban archipelago.

Island Tales

Sparked by culture buoys, the waterfront's loops and lilies provide bearings and direction to urban life. They're green—landscape and arbor—and orange—hardscape and enclosure. They include places to stop, see, snack, play, buy, listen, and learn. They're cool in the summer and warm in the winter. They make everything else look great. They engender activities, landscapes, and buildings. They slip in, around, and among the existing waterfront's currently illegible composition. They bring to Toronto a world apart that is part of its world: the island urbanism of Toronto's waterfront archipelago.

WASAW BRAIN TRUST

R. LOZANO-HEMMER — LIGHT ARTIST
R. PEISER — REAL ESTATE
MATHEWS NIELSEN — LANDSCAPE

WASAW PROJECT LEAD
SARAH WHITING
STAN ALLEN — SAA PRINCETON UNIVERSITY
WW PRINCETON UNIVERSITY
RON WITTE — WW PRINCETON UNIVERSITY
CARLOS ARNAIZ — SAA

D. ALLIN — TORONTO HISTORY
J. THOMPSON — ART CURATOR
S. KWINTER — THEORIST
A. SHORRIS — PLANNING
A. MANNING — ARCHITECT
BURO HAPPOLD — STRUCTURE
FRONT, INC. — SURFACES
J. GOMEZ-IBANEZ — URBAN ECONOMY
C. LEE — ARCHITECT
ARUP — TRAFFIC
S. BOCKING — ECOLOGIST
R.E. SOMOL — THEORIST
T. GOWER — ARTIST
J. ROSENBERG — LANDSCAPE
ATELIER 10 — SUSTAINABILITY
J. MAY — GEOGRAPHER
BIOENGINEERING — ECOLOGY
C. KUBISCH — SOUND & LIGHT ARTIST
C. WERTHMANN — GREEN SURFACES
D. LOPEZ-PEREZ — ARCHITECT
L. WYMAN — GRAPHICS
J. CHEON — ARCHITECT

Lily Pier, Portland Slip, with Culture Buoy (Museum) at head of slip

Culture Buoy (Zoo) at head of York Slip

Culture Buoy (Gallery), Jarvis Slip

Regenerating Economies
Essays

Active Forms

Keller Easterling

Some of the most radical changes to the globalizing world are not being written in the language of international law and diplomacy, but rather in the spaces of architecture and urbanism. These spaces are creating forms of polity faster than official channels can legislate them. They also prompt a contemplation of an expanded and unconventional repertoire for political activism.

Activists customarily rely on, among other things, resistance and refusal. Approaching the most powerful forces in the world with dissent frequently demands conviction and unity among those who have less power. It calls for assembly, the resolute condemnation of abusive policies, or the protection of others who are the target of abuse. For many, the vigilant maintenance of decency and justice requires strongly held beliefs, established principles, and forthright expression. Resistance, even in its most complex, artful, and viral forms, must often assume a critical, oppositional stance—an organizational disposition that faces off against authoritarian power. Though capable of striking at the heart of their opponent, explicit, small-scale antagonisms on the periphery are favored over collusion with the center. David must kill Goliath. These are classic techniques of activism that have, at certain junctures in history, required enormous courage to enact.

Yet meanwhile, the targeted power frequently escapes. Using proxies and obfuscation for protection, powerful players are rarely forthright about their aims, in part because they survive on fluid intentions. Finding the loophole to absolute logics or zero-sum games, power wanders away from the bull's-eye or wriggles out to take shelter in another ruse. Indeed, the notion that there is a proper realm of political negotiation usually acts as the perfect camouflage for this elusive behavior. Powerful players may then even come costumed as resistance. Goliath finds a way to pose as David, or multiple forces—assembling and shapeshifting—replace the fantasy Goliath of monolithic capital or corporate culture with even more insidious moving targets.

Dissent is then left shaking its fist at an effigy while the opposing powers mimic or confound with some other disguise. Activism that shows up at the barricade, the border crossing, and the battleground with familiar political scripts sometimes finds that the real fight or the stealthier forms of violence are happening somewhere else. The opponent of dissent becomes an even more mystical or vaporous force (e.g., capital, empire, or neoliberalism). Even those theories that admit to complicities and mixtures of power somehow still drift toward the epic heraldry and theme music of enemies and innocents (e.g., empire/counter-empire). In this way, the grand strategies of the left and the right share a combative structure. Expectations of proper techniques and territories for political work also supply some of activism's most significant internal constraints. Righteous ultimatums that offer only collusion or refusal might present a greater obstacle than any of the quasi-mythical forces that activists oppose. The architecture of global relations is not, of course, arranged as a series of symmetrical face-offs or head-to-head battlegrounds. There is ample evidence of overlapping networks of influence and allegiance. Moreover, it may be a mistake to disregard caprice—the subterfuge, hoax, and hyperbole that actually rules the world. The complex logics of duplicity may be more instructive than the straightforward structure of righteousness.

Still, an attempt to aid and broaden activism can even be interpreted as a betrayal of its principles. Manipulating the market is mistaken for collusion. Giving positive attention to agents of systemic change rather than negative opposition to a series of enemies is mistaken for an uncritical stance. Relinquishing the tense grip of resistance is mistaken for capitulation rather than a more precise parry or a more apt strategy. Answering duplicity with duplicity is mistaken for equivocation or lack of conviction rather than a technique to avoid disclosing a deliberate strategy. Preserving as authentic only some approaches to political leverage may foreclose on the very insurgency that activism wishes to instigate.

A political discourse in architecture and urbanism also frequently drifts toward tragic stock narratives. Architectural offerings within this discourse may be given a political theme and situated at a border crossing, battleground, or barricade. However apt or even sly the design may be, it is often relegated to the margins because it resolves all the world's dimensions into a single compatible utopia or because it makes too much sense. Alternately, likening engagement with collusion, the architect refuses to perform for fear of being co-opted by the market.

Encores of tragic arias about the impossibility of a political architecture support an enduring innocence.[1] As Jacques Rancière has said, "To ask, How can one escape the market? is one of those questions whose principal virtue is one's pleasure in declaring it insoluble."[2]

Perhaps the righteous and innocent should be allowed to remain perpetually pure and right. The dramas and tragedies of the Masonic order of architects give pleasure to many and need draw no further critique. While fully equipped with prodigious political craft, that craft should only be deployed in the arena of careerism and should not be burdened with another political responsibility. Rather, it should be allowed to remain undisturbed in the autonomous cul-de-sac that it has long requested. Similarly, dissent that would consider itself sullied by alternative tactics might remain exempt, freeze-framed in a moment of being right.

1 For instance, with its attraction to tragic ultimates and endgames, Manfredo Tafuri's critique of the "impotent and ineffectual myths" of a political architecture is apt if architecture sees as its only tools form as object and ideology. Manfredo Tafuri, *Architecture and Utopia: Design and Capitalist Development* (Cambridge, MA: MIT Press, 1979), 178, 182.

2 Jacques Rancière, "The Art of the Possible: Fulvia Carnevale and John Kelsey in Conversation with Jacques Rancière," *Artforum International* 45, no. 7 (Mar. 2007): 256–60.

Dissensus

I would rather talk about dissensus than resistance.
—Jacques Rancière

Yet a trap door out of these epic or tragic narratives is found in the very evidence they deny. In addition to direct, head-to-head political action, indirect techniques or aesthetic regimes may, after philosopher Jacques Rancière and others, generate *dissensus* rather than resistance.[3] While in common parlance dissensus is often used to describe the opposite of consensus, and is seen as a condition that

3 Ibid., 256.

needs remedy, Rancière has used the word positively, as the opposite of institutional isomorphism. Dissensus insists on considering what is "inadmissible."[4]

4 Jacques Rancière, *The Politics of Aesthetics* (London: Continuum, 2004), 85.

Indeed, change rarely follows sanctioned plotlines, but often pivots around hoax, hyperbole, and stray details. These phantom turning points are not easily placed within orthodox political logics. For example, Wal-Mart, the most egregious offender with regard to health care coverage of its employees, reappears as the purveyor of digitized health records. T. Boone Pickens, a former oil and gas executive and conservative Republican from the United States, is leading an effort to make wind a central, profitable source of energy. Some of the most advanced experiments in high-speed rail are being conducted in the Middle East, at the epicenter of oil. The infrastructures of transportation, communication, and business that are supposed to rationalize exchanges thrive on irrationalities of the market and the cults of management.

However invisible to political orthodoxies, such events may be the real cause of shifts in sentiment, changes in economic fortune, the escalation or suspension of violence, and swift epidemics. The biggest changes may result from a seemingly innocuous detail. The most productive move may be the selfishly motivated innovation of the most abusive player. Consensus, fooling many, may deliver the lowest and most destructive leaders. Fiction and stupidity, the cheerful friends of politics, are capable of stalemating the most reasonable advances or lubricating the most grisly forms of authority. Waters may seem to part inexplicably because of an indirect bargain made on a remote problem.

Inversions and outlying political evidence, with their fickle or underexplored logics, excite feelings of ingenuity. Here is a large field of mongrel events and category leftovers—butterflies that are not pinned to the board, because they do not reinforce customary political scripts or reset our accustomed narratives. Architecture frequently claims to be absent from the official policy table. Yet if it is the butlers, shills, proxies, and go-betweens who make many of the decisions about the way the world works, architects have long been seated at that table. Running through their fingers is this unorthodox, but extensive, parallel polity.

An expanded activist repertoire might be less self-congratulatory, less transcendent, less automatically oppositional, and more effective (and sneakier). Rather than tense resistance and competition, alternative strategies may ironically rely on the power of gifts, exaggerated compliance, rumor, misdirection, distraction, meaninglessness, comedy, unreasonable innovation, or contagions. For instance, with steamrolling sweetness, China offered two pandas to Taiwan—pandas whose translated names mean "unity." Or, as social scientist James C. Scott recalls from Milan Kundera's *The Joke*, when the prisoners in the novel deliberately and elaborately lose a footrace to the prison guards, their exaggerated compliance galvanizes their power and disarms their captors.[5] Instrumental meaninglessness lubricates displays in sports or tourism, even between fractious enemies. Comedy and distraction deliver critiques while diffusing tension. The entrepreneur pursues unreasonable innovations that will act as contagions rather than singular masterpieces (like those that architects train to create). Often the sea change supersedes the fight.

When Goliath and David are switching masks, and power is oscillating between different allegiances, many opportunities present themselves. While the notion of a tiny David and a giant Goliath is useful and empowering, it reifies both the fabled opponent and the activist underdog who provides small-scale antagonisms on the periphery, for fear of colluding with the center.[6] If it were possible to tinker with fables, might Tom Sawyer slip into David's role and use the gift and the briar patch while leveraging Goliath's size?

5   James C. Scott, *Domination and the Arts of Resistance: Hidden Transcripts* (New Haven, CT: Yale University Press, 1990), 139–40.

6   Alain Badiou, *Ethics: An Essay on the Understanding of Evil*, trans. Peter Hallward (London: Verso, 2001), 90.

Active Forms and Disposition

While for architects, authorship of form as object is a fundamental skill reliant on the aesthetics of profile and geometry, the discipline also has at its disposal an expanded set of techniques surrounding the manipulation of active forms, dispositions, and aesthetic practices, all of which serve dissensus.

Conceived as agency or within a spatial domain, active forms describe the protocols by which some alteration performs within a group, multiplies across a field, reconditions a population, or generates a network. If objective form operates in the nominative register, active forms operate in the infinitive. The designer of active forms is designing the delta, or the means by which the organization changes—not the field in its entirety, but the way it is inflected. They design not only the shape or profile of the game piece, but also a repertoire for how the piece can be played. So while perhaps intensely involved with material and geometry, active forms are inclusive of but not limited to enclosure, and may move beyond the conventional architectural site. These forms are not at odds with, but rather propel and expand, the power of form as object. As they ride larger organizations, they are instrumental to additional modes of authorship, with time-released powers and cascading effects.

For instance, the authorship of an individual house as objective form is different from the authorship of the protocol that created Levittown. The elevator is an active form and primary germ of urban morphology. Highway protocols similarly were active forms with the power to multiply across a field just as the spatial products for retail, tourism, transshipment, or free zones propagate in the world. The active forms for DNA replication involve explicit instructions with both chemical and geometrical substrates. The familiar geometric substrate is a double helix, but it does not stand for the process or for the millions of possible sequences that might result from these likely chemical behaviors. Similarly, the behavior of a virus is explicit on a small scale, but its epidemiological path through a population is unpredictable.

Active forms build disposition—an attribute that cannot be named, but only unfolded over time. For philosopher Gilbert Ryle, disposition, as agency or tendency, is latent until activated. It is not an event or object that can be named and verified. Disposition, for Ryle, was about knowing "how" rather than knowing "that." A person has the capacity or tendency to sing or smoke. The dog can swim. The rubber has a tendency to lose its elasticity. A ball on an inclined plane has a tendency to roll, and yet it need not move to possess this disposition. It is active because of its relationships—its relative position to other objects with very specific geometric attributes. Dispositional attributes sometimes remain as fuzzy imponderables within customary logics because they cannot be determined and they do not constitute an event, but must rather be observed over time as a potentiality, capacity, ability, or faculty. Ryle takes a particular delight in exposing the confusions that arise between naming and doing.[7]

7 Gilbert Ryle, *The Concept of Mind* (Chicago, IL: University of Chicago Press, 1949), 27–32, 43–44, 89, 116.

Architecture and urbanism offer similar confusions. Spaces are rarely considered to possess disposition. A building, landscape, or interior might be described in terms of its appearance, affect, geometrical composition, or visual pattern. Spaces are considered to be objects or volumes, not actors with agency or temperament that might even be evaluated for a quotient of aggression, submission, or exclusivity immanent in their arrangement. If asked to create something called active form, designers would naturally rely on what they are best-trained to create—a formal object themed, choreographed, or dressed to represent action. For instance, serialized geometric formations are used to create a placeholder for a process that cannot be named or fixed. A single enclosure is meant to represent, for instance, relativity or embryology. In grasping for apprehension of an evolving spatial field with changing components, the architect designs the field in its entirety. The more complex or agitated these tracings, the more "active" the form is meant to be. A more simple-minded confusion (made more powerful by being simple-minded) arises when action or activity is confused with movement or kineticism, as in a building that appears to be moving or a space composed of or populated by moving objects.

In active organizations of all types, from the scale of the city to the circuit, it is relatively meaningless to represent activity or disposition. For example, Savannah, Georgia, in its original plan was an assembly of active form reliant on geometry and designed to engender a political disposition. Its designer, James Oglethorpe, created a simple grid that looked like all the others, but it actually established a growth protocol not unlike that of a virus. To curb the problems caused by real estate speculation, the town was to grow by wards—where each ward was, like a mathematical function, an expression of interdependencies. Each ward contained a quotient of open space, and the lots around that green—expressed as tithings or percentages of the ward—were reserved for civic functions. Moreover, each ward automatically established a quotient of agricultural space outside of town. So while there were explicit geometrical instructions for each ward, the pattern of accumulated wards could not be predicted. Similarly, protocols for the internet yield a disposition that might be described as relatively open, redundant, simultaneous, and non-hierarchical. It would be meaningless to attempt to represent these dispositions, but powerful to author active forms that ride the network with very explicit instructions. In both these cases, there is nothing to see or represent in its totality, only something intensely formal to activate and replicate in a way that extends the reach of form as object.

Both objective forms and active forms offer artistic seductions. Indeed, they often work in tandem. Objective form, which presents shape and contour, can be attributed to and controlled by an author, and this is at least part of its seduction. Active form, on the other hand, takes pleasure in its ability to create ramifying effects. It does not wish to maintain a particular contour, but rather to maintain a behavior within an organization or a network. In theater, the actor loves the rhythm, sound, and content of the text, just as the architect takes pleasure in geometric contour. Yet the actor also takes pleasure in manipulating both the content of the text together with what the character is doing. Rarely relying on text alone, the actor does not play in the nominative (e.g., being a mother) but rather in the infinitive (e.g., smothering).

The aesthetics of active form and disposition, while inclusive of considerations of the object, extend to include aesthetic practices, like those that Jacques Rancière describes. Significantly, in *The Politics of Aesthetics*, Rancière does not discuss the aesthetics of politics, but the politics surrounding the reception of a work of art. For example, he describes not the pageant of goose-stepping soldiers in a zeppelin field but rather, for instance, the reception of Gustave Flaubert's book *Madame Bovary*—whose voice relayed to its audience a liberating disposition despite its roots in conservative politics. Rancière makes a distinction between aesthetics that concern what is being depicted versus what is being done.[8]

8   Rancière, *The Politics of Aesthetics*, 14.

With active forms, content and disposition may be discrepant. Names may be used, designations may be made, but they may not correspond to the dispositional activity of the form. Sociologist Erving Goffman used the word "disposition" to describe the entire performance—that is, the spoken words, gestures, postures, and facial expressions—that constitutes an individual's presentation of self.[9] He noted that these myriad subtexts often overwhelmed and were at odds with the stated text. Just as *Madame Bovary* communicated dispositional politics that were not textually expressed, an actor may speak the line "I love you" while playing an action or intention to murder with that love. A Levittown house may be called "colonial" even though its real composition is unrelated to the name. The home is only named colonial, but it has been composed as a serial set of building tasks performed across a field of houses. The homeowners who consume the name rather than the process end up buying something that never quite meets their expectations, just as the activist is left protesting at the wrong barricade. The content of rumor and gossip is less relevant than the way it behaves. During the U.S. presidential election of 2008, the rumor that Barack Obama was Muslim was effective precisely because it was so far from the truth. The rumor could be kept alive even longer and repeated twice as much—first to spread the falsehood and then to refute it. The hoax claiming that climate change was itself a hoax was effective for similar reasons. The bounce of the rumor or hoax may be instrumental in ways that are dislocated from content.

9   Erving Goffman, *The Presentation of Self in Everyday Life* (New York: Anchor Books/Doubleday, 1959).

A contemplation of active forms and disposition stretches disciplinary habits of mind to consider a common art for shaping the object as well as the way it plays—an art with enhanced faculties for conditioning material and immaterial parameters, aesthetic practices, and political trajectories, which may even be located at a remove in space and time. Further tutoring an expanded political repertoire, these active forms are capable of embodying discrepancies and slippery, undeclared forms of power.[10] Disposition is politically powerful in that it can

10   Max Kistler and Bruno Gnassounou, eds., *Dispositions and Causal Powers* (London: Ashgate Publishing Limited, 2007).

disappear and be discrepant, but it can also serve as the foundational medium that decides what survives—a conditioning substrate or an infrastructural chemistry immanent in organization. Yet dispositional techniques extend form-making into another, central and potent territory. They provide the means by which forms find new, time-released capacities and infrastructural territories that are the medium of power and polity. While some political traditions call for inversions and revolutions or some other annihilation of the preceding system, a lateral dispositional shift might be just as radical, but never permanent. The weather-changing, medium-changing, compounding capacities of dispositional activism make it among the most powerful tools of urbanism.

Some True Stories

Some True Stories: Researches in the Field of Flexible Truth, an exhibition at the Storefront for Art and Architecture in the fall of 2008, presented design research concerning global infrastructure. Rumor and comedy were useful techniques for the presenters. Each project was a mixture of fact and fiction—"faction," as they say in Hollywood. Since measure or reason rarely create epidemics of persuasion in the world, and since many of the most powerful operations are lubricated by obfuscations, the material of the show entered into this confidence game. Design is a hoax. The presentations deliberately avoided confronting the world with a forthright, righteous reform. Rather, as if attributing the ideas to others, they congratulated the world on having had the better idea all along. This design research swims in the dirty waters with all the other shills, looking for new points of leverage within fictions and persuasions. The collection favored agility, ricochet, and cultural contagion over prescription. It was attracted to spatial entrepreneurialism, unreasonable innovation, impure ethical struggles, and obdurate problems that continually resist intelligence. The following projects, included in the Some True Stories show, hoped to spread rumors that the world has changed and to operate with all the guises and none of the disadvantages of truth.

Gossip might be seen as the linguistic equivalent and forerunner of witchcraft.... Rumor is the second cousin of gossip and magical aggression.

—James C. Scott

[There is] no great idea that stupidity could not put to its own uses; it can move in all directions, and put on all the guises of truth. The truth, by comparison, has only one appearance and only one path, and is always at a disadvantage.

—Robert Musil

Project One: VPL ›› fig. 1

Researchers: Rustam Marc-Mehta, Thom Moran

fig. 1 ›› VPL

VPL is the product of unexpected economies and partnerships, resulting from hybridizing rail and air travel in a triangle of the Southwest that contains eight of America's ten fastest-growing cities and three of the nation's most congested airports. Like other beloved American acronyms, the airport code VPL will become the name for a vast development zone in the desert, equidistant from McCarran International Airport (LAS) in Las Vegas, Phoenix Sky Harbor International Airport (PHX), and Los Angeles International Airport (LAX). Facing a shortage of airspace and no opportunities for expansion, airlines merge with rail to link the three airports via a central hub in the desert. The move was a preemptive grab at high speed rail's 350 mile-per-hour sweet spot to free up runway space for valuable international flights.

While critics call the area planned sprawl, its proponents portray the plan in progressive terms. The young developers, speaking in the jargon of complexity theory and the business models of Las Vegas casinos, are planning a single-level, daylit enclosure several square miles in area to be shared between the three airports. Part airport city, part casino, and part suburb, the plan will be the first stateside installation of Japanese high-speed rail technology, which has already been exported to Taiwan and soon to China. Politically conservative businesses have rushed to invest in this "green" building, which is offering tailor-made subdivisions with inherently low carbon footprints that are an hour-long train ride from three of America's largest cities.

Project Two: Mecca ›› fig. 2

Researchers: Ashima Chitre, Mustapha Jundi

fig. 2 ›› Mecca

There are many familiar means of generating small amounts of electricity through pressure or absorption of sunlight, including piezo materials and fabrics embedded with photovoltaic strands. Mecca flexible rugs and tents—meant to be used in the holy city, located in Saudi Arabia—are the most massive experiment with these materials to date. During the height of the pilgrimage season, the tents and the mats underfoot leverage energy from the large volume of visitors. The epicenter of oil country is an unlikely place to experiment with new forms of electricity generation, and also surprising is the imagery of the tents, which merge with the Mecca megamall to become an iconic conglomerate used in billboard and bus advertisements.

Project Three: Floor ›› fig. 3

Researcher: Keller Easterling

fig. 3 ›› Floor

The ordinary floor is changing the terms of architectural design. Transportation designs frequently range from elevated utopian remedies (less interesting to us) to the slightly mad visions of amateur enthusiasts. Projected designs often depict a complex and responsive new circuitry of infrastructure intersections. The floor drawing in this installation does not belong with those of Norman Bel Geddes, Lawrence Halprin, Geoffrey

Jellicoe, or Brian Richards. Instead, parts of it first appeared on one of the web's popular AutoCAD exchange networks. Members of these networks generously share drawings named, for instance, "Andrew.dwg," "do not delete.dwg," or "Elks club parking lot.dwg," because...someone might need them someday. The found drawing, together with its text, is particularly impressive because there is nothing futuristic or visionary about it. Rather, it presents an exuberant rehearsal of existing transport technologies, for which the floor is a navigational surface. Additionally, it explores the merger of the car and the elevator, as can be seen in warehouses, ports, and other logistics environments. New automated vehicles read floor graphics and signals for instructions. The drawing does not depict a clichéd dream of omnidirectional movement, but simply an expanded repertoire for the common floor. Note also that the floors and columns of Le Corbusier's Maison Dom-ino have been redefined as both structure and passageway. The new floor, like the elevator, is depicted as a highly contagious germ or multiplier of urban morphology. Like many drawings found in the AutoCAD exchange networks, this one appears to have been lovingly created with some affection for the floor's new graphic excesses.

Project Four: Section 27-751 ›› fig. 4

Researchers: Gabby Brainard, Jacob Reidel

New York City Building Code:
§[C26-1205.7] 27-751: Minimum Dimensions of Habitable Rooms
Habitable rooms shall have a minimum clear width of eight feet in any part, a minimum clear area of eighty square feet, and a minimum clear ceiling height of eight feet.

fig. 4 ›› Section

§[C26-201.0] 27-232: Definitions

Mezzanine: An intermediate floor between the floor and ceiling
of any space. When the total gross floor area of all mezzanines
occurring in any story exceeds thirty-three and one-third percent
of the gross floor area of that story such mezzanine shall be considered as a separate story.

The New York City building code defines habitable space as any room
with an eight-foot ceiling. But in fact, the market will accept ceilings that
are a few inches lower. Brooklyn architect Robert Scarano has capitalized on the difference between code and reality, and parlayed it into a
building type that has transformed his native borough.

Scarano is best known for the glassy luxury condominiums that
have sprouted all over Brooklyn's "up-and-coming" neighborhoods in
recent years. These buildings, which literally stand head and shoulders
above their neighbors, are evidence that his team has mastered the art
of maximizing building envelopes up to (and sometimes beyond) the
limits allowed by code. Scarano's signature move is designing double-
height living spaces with mezzanines whose ceilings are just shy of eight
feet high. In permit applications, he claimed that the mezzanines were
not "habitable" and subtracted their square footage from the overall
area. This enabled him to build bigger while also creating the airy, loft-
like apartments buyers wanted. The result is a new building type—the
mezzanine loft—that takes its place alongside the mansard roof and the
setback skyscraper as a typology born of building regulation and development pressure.

Scarano's ability to exploit code loopholes has made him popular with developers, but it has also drawn fire from local community
boards and the press, not to mention the law (several of his buildings
are under investigation by the Department of Buildings). Despite the
controversy, we see Scarano as a compelling example of an architect
on the make—twisting, tweaking, and reshaping the rules by which he
operates. Much has been made of architects' lack of power in the design
and construction process, and the ways their actions are constrained

by clients, codes, and contracts. By manipulating all three, Scarano has turned limitations into opportunities. We present his story here as an inspiration to the profession.

Indeed, a new generation of architects is already following Scarano's lead. In Hunters Point, Queens, the young practice called United States Architects (USA) plans to use the mezzanine loophole in high-rise construction for the first time. In USA's proposed tower, the mezzanines take the form of prefabricated, high-end residential units inserted into a conventional framework of high-rise affordable apartments. The prefab "pods," which can be completely customized by their future owners, are used to leverage more space for affordable housing, in essence inverting the typical ratio of market-rate to affordable units in a project of this type. The result is an iconic residential tower that the developer, Mirax Group, hopes will "initiate an era of enlightened high-rise construction in the neighborhood." To date, the USA design has not received the same criticism as Scarano's projects, perhaps because of Mirax's politically astute approach to affordable housing, or maybe because New Yorkers have finally accepted the mezzanine typology as a turn-of-this-century addition to the city's skyline.

Exhibit drawings were provided courtesy of Scarano Architect PLLC. and United States Architects.

Project Five: Amazone

Researchers: Carol Ruiz, Santiago del Hierro

The Napo River in Ecuador has been proposed as a means of extending the Amazon to the Pacific to create a transoceanic corridor that would bypass the Panama Canal and facilitate a new set of trade alignments for South America. These new global trade expectations compete for influence with oil exploration, fragile rainforest reserves, and dispersed indigenous communities in a region already packed with myths and political unknowns. The Napo, with its multiple interests, could be the site of business as usual, or an experiment in leveraging and orchestrating trade-offs between extraction and preservation.

The film *Negociamos* (2008) presents the contradictory tales of these manifold interests in the same sloppy way that they are encountered in the field. It tells the story with the original amusement of discovering facts and data that seem to have been hidden from the public. None of the documents, maps, and videos can found in an organized database. Consequently, each of them presents just one piece of a growing puzzle.

Project Six: Cable ›› fig. 5

Researchers: Keller Easterling, Mwangi Gathinji

fig. 5 ›› Cable

East Africa is one of the last places on earth that has not been served by submarine fiber-optic cable. In the last few years, several competing plans for submarine cable may help to avoid the monopoly controls that have made broadband cable in both east and west Africa typically cost ten times what it does in the United States. The road between the cities of Mombasa and Nairobi in Kenya is receiving a terrestrial extension of the fiber-optic cable and serving as a test bed for new urban outcroppings of the technology, from free zones to digital villages.

Cities without Centers and Edges

Michael Dear

The way we make cities is changing radically. No longer are cities being built from the inside out (from core to periphery), but instead from the outside in (from hinterlands to what is left of the core). As a consequence, urban theory, practice, and policy-making require revision, but for this to happen we also need new ways of seeing the urban, even a new vocabulary for discussing the "city."

Peripheral urban developments in Southern California have long occurred without conventional downtowns, which are sometimes added later for aesthetic and identification/branding purposes or simply to augment consumption opportunities. In such cases, "downtowns" or "town centers" become, in effect, externalities of the urban process; they are no longer functionally constitutive of the city, but merely incidental side effects. Consequently, does it really make sense to promote mega-projects for downtown renewal when the principal urban dynamic has everywhere shifted to the periphery? Of course, it is possible to defend downtown revitalization on the basis of efficient reuse of the physical and social infrastructural investments already in place. However, such policy must be recognized for what it is: a hugely risky investment strategy that is predicted (by theory) to fail. If we take seriously the theory-practice link, then the altered urbanism I outline in this essay will necessarily require innovations in architecture and planning practice.

Consensus has it that we have entered a global urban age because the majority of the world's population now lives in cities. Yet there is precious little understanding about what this trend entails, beyond the customary Malthusian-inspired fear of apocalypse. Attempts to clarify this profusion of nomenclatures by situating the urban process within a wider social dynamic are confounded because this dynamic is itself an unstable, multifaceted prism that incorporates the following: *globalization*, including the emergence of a small group of world cities as centers of command and control in a capitalist world economy; *network society*, including the rise of the "cyber cities" of the information age; *polarization*, the increasing gap among rich and poor nations, between different ethnic, racial, and religious groups, between genders, and between those on either side of the digital divide; *hybridization*, the fragmentation and reconstruction of identity and cultural life brought about by international and domestic migrations; and *sustainability*, including a widening consciousness of human-induced environmental change.

Taken together, these categories provide a powerful, though not exhaustive, framework for the problematics of both global and local politics (for brevity, call it neoliberalism, although this term already carries too much baggage). And while these tendencies may find formal equivalence in previous eras (e.g., earlier manifestations of globalization), the present concatenation is different because they have never before appeared in concert, never before penetrated so deeply, never before been so geographically extensive, and never before overtaken everyday life with such speed. In short, there has never been anything as globally universal as the rise of the information age. In my judgment, it is likely to prove as profoundly altering as the advent of the agricultural and industrial revolutions of earlier times.

This new world order is already manifest in an altered urban structure that, according to urbanist Bruce Katz, possesses five principal characteristics: increasing scale and size of cities; accelerating speed and velocity of urban growth; new levels of mobility and migration among diverse populations, both within and between nations; increasingly complex socioeconomic, political, and cultural arrangements; and unprecedented connectivity among peoples, firms, and places.[1] The local urban outcomes associated with these global adjustments have puzzled analysts, who for more than two decades have groped for meaning by reading the texts of the burgeoning urban landscape. Manifestations of change include edge cities, privatopias, heterotopias, theme park–ization, malling, surveillance spaces, the erasure of public space, and so on.[2] Urban historian Dolores Hayden's 2004 field guide to urban sprawl is perhaps the most systematic taxonomy of contemporary urban

1   Bruce Katz, Andrew Altman, and James Wagner, "An Urban Agenda for an Urban Age" (paper presented at the Urban Age Conference, Berlin, for the Brookings Institution, 10 Nov. 2006).

2   Michael Dear, *The Postmodern Urban Condition* (Malden, MA: Blackwell Publishers, 2000), chapter 7.

form. Her catalog contains about fifty categories ranging from alligator to zoomburg, along with more established terms such as mall, privatopia, and theming.[3] Edward Soja goes beyond classification to link emerging urban forms with an underlying political economy, including a changing geography of economic restructuring, globalization and the rise of world cities, and the growing gap between rich and poor.[4] Other researchers have described contemporary urban process as being polycentric, postmodern, a patchwork, splintered, and posturban. The places manufactured by these altered processes are variously labeled as city-region, micropolitan region, exopolis, edge cities, and metroburbia. The proliferation of neologisms describing emergent urban forms is indicative of confusion rather than intellectual mastery.

3   Dolores Hayden, *A Field Guide to Sprawl* (New York: Norton and Company, 2004).

4   Edward Soja, "Los Angeles 1965–1992: From crisis-generated restructuring to restructuring-generated crisis," in *The City: Los Angeles and Urban Theory at the End of the Twentieth Century*, ed. Allen Scott and Edward Soja (Berkeley: University of California Press, 1996), 426–62.

Los Angeles and Urban Theory

The Los Angeles region demonstrates great significance as the progenitor of urban change throughout the United States. If the tendencies manifest in the Los Angeles area were better understood, this would be tantamount to developing a science of urbanism and a substantive basis for public policies.

—Arthur Grey

Current urban transformations are thrown into especially high relief in Los Angeles. Let me immediately make clear that I do not claim that they are unique to L.A. nor that they lack historical precedent. However, together they amount to a revolution in urban place-making that is affecting many cities across the world (albeit not in equal proportion). L.A. is simply one of the best currently available counterfactuals to conventional urban theory and practice. As a result it is a valuable foundation for excavating the future of cities everywhere. Since economist Arthur Grey wrote about the city in 1959, the principal dimensions of urban change in L.A. have become well known.[5]

5   Arthur Grey, "Los Angeles: Urban Prototype," *Land Economics* 35, no. 3 (1959): 232–42. For some representative overviews of recent work, see Michael Dear, H. Eric Schockman, and Greg Hise, eds., *Rethinking Los Angeles* (Thousand Oaks: Sage

Publications, 1996); Scott and Soja, *The City: Los Angeles*; Roger Waldinger and Mehdi Bozorgmehr, eds., *Ethnic Los Angeles* (New York: Russell Sage, 1996); and Jennifer Wolch, Manuel Pastor Jr., and Peter Dreier, eds., *Up Against the Sprawl: Public Policy and the Making of Southern California* (Minneapolis: University of Minnesota Press, 2004).

6   Michael Dear, ed., *From Chicago to L.A.: Making Sense of Urban Theory* (Thousand Oaks: Sage Publications, 2002).

The detailed, empirical analyses by contributors in the 2004 book *From Chicago to L.A.* reveal multiple shifts in the practices of urban place production: demographic, economic, political, social, cultural, and virtual.[6] These include, inter alia, the observations that population diversity is becoming the norm in contemporary cities, and that the conventional divide between black and white in many American cities is being submerged by a minoritizing polity; that waves of immigration are altering practices of community and citizenship; that the principal tropes of contemporary urbanism include edge cities, privatopias, and other mutant urban forms that I just described; that the rise of post-Fordism and the "network society" are transforming urban economic geographies everywhere; that religious affiliations are atomizing as diverse, multicultural populations with transnational ties recreate spiritual traditions beyond conventional religions; and that the crisis of sustainability is a key component of the urban question. The book's contributors also convincingly show that altered ways of reading and representing the city are needed if we are to recognize and gather evidence measuring urban change and plan effectively to manage it.

The Los Angeles School of Urbanism refers to a loosely affiliated group of international scholars who, since the 1980s, have made L.A. their research focus. Initial work highlighted the emergence and consequences of economic restructuring in Southern California, but quickly broadened to consolidate the knowledge base for what had hitherto been a relatively neglected city-region. Almost concurrently, a subset of researchers recognized in L.A. a particular form of urban transition characteristic that they labeled "postmodern urbanism." Finally, by the late 1980s, the realization came that many lessons from L.A. were relevant to scholars beyond Southern California, and the aggregate of these findings became tentatively codified as the L.A. School of Urbanism. In my view, the L.A. School's account of postmodern urbanism offers an especially productive template for generating alternative urban theory. During recent decades, the term "postmodern" has accumulated so many meanings that it has reached the limits of language. However, this should not detract from its three enduring interpretive propositions: postmodernism as a series of distinctive cultural and stylistic practices that in and of themselves are intrinsically interesting and consequential; postmodernism as epoch, or the totality of emergent practices viewed as a cultural ensemble characteristic of contemporary capitalism—often referred to as postmodernity; and postmodernism as philosophy/ method, representing a set of discourses that are antagonistic to foundational constructs of whatever persuasion and—most particularly—the hegemony of any single intellectual persuasion.

All three approaches are germane to contemporary urban analysis. For instance, theme parks and other urban morphological texts may be read as stylistic evidence of discontinuity in urban practices, the rise of cyber cities as manifestations of epochal change, and the collapse of master planning as proof of the demise of previous urban rationalities. Implicit in all three propositions is the notion of a radical break—a fundamental nonconformity between past and present practices. For now, at least, it would be unwise to corset these emerging urbanisms within existing but obsolete analyses (such as New Urbanism or modernism) that are simply inadequate to encompass contemporary urban realities.

The central conceit of postmodern urbanism is that, just as the core beliefs of modernist thought have been displaced by multiple ways of knowing, so has the notion of a universal urban process been dissolved by the multiplying logics that are transforming city building.[7] At the core of this transformation is the altered relationship between city and hinterland. In modernist urbanism, the impetus for growth and change proceeded outward from the city's central core to its peripheries. In postmodern urbanism, this logic is precisely reversed: the evacuated city core no longer dominates its region; instead, the hinterlands organize what remains of the center. By this, I mean that urban space, time, and causality have been altered. Thus, the heterogeneous spatial logics that characterize contemporary urban development derive from the outside-in, not inside-out, as in modernist urbanism. Furthermore, in the sequence of urban development, a center—if one (or more) ever emerges—appears chronologically later than the peripheries.

7 Dear, *The Postmodern Urban Condition*, ix.

The direction of causality is from periphery to center (even if, as often happens, this finds expression as an absence of pressure or direction). As a consequence, the urban core (if it exists) embodies altered structural and functional relationships with the surrounding city-region that are radically different from those in the modernist city.

The distinction between modernist and postmodern urbanisms is at its strongest in the examples of Chicago and Los Angeles. For me, the industrial Chicago of the late-nineteenth century remains the foundational example of a modernist city. The core-to-hinterland causality of modernist urbanism was best captured in sociologist Ernest W. Burgess's 1925 account of the evolution of differential urban social areas within the city.[8] Burgess and other adherents of the Chicago School observed that as distance from the urban core grew, the city would take the form of a series of concentric rings of diminishing density.

8   Ernest W. Burgess, "The growth of the city: An introduction to a research project," in *The City*, by Robert Park, Ernest W. Burgess, and Roderick McKenzie (1925; repr., Chicago: University of Chicago Press, 1967): 1–14.

Now imagine a city where fragmentation (i.e., geographical nonadjacency) and decenteredness (polycentrism) are the primary urban dynamics: there would be many urban cores, not one. Independent edge cities will spring up with no allegiance to a city center; conventional town centers will no longer be at the heart of the urban process. Suburbs, understood as peripheral accretions to existing urban cores, will no longer exist, and the agglomeration dynamics that historically produced cities will be sufficiently altered so as to bring into question the whole concept of a "city." This is the world of postmodern urbanism; this is what Steven Flusty and I have called "keno capitalism."[9] » fig. 1

9   Michael Dear and Steven Flusty, "Postmodern Urbanism," *Annals of the Association of American Geographers* 88, no. 1 (1998): 50–72.

Keno capitalism assumes a world of ubiquitous connectivity courtesy of the information age. Urbanization occurs on an undifferentiated grid of opportunities, where each land parcel is (in principle) equally available for development as a consequence of access to the information superhighway. Capital settles on a land parcel while ignoring opportunities on adjacent lots, thus sparking uneven urban development. The relationship between development on one lot and another is a disjointed, unrelated affair, because

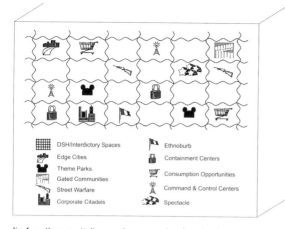

DSH/Interdictory Spaces
Edge Cities
Theme Parks
Gated Communities
Street Warfare
Corporate Citadels
Ethnoburb
Containment Centers
Consumption Opportunities
Command & Control Centers
Spectacle

fig. 1 ›› Keno capitalism, or the geography of postmodern urbanism

conventions of urban agglomeration have been replaced by a quasi-random collage of noncontiguous, functionally independent land parcels. After considerable time and further development, these isolated parcels may collide with other developed lots and take on the appearance of what we conventionally regard as a "city." However, there is no necessity for such an agglomeration to occur, because the grid of keno capitalism's urban card is infinitely expandable in any direction, allowing a fragmented urbanism to occur piecemeal for as long as potential development parcels remain wired.

The notion of a quasi-random urban process only tangentially related to previous urban conventions does not imply that such a process is alogical, but rather that it is composed of multiple rationalities that displace or mask those earlier conventions. Nor does it mean that modernist urbanism is dead, although it may be ailing. Just as some places in the American West and Southwest are already postmodern in their urban processes, many older cities in the Northeast and Midwest retain their residual modernist ways. However, even places of persistent modernism (including Chicago) are now being overwritten by the texts of postmodern urban process, which provide compelling evidence of urban and social change. Think of Chicago's O'Hare International Airport *metropole* or the contradictions surfacing in the city's downtown Loop. One does not have to become postmodernist to accept the challenges of postmodern urbanism. There are plenty of ways to name the present: choose the one you prefer, and let us move to the substance of debate.

The Altered Urban Lexicon: Categories, Politics, and Policy

Adjustments in the size, spacing, and internal structure of cities are textual clues to fundamental change in urban process, including the agglomeration of forces that brought the modernist city into existence.

If we are to understand these manifest material changes, adjustments to the way we see cities are also necessary. Chief among the consequent epistemological and ontological challenges is the need for a new urban lexicon that redefines the categories of urban analysis. For instance, a single, dominant "downtown" core is best understood as a historical expression of modernist urbanism; in no way can it be construed as the nerve center of a postmodern city-region. By extension, there is no such thing as "suburbanization," understood as peripheral accretion in a center-led urban process. Edge cities may look like suburbs, but they most certainly are not.

Perhaps the most pressing categorical revision in my dictionary relates to the term "sprawl." For some, this much-maligned appellation invokes all that is bad about uncontrolled urban growth, yet for others it is the benign realization of millions of American suburban dreams. What could possibly be wrong with that? In my new dictionary, the definition of sprawl as uncontrolled suburbanization is a secondary, even antiquarian usage. Instead, its primary meaning would describe the principal formal expression of contemporary (call it postmodern, if you will) urbanism. Sprawl is an urban theoretical "primitive": the most fundamental category for describing the way urbanism takes place. One important consequence of reframing sprawl in this way is the positioning of sustainability at the core of the urban question. Until very recently, conventional urban practice relegated environmental issues to the status of an environmental impact review (EIR) checklist. But now that cities have broken their boundaries, habitats are being destroyed and species have been eliminated. The viability of life on earth is truly under threat, though this realization is desperately slow in dawning.

Another important lexical recategorization pertains to the convention that earlier distinguished intracity and intercity structure. Urbanists in the latter half of the twentieth century uncovered many systematic ways to describe urban form and process at both scales, based largely on the assumption of distinct geographies of internal city structure and the structure of networks of cities. It was no accident that quantitative urban geography after the 1960s catalogued a wide variety of statistical regularities that found expression in "laws" of urban structure both at the intraurban and interurban scales. These empirical consistencies included the rank-size rule (relating to the primacy of a single major city in the urban hierarchy of each nation) as well as central place theory (referring to regularities in the size and spacing of cities).

Most if not all of the statistical regularities that characterized our twentieth-century understanding of cities are now being challenged by the revised geographies of American urbanization. Across the country, the fastest-growing urban areas are those "micropolitan" districts outside established cities, a trend that represents a radical flattening in the hierarchy of American urban places. In short, the traditional geography of interurban size and spacing is being erased. At the intraurban scale, I have already described some disaggregated manifestations of change under the rubric of keno capitalism. In aggregate, the splintering of internal city structure and the multiplication of sprawling urban hinterlands are producing a radically altered urban structure that collapses the scalar distinction between internal city structure and system-wide urban structure. They have become a single integrated form that concretizes a multiplicity of urban processes. They are, in a phrase, cities without edges or centers.

Previous analytical conventions of urban scale have been obliterated by the empirical realities of sprawl. Urban space is now a single, continuous plane, even though land and property developments remain geographically uneven (as per the expectations of the keno capitalist model, shown on p. 232). One of Southern California's most prescient observers, Carey McWilliams, foresaw this trend six decades ago:

> Southern California constitutes a single metropolitan district which should be characterized as rurban: neither city nor country but everywhere a mixture of both. Just as Southern California is the least rural of all the regions in America, so, paradoxically, Los Angeles is the least citified of all the cities of America.[10]

10 Carey McWilliams, *Southern California: An Island on the Land* (1946; repr., Salt Lake City: Peregrine Smith Books, 1973), 12–13.

And Grey anticipated the practical consequence of sprawl: "By 1970 the territory from Santa Barbara on the north to Baja California, is expected to coalesce into a single metropolitan

11   Grey, "Los Angeles: Urban Prototype," 240.

area."[11] Such anticipations regarding the future of Southern California were farsighted; nevertheless, they remained exceptional for most of the remainder of the twentieth century. It is only now that the theoretical and political frames of L.A.'s urbanism are being accepted as a theory of widespread relevance. In the meantime, the colliding metropolises in Southern California and Baja California, Mexico, have already produced a world city I call "Bajalta California."[12]

12   Michael Dear and Gustavo Leclerc, eds., *Postborder City: Cultural Spaces of Bajalta California* (New York: Routledge, 2003).

13   Wolch et al., *Up Against the Sprawl.*

Sprawl affects urban politics overwhelmingly, just as politics influences sprawl.[13] This much is obvious from myriad studies of minoritization; changing notions of community, identity, and citizenship; and the ubiquitous presence of NIMBYism (short for "not in my backyard"). In some fundamental way, the futures of electoral politics, representative government, and even the possibility of local democracy have been brought into question. We are only now coming to grips with a politics of urban pathology. The pioneering work of political scientist Evan McKenzie on the rise of privatopias is indicative of what I regard as a pathological urban form—a perverse doctrine of anti-democratic residential apartheid that now comprises 18 percent of America's housing stock and houses one-sixth of the nation's population. Underwritten by the politics of privatization, common interest developments (CIDs) are described by McKenzie as maturing into an orchestrated attempt to replace public municipal government with unaccountable private agencies.[14] Another frequent form of secession, in Los Angeles at least, has been the incorporation of new cities—about thirty around L.A. since the late 1970s—in which political boundaries become the jurisdictional walls separating "us" from "them." Such political geographies of privatization, secession, and balkanization represent profound threats to the urban polity and should be recognized as such.

Paradoxically, sprawling cities also provide enclaves where intense local autonomies are possible, enabling communities-of-interest to realize their goals below the radar of formal politics.

14   Evan McKenzie, "Emerging Trends in State Regulation of Private Communities in the U.S.," *GeoJournal* 66 (2006): 89–102. For a global account of these phenomena, see Georg Glasze, Chris Webster, and Klaus Frantz, eds., *Private Cities: Global and Local Perspectives* (New York: Routledge, 2006).

Such movements include the activities of the much-vaunted creative classes and advocates of green urbanism. In addition, the potential of revitalized local social movements, globalization from below, and recovered human agency all point optimistically to a grassroots political renaissance.[15] Local governments themselves find incentives and opportunities to experiment. For instance, in Southern California, Riverside County has been attempting to manage rapid urban growth by invoking federal endangered species legislation. In Ventura County, similar land-use management objectives were sought through a broadly based coalition of grassroots movements: same goal, different political means.

Stated plainly, urban geography has trumped local politics. By this I mean that altered geographies of postmodern urbanism are redefining the meaning and practice of urban politics and planning. This extension of cities beyond conventional political jurisdictions negates the notion of representative democracy, compromises the ability of the local state to serve the collective interests of its constituents, and may even intensify the subordination of the local state to plutocratic privatism. The tendency for geography to outgrow government may appear to be a restatement of a familiar problem: namely, the search for a viable regional planning and government apparatus in a fragmented metropolis. Arguments in favor of supracity government have long been advanced, provoking many rebuttals championing the proliferation of small urban jurisdictions on the grounds that interjurisdictional competition and differentiation maximizes residential choice and promotes efficient public service delivery. Today, however, jurisdictional fragmentation in mega-city-regions has become a pathological, iatrogenic condition: the clash between urban hypertrophy and obsolete government itself causes new problems and prevents the local state from meeting its obligations. This is a world in which the dreaded NIMBYism is being replaced by the gridlock of BANANA (for "build absolutely nothing anywhere near anybody"). The sheer scale of urban management in these city-regions is mind-boggling: in Southern California, a five-county region (Los Angeles, Orange, Riverside, San

15   Roger Keil, *Los Angeles: Globalization, Urbanization & Social Struggles* (New York: Wiley, 1998); Steven Flusty, *De-Coca-Colonization: Making the Globe from the Inside Out* (New York: Routledge, 2004); and Michael P. Smith, *Transnational Urbanism: Locating Globalization* (Malden, MA: Blackwell Publishers, 2001).

Bernardino, and Ventura counties) contain about 17 million people in 177 cities spread over 14,000 square miles and subdivided into more than 1,000 special districts. In Los Angeles County, there are only five supervisors representing more than eight million inhabitants. Daily life in L.A. testifies to the notion that its local government is fundamentally undemocratic and dysfunctional. Its practitioners lack both the capacity and the will for collective political action. Federal and state governments, committed primarily to denying the funds for authorized public programs, stymie even sympathetic local politicians. Needless to say, effective urban democracy has always been problematic; the difference nowadays is that it may be mortally wounded by deliberate agents of destruction.

For many, the central, normative question in urban political geography pertains to the appropriate scales of (re)territorialization of local governance. What is the optimal scale of regionalization to ensure effective representative democracy and efficient public service provisions in the hyperextended metropolis? Existing theories have failed to come up with effective answers to this question, and indeed, today the question slumbers in too many academic minds (important exceptions include sociologists Neil Brenner and Chantal Mouffe).[16] In the meantime, millions of people are effectively disenfranchised, unserved, underserved, or even actively harmed by these failed local states. But because the city has already superseded political geography, the principal normative issue may no longer be reterritorializing local government. Urban politics in the information age operate simultaneously on global and local scales in both material and virtual worlds. Without incorporating this shift, we will continue to invoke obsolete policies, in the hope that central-city/suburban political alliances will cure urban fiscal imbalances, unify disparate constituencies, and facilitate regional planning. How impossibly archaic this favored panacea sounds in hinterland-driven urbanism!

16 Neil Brenner, *New State Spaces* (Oxford: Oxford University Press, 2004); and Chantal Mouffe, *On the Political* (London: Verso, 2005).

Architecture for a Hinterland Aesthetic

> Transformations of the city exceed our ability to control them...
> we arrive at results seemingly by fast-forward, without clear grasp
> of how we got there. Though not necessarily temporally fast,
> change occurs as a set of discontinuous jump cuts: urban devel-
> opment is not progressive, but it can never turn back; design is
> increasingly regulated without ever showing improvement.
>
> —The cityLAB manifesto

The cityLAB manifesto conjures up every professional's nightmare: lack of control, nonlinear process, pathological outcome, dysfunctional regulation, and aesthetic implosion. Yet its vision seems fully consistent with the outline of postmodern urbanism I have portrayed in this essay. How will the architectural palette of time-space, built form, aesthetics, and money confront a world of fast-forward urbanism?

To begin, let me emphasize that traces of a fragmented urbanism have been with us for a long time, although they may not have been universally acknowledged or understood in anything remotely resembling the terms of this essay. I have already mentioned the examples of Grey (1959) and McWilliams (1946). Elsewhere, historian Eugene P. Moehring described the phenomenon of "leapfrog growth" in mid-twentieth-century Las Vegas, referring to the tendency for development to occur in disjointed, noncontiguous parcels.[17] This produced what economist Charles Paige called a "checkerboard effect dominated by large residential subdivisions connected by commercial strips along major streets and separated by equally large squares of undeveloped land."[18]

These cases do more than remind us not to overlook the past; they also underscore how important it is to ask the right questions about past and present to avoid easy acceptance of existing analytical categories. In my view, the necessity for something new in urban theory is being demonstrated on an ongoing basis by multidisciplinary

17 Eugene P. Moehring, *Resort City in the Sunbelt: Las Vegas, 1930–1970* (Reno: University of Nevada Press, 1995).

18 Ibid., 238.

efforts in the burgeoning field of comparative urbanism, which has systematically begun to explore the similarities and differences among contemporary cities across the world.[19] In a comparison between New York City and Los Angeles, for instance, sociologist David Halle concludes that L.A. highlights the changing relationship between core and periphery and argues that this shift is pertinent to other American cities.[20] Geographer Richard P. Greene finds evidence that Chicago's modernist urbanism is presently being overlain by a postmodern scrim.[21] Urban planner Klaus R. Kunzmann has described the emergence of "patchwork" urbanism in the city-regions of Europe.[22] And in their work on the intersection of cities and network society, urbanists Stephen Graham and Simon Marvin explicitly invoke the keno capitalism icon in their concept of "splintering urbanism."[23] It is too early to regard these investigations as evidence of a theoretical convergence. Indeed, an early closure on emerging debates would be counterproductive. However, to me, these first signs of convergence (not closure) are indicative of a widening acceptance of urban transformation.

When architects and urban designers focus on a grounded theory of architecture, that is, the material context into which built form fits (or not!), they come very close to the concerns of this essay. Helpful examples abound. Thus, Nan Ellin's notion of "integrated urbanism" engages many topics that match my concerns, including time and space, morphology, and scale and hybridity.[24] (Even though her holistic account of an integrated urbanism ends up in a place quite different from mine.) Similarly, Alan Berger's "drosscape" is a visually stunning analysis of the production, obsolescence, and recycling of urban and nonurban waste landscapes across America.[25] Operating with multiscalar frames, Berger shows how places—from city-regions to individual plots—are part of a disjointed process of use, abandonment, and (sometimes) reuse that casts original light on contemporary

19   For more on comparative urbanism, see Janet L. Abu-Lughod, *New York, Chicago, Los Angeles: America's Global Cities* (Minneapolis: University of Minnesota Press, 1999); and Michael Dear, "Comparative Urbanism," *Urban Geography* 26, no. 3 (2005): 247–51.

20   David Halle, ed., *New York & Los Angeles: Politics, Society, and Culture* (Chicago, IL: University of Chicago Press, 2003).

21   Richard P. Greene, "Strong Downtowns and High Amenity Zones as Defining Features of the 21st Century Metropolis: The Case of Chicago," in *Chicago's Geographies: Metropolis for the 21st Century*, ed. Richard P. Greene, Mark Jansen Bouman, and Dennis Grammenos (Washington D.C.: Association of American Geographers, 2006), 50–74.

22   Klaus R. Kunzmann, "World City Regions in Europe: Structural change and future challenges," in *Globalization and the World of Large Cities* ed. Fu-chen Lo and Yue-man Yeung (Tokyo: The United Nations University Press, 1998), 37–75.

23   Stephen Graham and Simon Marvin, *Splintering Urbanism: Networked infra-structures, technological mobilities and the urban condition* (London: Routledge, 2001).

urban process. As a final example, Dana Cuff's notion of a "provisional city" foregrounds scale and the politics of property in ways that extend and are consistent with my project.[26]

This said, it is hard for me to imagine a revitalized urban aesthetic under the circumstances of keno capitalism. Is there a "hinterland aesthetic" analogous to the modernist ideal of a downtown core, with its collection of heroic testaments to democracy, culture, and corporate wealth? For now, the hinterland seems capable of producing only a radical aesthetic flattening, a pastiche of homogeneous brands and functions in tenuous adjacency. As a corollary, what would a revitalized "core-city aesthetic" look like? Currently, an architecture of serious spectacle continues to provide an irresistible narcotic for clients and designers everywhere, in the horrifying prospect of seventy-story, freestanding towers looming over Chapultepec Park in Mexico City; in Middle Eastern oil states that rush to design a future without oil by creating new cities of spectacle; or in China's chaotic—and possibly ruinous—sprint toward first-world status. But the Dubai urban circus proves only that modernist megaprojects remain a fashionable fetish among autocrats and plutocrats. And one-third of Shanghai's apartment complexes are subdivided into "collective rentals" (where a single unit can house ten or more people and architecture masks an affordable housing problem of colossal proportions). Meanwhile, at home in hinterland and core alike, public art and architecture dwindle, landscapes of security and surveillance permeate, and privatism winks at the demise of the public realm.[27]

I think of architecture as a wayfinding device in this new world of urbanism. Visionaries are needed who understand a nonlinear world, who will invent a hinterland aesthetic and a revitalized professional practice not confined to ambitions of plutocratic spectacle. They will help recover local democracy by opening up autonomous public spaces, virtual and real; they will empower urban informality and the kind of spontaneity and connectivity observable in Tijuana; and they will encourage street-level presences

24 Nan Ellin, *Integral Urbanism* (New York: Routledge, 2006).

25 Alan Berger, *Drosscape: Wasting Land in Urban America* (New York: Princeton Architectural Press, 2006).

26 Dana Cuff, *The Provisional City: Los Angeles Stories of Architecture and Urbanism* (Cambridge, MA: MIT Press, 2000).

27 Mike Davis and Daniel B. Monk, eds., *Evil Paradises: Dreamworlds of Neoliberalism* (New York: The New Press, 2007).

and remembrances just as the community history Power of Place (PoP) projects in L.A. have done. They will make environment a prime directive. And they will understand that architectural theory and practice are not involved with aesthetics, but must be grounded within a broader theory of urban form and process if they are to understand and invent the urban future.

Strange Attractors, or the Catalytic Agency of Form

Roger Sherman

With cities developing today at a rate that outpaces architects' and planners' efforts to shape them, there is no longer sufficient time to plan. Both the Katrina and 9-11 disasters revealed the time-honored master plan's incapacity to provide the resiliency and authority necessary to attract investment and serve as a vehicle for instigating and shaping urban futures. In the atmosphere of risk posed by today's unpredictable political economy, real estate investors and municipal officials alike instead rely increasingly upon individual, catalytic projects, in which control is consolidated and uncertainties are minimized. Encouraged by short election cycles, real estate investment trusts (REITs), and onerous entitlements processes, these projects exploit, like arbitrage, emerging or latent markets and protocols. Symptomatic of the dominant role played by the private sector in the development of the American city, this new business model is at once opportunistic and speculative: its charge is to tilt the risk:reward ratio in its favor by considering every project a destination in itself. Architecture has, in this context, become as much a part of brand identity as merchandise or services, aimed at appealing to the insatiable appetite of the public-at-large for new and different forms of experience, and developing new constituencies in the process.[1] Visceral stimulus packages as much as economic ones, their designs are characterized by uncanny visual effects, cunningly strategized to attract visits by generating the buzz of an urban legend in the making.

Indeed, our top architects have greatly profited from the must-see environment of today's identity-obsessed culture, exemplified in the famous "Bilbao effect"—wherein a signature work is plunked down as the ante in a high-stakes gambit to leverage future urban investment through sheer notoriety. However successful as an economic or media strategy, the Bilbao phenomenon is a limited model

1   B. Joseph Pine and James H. Gilmore, *The Experience Economy* (Cambridge, MA: Harvard Business School Press, 1999).

by which to reassert the instrumentality and value of architecture as an urban one, principally because it depends upon the catalytic power of the (preferably notable) architect's *own* identity instead of those of the constituencies it might attract, or of the larger scenario it is interested in catalyzing. In a Faustian bargain, it trades architecture's ability to channel cultural images and orchestrate new operating systems, settling instead for the short-term commodity value of its celebrity association. However prescient they may appear, such designs ultimately fail to suggest, let alone shape, how the future might unfold. This essay argues for and presents several means by which architecture can attract and capture the popular interest and following—its mojo, if you will—that is today a prerequisite to the success of any new business model, or design strategy, that operates in the urban marketplace.

At a time when the culture-at-large is obsessed with identity and its natural corollary, notoriety, the "stickiness" of form and imageability is central. In the urban game, this quality is less a product of the architect's proprietary formal gestations than of an almost pheromonal approach, keyed to specific subcultures and audiences, and the unique values they carry and lifestyles they attract (see Claritas Corp.'s demographic profiling by cluster/lifestyle group). There is growing agency for this mode of design thinking, one that recognizes that urbanism has at one level become a form of entertainment, wherein the architect-planner's role is not unlike that of a Disney imagineer, creating captivating—but also potentially genuine and interactive—forms of pleasure that employ market savvy to engage the politics of identity. A netherzone of design practice that collapses the traditional distinction between architecture and urbanism, it recognizes that for many today, the city and its varied amusements offer those who dwell in it an opportunity to participate—even if provisionally—in a range of forms of collective life.

Private sector entrepreneurs have long since come to this realization, choosing to provide their own urbanisms (what Reyner Banham coined as enclaves), having seen firsthand (beginning perhaps with Disney) how such experiences provide a means of expanding one's brand and audience beyond the expected catchment area. Symptomized in districts of exclusive and homogeneous identity, these are referred to in planning parlance as overlay zones (or O-Zones), often stewarded by quasi-public institutions such as business improvement districts (BIDs) and homeowners' associations (HOAs). Their highly orchestrated tracts of homes, offices, factories, and shopping malls constitute veritable sec-ond cities—*new natures* whose specialized orientation ranges from "com-munities" for golfers to "parks" for dog lovers to "streets" for bargain hunters.[2] Design strategy operates cunningly hand-in-hand with

2   Dana Cuff, Roger Sherman, and R. E. Somol, "O-Z.LA: A New Operating System for Los Angeles 2107," for the History Channel's *Engineering and Empire* series (Dec. 2007).

fig. 1 ›› O-Zones come in different guises, ranging from those that dictate an utter singularity of character (e.g., the golf community, top); others that pretend to offer the organic (e.g., the ersatz urbanism of Universal CityWalk, middle), but ironically always the same version of it as others that do the same; and those that are simply directed at resisting change (the historic preservation overlay zone, bottom).

a business plan, as bait and hook. In other respects, however, they play it safe, securing their future (and property values) through strategies of exclusion and the reductive narrative of theme. Employing closed and finite organizations, they target predetermined demographics, often, paradoxically, in contrast to representations of self-organized urban variety.[3] The political equivalent of black holes, O-Zones absorb interest and income while offering little or no collateral benefits to the cool residual field in which they are indifferently distributed. ›› fig. 1

While for some this trend is a sign of the dissolution of civic life, it could instead be argued to represent an alternative: namely, the emergence of an unprecedented number of new and highly particular forms of collectivity. Given their undeniable popularity and economic success, however, it is unrealistic to imagine that the attraction of urban denizens to such pleasure zones, as Robert Venturi called them in *Learning from Las Vegas*, can be resisted.[4] Rather, the challenge for architects is to explore how the larger cultural desires of which the O-Zone is a symptom may be harnessed toward the constitution of urban communities that achieve viability by undermining previous models of identity politics and special interests, rather than reinforcing them.[5]

By doing so, architecture would create for itself an opportunity to recover a political relevance and agency it has lacked since modernism. The politics of that movement were driven by a vision of social equality based upon a uniform, idealized subject, embodied by an aesthetics of optimization. Today, in contrast, it is the desire for social distinctiveness—what *else* one can be or do—that matters: a politics of difference, with identity as its lure. This suggests a concomitant shift in the program of architecture from one concerned with *how best things might work* to one that instead queries how else they might be orchestrated.

This demands that we recognize what entrepreneurs and politicians have understood long before us: namely, that in today's identity-inflated culture, greater value is added by the power of

3   O-Zones generally fall into one of two categories. The first is that of singular identity (usually gated, of which golf or retirement communities are well-known examples), which constitute the predominant model of residential development today. The second, the darling of commercial developers, is characterized by a hyper-differentiation—a kitchen-sink urbanism descendant from the theme park, whose success as an attraction has led to its replication on other urban sites throughout the United States (in Los Angeles, Citywalk and the Grove are known to every Angeleno). In the first case, the identity of the place is unique, but the problem is that it excludes wider and unscripted public participation. The other model pretends, through its scenography, to be diverse, organic, and open, when in fact public access is as highly controlled as in the former case; the vibrant urban experience it promises is one that never exceeds style.

4   Robert Venturi, Denise Scott Brown, and Steven Izenour, *Learning from Las Vegas* (Cambridge, MA: MIT Press, 1972).

5   Cuff, Sherman, and Somol, "O-Z.LA."

6   R. E. Somol, "Yes is More," foreword to *L.A. Under the Influence: The Hidden Logic of Urban Property*, by Roger Sherman (Minneapolis: University of Minnesota Press, 2010), xvi.

7   Venturi, Scott Brown, and Izenour, *Learning from Las Vegas*.

contrivance than by that of beauty—in the stickiness of a cunning conceit more than in its technical virtuosity. Theorist R. E. Somol (in reference to Ed Ruscha before him) calls this the "What?— Wow!": a mode of design strategy possessing the power to elicit the intrigue that is a necessary precondition to attracting interest to a location that otherwise has no intrinsic value.[6] Venturi and company's "duck" achieves notoriety this way, through the eye- (or i-, as in interest or investment) catching power of anomaly.[7] Like the rebranding of an otherwise valueless rock, this may be found in a series of techniques, largely borrowed from the set design and advertising fields, that as we shall see are simultaneously formal and semantic. ›› figs. 2 + 3 Their unique allure is sourced not in their formal complexity or elaboration, but in their estrangement of the familiar and their concealment of the mechanics that underlie their uncanny visual effects. Unlike the "everyday," which argues merely for a replication of the commonplace, the popular appeal of the decoy lies in the transformation of the familiar to a near fictive state, verging on the incredible.[8] It promises to evoke and deliver another way of being in the city/world— what today has even received its own moniker: that of *extreme experience*.

8   John Chase, Margaret Crawford, and John Kaliski, eds., *Everyday Urbanism* (New York: Monacelli Press, 2008).

fig. 2 ›› Cover of *Stone Soup*, by Marcia Brown (New York: Aladdin Paperbacks, 1997); fig. 3 ›› The Pet Rock, invented by Gary Dahl, 1975

To leverage spectacle into more than mere notoriety, however—that is, into a bona fide destination capable of sustaining public engagement beyond vicarious online interest—requires embedding superficial appeal with a material and logistical intelligence. In other words, the duck must become a *decoy*, a sight that is also a site: one inviting membership and participation.» figs. 4 - 6 The decoy demands further inspection,

figs. 4 - 6 » Venturi's duck must become a decoy, shaped as much by the audiences it wishes to attract as by what it has to sell. Unlike the duck, the decoy possesses externality effects, catalyzing behavior beyond itself: fig. 4 » Long Island Duckling, from *Learning from Las Vegas* fig. 5 » Cormorants attracted to their decoys fig. 6 » The rooftops of Wrigleyville, beyond the right field wall of Chicago's Wrigley Park, whose bleachers extend atop them

conflating an uncanny appearance with inventive operational regimens as a kind of trap to lure and capture audiences beyond its ordinary catchment area. Such is the case with San Francisco's Lombard Street, branded the "crookedest street in the world." In 1922, the little-used street, with its steep, 27 percent grade was redesigned by the developer who owned the land on either side of it to include eight switchbacks in its one-block descent.[9] » fig. 7 This pragmatic if inefficient solution made Lombard Street accessible to automobiles, and at the same time increased the desirability and value of the adjacent lots. It also resulted in the creation of a singular identity for the street, one that on account of its steep slope "naturally" advertises itself to the city below—and more recently to Google Earth. The "accidentally" picturesque street configuration is reinforced by Technicolor material arrangements that dominate the ground-level experience: brick pavers and unnaturally colored, abundant flower beds that fill the triangular residual areas between zigzags. At eye level, these obscure the path

9   See www.aviewoncities.com/sf/lombardstreet.htm.

fig. 7 ›› Various views of Lombard Street, including a
scene from the BYOBW event and viral marketing that
the event has generated.

of the road beyond each turn, immersing the driver in the fantastical
atmosphere of the right-of-way, like Dorothy in the poppy fields of Oz.

Lombard Street represents the triumph of plot over plan; it takes
hucksterism seriously, conflating planning with entertainment.[10]

10   Somol has called this
"entertainment planning." See
this essay's lexicon for further
definition.

In contrast to the conventional streetscape project, which merely restyles an existing thoroughfare, the ingenuity of Lombard lies in the way that it "hacks" the familiar street grid. It distorts and distends the right-of-way in a manner that reinvigorates the mundane act of driving, introducing conditions that challenge the driver's skill and demand heightened attention. Lombard is DIY (drive-it-yourself) urbanism: one that must be performed to be believed. It is also a form of membership initiation— a quite literal rite of passage. Everyday functions (parking, trash pickup, parkway) run through it, but are rescripted.

At the same time, the block manages to be anomalous without being exclusive. In addition to serving residents themselves (the value of whose properties are also greatly enhanced), Lombard is a photo-op Mecca for out-of-town visitors; a weekend venue for neighborhood exercise enthusiasts; and perhaps most intriguingly, the scene of BYOBW (Bring Your Own Big Wheels), a citywide Easter spectacle that has generated its own website, identity, and cult following—in spite of lacking any commercial agenda. Rather than hedging its bets, Lombard Street instigates the outcomes it desires, employing an audacious, supply-side approach aimed at creating its own market. In fact, its public notoriety today belies the fact that it was originally the result of a real estate gambit developed entirely by private interests. Instead of waiting to act until the area's market and context "arrived," its developer engaged in the reconfiguration of the street in order to increase the value of his larger property. In doing so, he knowingly or unknowingly built a Trojan horse: a lasting public presence at the heart of an otherwise private venture.

However unpremeditated the full consequences of its sponsor's scheme, Lombard Street demonstrates how, if properly conceived, design can be cleverly if not ironically embedded with a conceit to expose the unlikely ties that bind diverse constituencies. Somol argues that this offers architecture the opportunity "to be at once commercial and critical."[11] At a moment when nature has been supplanted by culture, biology information, and ecology logistics, he says that architecture's agency lies in "hybridizing signifying regimes with the pursuit of new institutional arrangements," producing a new

11 R. E. Somol, "Urbanism without Architecture," in *Points + Lines*, by Stan Allen (New York: Princeton Architectural Press, 1999), 140–43.

kind of machine distinct from that of its modernist predecessor: a socio-political one, capable of eliciting new forms of collective life, soliciting audiences that cut across existing social and spatial statics.[12]

At a time when a project's context is defined more by a mix of capitalism and NIMBYism than by its immediate physical surroundings, architecture must be strategized to operate like a Trojan horse: one that can attract both the vagaries of private investment and competing interest groups, and at the same time leverage an expanded public realm.[13] This is especially pertinent to American cities, where new development is already in fact required to provide some public improvement as a part of the quid pro quo of the entitlement process. Most commonly, these take the form of so-called mitigation measures, such as low-grade infrastructure improvements (e.g., widened streets or upgraded sewer lines). In light of the intermingled relationship today between private investment and public interest, architecture would do well to assume a more opportunistic approach to such trade-offs.[14] By crafting design strategy in such a way as to attract wider participation, it demonstrates its more robust and visible public (and, as it turns out, private) value, changing the urban game from one in which architecture pays for public life (e.g., sewers) one where it *plays* for public life.[15]

Lombard Street's fantastical imageability, combined with its logistical novelty, are the bait and hook, respectively, of its strange attraction. In a way that neither is able to achieve alone, they together offer the opportunity to sample an "altered state" of being, whose pheromone-like appeal, well-understood in the field of entertainment, is to be "played." Lombard succeeds because its imageability is not produced by the optimization of function (the parametric project), but by its *eccentricity*. This also lends it a certain quality of undecidability (How does it work?) that leaves it open to not one, but a range of, scenarios. The same may be said to apply to its complex and uncanny imageability, which is a difficult-to-unravel mash-up drawn from an equally unlikely assortment of sources. Lombard Street's notoriety is a product of enigma rather than of finesse, of its anomalization of performance

12 Cuff, Sherman, and Somol, "O-Z.LA."

13 Ibid.

14 Charles Moore, "You Have to Pay for the Public Life," *Perspecta* 9/10 (1965): 57–97.

15 Ibid.

rather than its optimization. As a decoy, it presents itself as a *perceptual puzzle*, designed to both literally and figuratively elicit a double take from the passerby—one that invites and at the same time requires closer and often repeated inspection in order to divulge its secrets (logic). As opposed to parametric processes, which are aimed at the expression and exhibition of technique, the decoy's powers of attraction lie precisely in the *concealment* of its methods of production—sometimes even deliberately misdirecting the knowing viewer. As in magic, that sleight-of-hand is a necessary precondition to eliciting a "How did they…?" sense of curiosity and estrangement in the spectator.

Found in certain alternative histories and "outsider" practices of architecture (the folly and the work of the SITE organization are two that come to mind, in addition to Venturi's projects), this modus operandi is principally native to the languages of advertising and the theater arts. » fig. 8 Essential to the ad man's métier is the savvy ability to

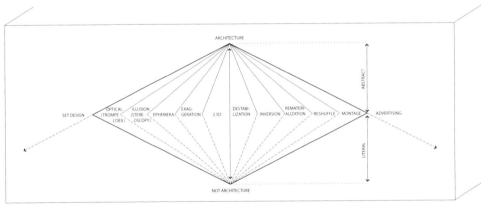

fig. 8 ›› Expanded Field diagram (revised, with apologies to Rosalind Krauss), showing the gravitional pull exerted on architecture's disciplinarity by the fields of advertising and set design, and the techniques they offer by which to recover architecture's popular mojo

convey identity and message interchangeably, specifically through the unapologetic use of the literal. Not the obdurate, inarguable, assertive dimension of the literal as discussed by Mark Linder, but rather its dry, derisive, preposterous potential: like Beckett, it has the power to make

16   Mark Linder, *Nothing Less Than Literal: Architecture After Minimalism* (Cambridge, MA: MIT Press, 2004)—with thanks to Linder for his email comments to the author about Beckett.

some laugh and others cry.[16] Set design, on the other hand, melds visual and emotional effect, delivered through the use of exotic ephemeral and illusory phenomena. Ephemera carry the "I was there when it happened" allure of the temporary, while illusions elicit a "How did they do that?" response as their hook. In the case of both fields, the aim is to make the viewer do a double take, accompanied by either a certain awe or amusement.

The literal arts is particularly interested in manufacturing a "What's wrong with this picture?" impression. It achieves this through techniques such as exaggeration, destabilization, and various forms of montage, including inversion, reshuffling/substitution, and rematerialization. Exaggeration attracts note through the superlative: the (world's) largest/smallest, longest, most, and so on.   ›› figs. 9 - 11 Its

figs. 9 - 11 ››   The use of exaggeration is not so much to actually fool the eye as it is to stimulate and amuse, bringing the scaleness and untamed environment of the virtual into real space: fig. 9 ›› *la D.S.*, Gabriel Orozco; fig. 10 ›› *Tree*, Axel Erlandson; fig. 11 ›› *Disco Ball*, Michel de Broin

variant forms include distortion and contortion—such as the distension of a recognizable figure (e.g., Lombard Street's sharp, steep turns). The spectacular power of instability (destabilization) is perfectly embodied

by the Tower of Pisa, which is renowned not because it is the best of its kind typologically (towers), but because, even if due to accident rather than design, it does something none of the others do (defy gravity), to the point that its precarious state begs not just to be seen, but verified in person, to experience for its vertiginous effects. ›› fig. 12 Montage operates like a visual-linguistic pun whose message is embedded in the oscillation between the

fig. 12 ››   The Tower of Pisa is an object lesson in the power of the eccentric, unstable, or almost dangerous.

figs. 13 – 15 ›› Montage makes savvy use of substitution in order to grab one's attention through the subtle but jarring subversion of the familiar. Examples include: ›› fig. 13 image-source incommensurability (stone house, Guimares, Portugal); fig. 14 ›› inversion (*Upside Down Mushroom Room*, Carsten Holler; and fig. 15 ›› dissociation of figure and material constitution (*Staircase V*, Do-Ho Suh).

assumed and the unexpected, through the "trick" of substitution. This sometimes involves reversing conventional roles or places (inversion); at other times requires changing up the conventional order of things; and at yet other times involves pairing familiar but disassociated forms and materials. ›› figs. 13 - 15 The goal in all these cases is to achieve a kind of double agency, in which the new is experienced through an unexpected combination of identities and the radicalization of the operating systems with which each is conventionally associated.

The popular drawing power of illusion lies in challenging conventions of spatial perception in ways that are both entertaining and riveting—particularly at a moment at which our experience of the world is increasingly mediated through, and dominated by, the view through a monitor-window. One such technique, common to set design but increasingly employed outside the world of the stage (primarily through the medium of outdoor advertising), is 2.5-D: a beguiling optical transgression in the relationship between flatness and

depth. ›› fig. 16 A contemporary and freestyle redux of the baroque trompe l'oeil, 2.5-D's sense of impossibility seems all the more startling when taken out of the controlled interior environments (churches, theaters) that once limited its use and redeployed in the open urban environment, often as an apparent (though in fact highly contrived) visual "accident."

fig. 16 ›› 2.5-D acquires its visual power by transgressing the bounds of the mostly two-dimensional media by which information is transmitted to us. It asserts the possibility for messages to interact with lived experience.

figs. 17 – 19 ›› Popularly employed in outdoor advertising ›› figs. 17 + 18, as well as by artists such as Ed Ruscha in his work *Pay Nothing Until April* ›› fig. 19, lenticular optics are capable of carrying up to three separate images, enabling them to communicate through the relationship that one has to the next. Images may also be viewed transposed.

fig. 20 ›› Artist Felice Varini's makes extensive use of anamorphism to pose puzzles that challenge the viewer to use both her mind's eye and (moving) body to "solve" them (*Cardiff Bay Barrage*, Wales, 2007).

More proprietary to the theater arts is the exploitation of stereoscopic techniques such as anamorphism and lenticularity, in which a single object or image changes in appearance depending upon the angle from which it is perceived. ›› figs. 17 – 20 Importantly, both require a "see it (in person) to believe it" inspection that is essential to sustaining intrigue and ultimately building membership. Moreover, in assuming a seemingly different identity depending upon the point from which it is being seen, the i-catcher literally addresses multiple points of view—and by extension, the different audiences with which each might be associated. This seems exceedingly relevant today, given the new and multiple vantage points from which information and even a given site are now accessible—whether from the satellite view Google Earth, the passing glance from the elevated freeway or high-rise window, or the time-honored "on the ground" encounter. »» fig. 21

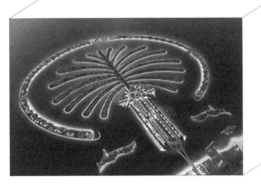

fig. 21 »» Dubai's palm islands, savvily designed to market themselves to the global audience of Google Earth

Like the stereoscopic, the ephemeral is also tied to change—in this case not as a function of the position of the spectator, but rather in relation to time and/ or environmental conditions. Of all the above-discussed methods, the ephemeral is the one that most directly challenges architecture's conventional dominance over other design mediums (e.g., landscape, lighting, and graphics), requiring a more robust, transdisciplinary approach. Artist Olafur Eliasson's *Weather Project* at the Tate Modern (2003) is a signal illustration. »» figs. 22 - 24 Immersive and sensorial rather than articulate and legible, it is defined not by solid and void but by conditions and effects. Color, light, reflection, mist, and so on are treated with greater importance and substance than traditional materials. Eliasson was not interested in revealing the underlying truth regarding how the project's uncanny ambience was actually produced. (This is to be distinguished from the so-called parametric project, whose avowed interest in atmospherics seems to be the latest rationalization for work that is actually vested in a particular type of formal expressionism). In the case of the Tate installation, these effects were deployed in service of creating a "palm latitudes" ambience that was cunningly conceived to attract to the museum those who would not ordinarily be found there (beachgoers, clubgoers). *Weather Project* operated on the premise that new audiences would be drawn there by

figs. 22 – 24 ›› Olafur Eliasson's *Weather Project* (Tate Modern, London, 2003)

the promise of experiencing the foreign (strange)—in this case, an oft-yearned-for climate—without having to leave London. The intelligence of the work lies in the fact that its craft and mechanics are sublimated to its effects, which were created through the borrowing of light from the very atmosphere with which it is intended to contrast. This caused the museum's interior to change in mood depending upon the time of day, season, and weather outside—an important inducement for return visits, as well as a means of broadening membership. Documentation of the actions of spectators over the period of *Weather Project*'s existence more than validate this premise: behavior ranged from the planned (picnics) to the improvised (the grouping of bodies into formations to be "read" by the larger collective of patrons in the mirrored ceiling above).

Plying the familiar rather than the abstract, the decoy's identity is not tied directly to one specific referent (this is this), but rather is suggestive (this could be this) and conditional (sometimes it looks like this) in its associations. Its undecidable identity—often appearing to be a cross between vaguely recognizable figures and/or associations—is characterized by a certain *indifference* with respect to the range of prospective scenarios it supports. It is this indifference—or ambivalence—that lends the decoy the same eccentricity to its logistical arrangements that it possesses in its imageability, one that challenges the routine in ways that prove both new and entertaining. It accomplishes this by applying many of the just-discussed operations (exaggeration, inversion, and so on) to existing protocols and conventions of use, producing the new not from scratch, but through the rejiggering of the familiar. Without an equally cunning operating system, the new markets that its outward appearance (the bait) seeks to attract will be unsustainable. A clever conceit, however buzzworthy, cannot ultimately provide the long-lasting degree of engagement that merits repeat visits. This means that, in order to succeed, those arrangements must be intelligently conceived to support multiple prospective scenarios of use (like Lombard Street). Given the climate of uncertainty that characterizes cities today, architecture must possess the (built-in) intelligence to exhibit varied capacities or values to multiple audiences, not only at the same time, but at different ones.

This is not to suggest that a building needs to actually physically transform in order to be operative. Indeed, change and adaptability are not synonymous with changeability in the literal sense. Rather, what matters, Somol points out, is not the desire for contingency, but the recognition of contingent desires.[17] Instead of being premised upon one particular scenario or audience that may or may not materialize, the decoy possesses a valvelike diagram of organization that supports several plausible scenarios of use. This does not mean that it merely accommodates itself to whatever may transpire (exemplified in the one-size-fits-all genericness of the multipurpose room). Instead, it involves looking for a singular conceit than can contain alternative organizational patterns and pathways. ›› figs. 25 - 27

17 R. E. Somol, comments at the "Fast Forward" symposium, held at UCLA in the spring of 2007.

figs. 25 - 27 ›› Allan and Ellen Wexler's *Tables of Content* project (Douglas Park, Santa Monica, 2001) consists of a single formal "primitive" based on the classic picnic table, cleverly adapted to act in alternative contexts of use: as a bridge, a playhouse, and a climbing platform.

Material arrangements that are only incidentally related to prospective uses, rather than optimally engineered in relation to a single preferred one, yield formal complexity through a process by which the primitive is successively adapted, through a process of design-as-testing, to each particular contingency. In this approach, shape, material, and/ or surface characteristics constitute a crucial point of tangency—literally—between the unlikely combination of (possible) audiences they are designed to attract.

This is not meant to argue for the uncoupling of form from use altogether, but rather for a kind of *functional ambivalence*, or even indifference: one that negotiates between a range of potential purposes. In contrast to the form-finding process of the parametric, the literalism of the decoy is dedicated more to the recognition of identity than it is to the expression or elaboration of function. This conspicuous indirectness in the relationship between form and purpose in the decoy not coincidentally parallels the concealment of means and methods in its imageability. This approach bears a strange kinship to those of Venturi, who famously argued that (formal) complexity is a productive outcome of the contradiction, or frisson, between use and composition (most often expressed at the interior–exterior interface). Venturi's double-functioning element is likewise defined strictly in terms of its semiotic value to an educated audience. In the decoy, that complexity is politicized, produced instead by the formal negotiation between contingent desires. By making its association with use more ambiguous, the semiotic value of form is allowed to remain open to not only other imagined readings, but other scenarios of use, by other publics, at other times. Again like a Trojan horse, the performative dimension of the of the signifier only reveals its underlying intent (intelligence) over time, waiting to unleash an embedded political potential through the agency of identity.

Semiotics and performance come together in Trail Mix, a 2005 proposal for a public space in Toledo, Ohio, by Roger Sherman Architecture and Urban Design. ›› figs. 28 - 30 Trail Mix acts as an urban wayfinding machine and also serve as a drive-through recycling center. It reconfigures an archipelago of traffic islands at a major street intersection, sorting the forty thousand vehicles that pass through the intersection every weekday morning into a series of dedicated "exit" lanes. Threading between and separating the lanes are a series of banana-shaped medians, each banked on one side (on the other is the frontage out of which drop-offs/pickups are made). Covered in locally manufactured materials, as well as a sampling of those being exchanged on-site, the embankments might recall to some the loaded barges that once passed through the Erie Canal—whose path the roadway now fills—or to others the region's numerous Indian burial mounds.

Trail Mix changes both its operation and appearance, depending upon the hour or day as well as climatic conditions. The through-lanes of the recycling center open and close at different times and seasons as

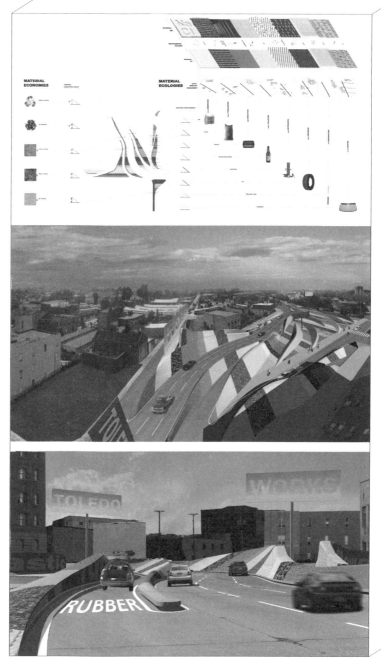

figs. 28 – 30 ›› Trail Mix (Gateway Park), Roger Sherman Architecture and Urban Design, Toledo, Ohio, 2005, from top to bottom: bird's eye view, ecologies/economies diagram, diagram of circulation relative to time of day, and roadside view of loading/unloading area

a function of the availability of certain materials for sale (mulch in the fall, road salt in winter, flowers in spring) or hours of collection. Each material is grown, stored, sold, or collected in one of the embankments. In addition, the materials on the embankment surfaces themselves turn "on" and "off"—visually and in some cases programmatically activating in response to different environmental stimuli: rain, snow, headlights, mud hens, and so on. Economy is merged with ecology. The experience of the site—its appearance and performance—is seldom the same from one encounter to the next, continually refreshing its interest as it does its inventory. The routine (the weekday commute, the pickup and drop-off of recyclables) is made entertaining, to the level of becoming a new form of public space as well as spectacle.

The decoy emblematizes the catalytic agency of architecture-as-urbanism, using the power of the literal to act as a Trojan horse: at once a lure and a strategy, a means of capturing interest/investment, and also of influencing that which is in its proximity. In contrast to the futility master plan, which promises what's next, the decoy induces progress through the allure of what's new (different): its effects (appearances) are inextricably tied to that which it seeks to affect. Rather than being satisfied with indexing data or elaborating existing conventions, the architecture of the decoy marries real estate speculation with conceptual speculation, managing risk by strategizing how to anticipate and secure its own reception. At a time of rapid change, it shows us that the lack of predictability represents a window of opportunity for new business models, social scenarios, and images for urban life, and in turn, the formal invention that they might instigate. In this respect, not just set design and advertising, but a host of other disciplines outside of architecture (e.g., hydrology, farming, new transportation forms) represent a rich repository of other operating systems—alternative protocols, logics, and parameters—from which to draw on as a means of enabling architecture to add value—not to mention recover its popular mojo. In the end, though, it is not program alone—however unique—but rather architecture itself that sets the trap: namely, in the form of specific, highly imageable and sticky architectural elements that have both a provisional value (use, marketing ploy, and so on) but also sow the seeds for a variety of plausible futures, which they are designed to support and suggest.[18] The lexicon below outlines in greater detail several of the key aspects of catalytic design thinking discussed in this essay.

18   Roger Sherman, "If, Then," Log 5, ed. R. E. Somol and Sarah Whiting (Spring/ Summer 2005): 50–58.

The Tradeoff: A strategy of embedment, aimed at winning the support of NIMBYists and public agencies that as a rule oppose development. Rather than assume the more conciliatory ("just blend in") approach to gaining public trust, emblematized through contextualism, the Tradeoff is predicated upon the assumption of a high risk/higher reward approach. It shamelessly builds in, through design, collateral benefits that "sweeten the pot" for stakeholders by appealing to their self-interest in exchange for their support. Design strategy may be conceived to "play" this dynamic logic by crossing the political and economic objectives of property owners, neighbors, merchants, and city agencies with a finite set of available options.

Trojan Horse: A particular type of Tradeoff by which to assuage community/political opposition. Whereas typically the pros of a project are limited to abstract statistical benefits (e.g., increased tax revenue) against which cons seem great because they are often directly experienced (traffic, loss of sun, and so on), the Trojan Horse proffers something entirely more tangible on the "pro" side. New York's Central Park was a Trojan Horse, in that it was strategized to give a different guise to the massive development project that was planned to follow it. Importantly, however, the park also continues today in a different dimension of the same role. Namely, it has come to serve as a built-in antidote of openness to what would otherwise be an exclusive and privileged enclave.

The Tie that Binds (Hotspots): If the undeniable economic success of the enclave is to be accepted rather than dismissed out of hand, the challenge then lies in co-opting its formal singularity to become a zone of radical inclusion, or Hotspot, rather than its inverse, as is currently the model. This requires the invention of formal and material arrangements that are embedded with semiotic associations and programmatic capacities that cleverly crosscut thorough differing demographics and social statics. The Tie That Binds refers to a design strategy that follows from a single conceit, but at the same time deliberately sends mixed signals that will attract—like an intelligent decoy—not one but a combination of species, each of which sees something of themselves in it. (For example, the simple use of water as a material conceit has the potential to attract those who seek to play in it, others who seek to garden with it, and yet others who seek health benefits from it.)

Entertainment Planning: A radically reconstructed type of theming, Entertainment Planning is a form of design thinking that learns from the power of extreme forms of pleasure practiced by special effects designers, but is treated with suspicion by architects and urbanists alike. It dispenses with the shallow narratives that characterize the many ersatz versions of urbanism (often based upon the same neotraditional model) that mistake style and motif for engagement, and instead focuses upon simply scripted, sticky, amusing logistical and material arrangements geared toward the orchestration of one-of-a-kind encounters that offer new ways of being in public.

Ploy: An ingenious or novel device, scheme, or stratagem that is designed to attract attention or increase appeal, a Ploy is a concealed, usually devious aspect or feature of something, as in a plan or deal. It is also a device by which an investor manages risk—a maneuver in order to gain advantage.

i-Catcher: Like its namesake (the eye catcher), which refers to the follies/sham ruins that were objects of contemplation in the English Picturesque gardens of the eighteenth century, the i-Catcher (another name for the decoy) is cunningly designed and imaged as an essential component of a business plan, whose intent is to attract investment and notoriety through internet buzz (viral marketing).[19]

19 Here I must credit the research work of the nine students in a studio I led at UCLA in early 2010, entitled Literal Arts: Double Takes to Double Agency. The following provided indispensable assistance in finding, culling through, and ultimately helping develop the techniques of public engagement that are discussed: Vuki Backonja, Sofia Borges, Mira Henry, Andrew Heom, Molly Hunker, Rona Karp, Heather McGinn, Karin Nelson, and Daniel Poei.

Regenerating Economies
Projects

Simming Brooklyn

Brooklyn, New York
Edward Mitchell Architects

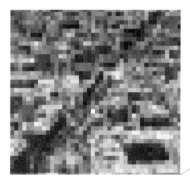

Gerhard Richter's painting *Townscape Madrid*, shown in decreasing levels of resolution

Gerhard Richter's 1968 painting *Townscape Madrid* not only represents a city—it also behaves like a city. Made from self-similar brushstrokes in a limited palette, the image of the city builds by local adjacencies, forming larger entities that we recognize as buildings, blocks, and neighborhoods without any apparent substrate or armature. A tool with this degree of refinement might be speculated upon. Rather than the gross generalizations offered by conventional tools like zoning, a refinement might be brought to the scale of the detail, addressing the local scale in which specific decisions are made.

In order to forecast a more dynamic logic, Edward Mitchell Architects created a genetic algorithm similar to the baseline standards used in SimCity. That game is dynamic with respect to markets and political will, and therefore closer to the processes and procedures of urban development. Conventional planning and zoning— no matter how refined—must generalize from fixed spatial and temporal projections. Studios at Yale's School of Architecture tested these gaming strategies, tabulating program formulas, density ratios, and potential synergies between urban "players." These statistical studies were turned into elements, or "tiles," used to construct an urban fabric for two neighborhoods in Brooklyn, New York: Williamsburg and Greenpoint. In these neighborhoods, the fine-grained distribution of naturally developing programs contrasts with existing zoning, which, though sympathetic with the ad-hoc mix, sought to leverage large-scale development at the waterfront.

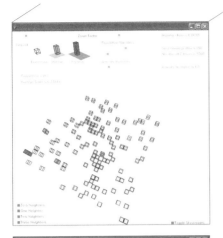

Screen captures of the dynamic models, in order:
"zero neighbor" tiling preference, "four neighbor"
tiling preference, and "four neighbor" tiling
preference with FAR limits

The research model demonstrated a number of interesting generalizations. Restrictive codes like floor-area ratios were prohibitive of the intelligent, individual agency that operates under self-optimization. One might build a tall building directly next to another tall building, but the lack of daylight would not forecast a positive outcome for the developer. The simulation's lessons were used in conjunction with studies of the local infrastructure and real estate practices. Predictions were made as to what factors might affect specific building form. For example, value lies in the first two floors and upper floors of high rises, meaning that tall buildings might be holey in the middle floors or, like a plant, bend to optimal light and view situations.

Finally, the study showed potential development sequencing. Its "forecast" correctly predicted that properties surrounding McCarren Park would be the most fertile for development; that swapping public land at the center of the infrastructure for less desirable properties would lend access and equity to upland parcels to connect them to the waterfront; and that brownfield sites along the water might be land-banked for future development.

Contributors: Jason Van Nest, Andrew Lyon, Roy Griffith, Keith Krumwiede, Sarah Stevens, and Chris Rountos, with grant support from the Boston Society of Architects and additional student research contributions from students from the Yale School of Architecture

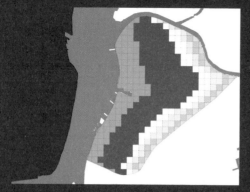

Diagram of typical program distribution for New York
City neighborhoods, superimposed on Greenpoint

Diagram of desired program distribution for Greenpoint

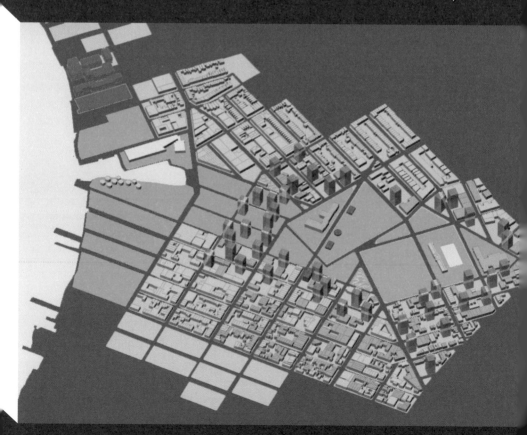

Predicted development around McCarren Park based on the algorithmic model

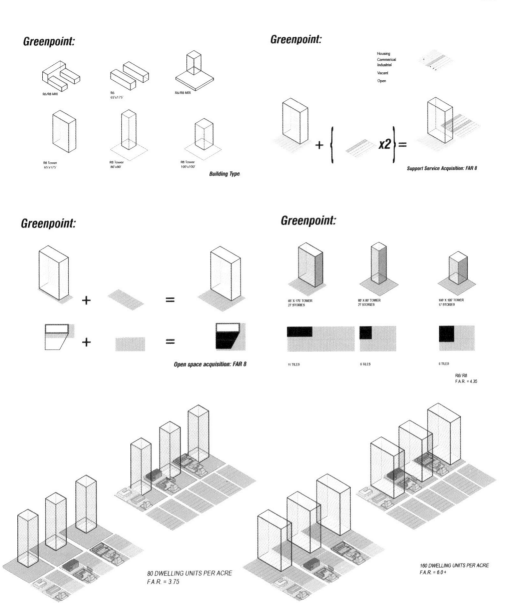

Program tiling samples based on correspondence of residential density to public and commercial amenities

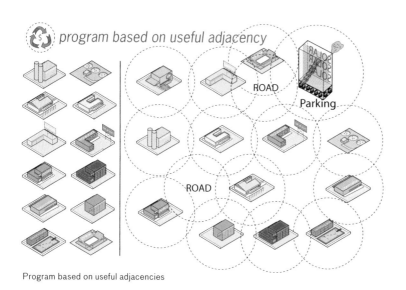

Program based on useful adjacencies

Urban cluster

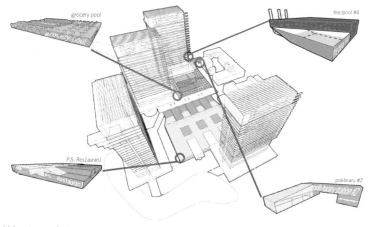

Urban tower cluster

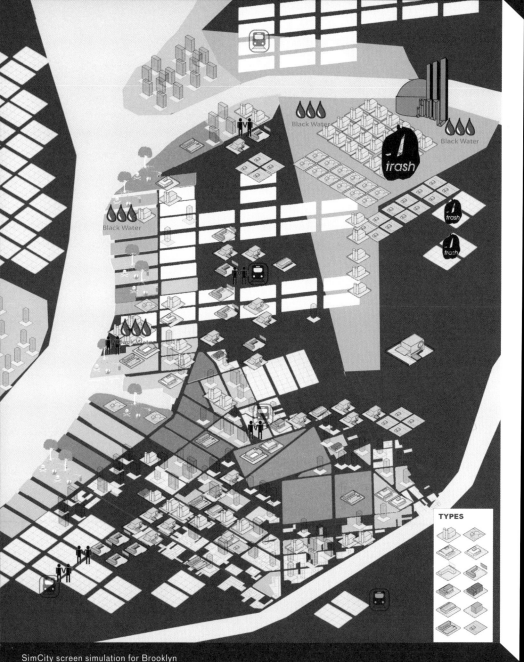

Black Water

Black Water

trash

Black Water

trash

trash

Black Water

TYPES

SimCity screen simulation for Brooklyn

Duck and Cover: Thinking Out of the Big Box

Tracy, California / Phoenix, Arizona / Brooklyn, New York

Roger Sherman Architecture and Urban Design / Greg Kochanowski

Duck and Cover—named in honor of the discourse first introduced in Robert Venturi's landmark book *Learning from Las Vegas*—puts forth an architectural strategy-cum-business plan. It harnesses the vagaries of private investment and NIMBYism to act as a Trojan horse that proffers a new politics of urban community and public space. The community of affiliation it produces cuts across—rather than reinforces—existing social divisions, undermining previous models of theme, identity politics, and special interest. Big-box retailers, with their strong brand identities and large tracts of underutilized land, represent the next frontier of opportunities for this new paradigm. With the recent and dramatic increase in the value of real estate in many U.S. cities, their "stand-alone" formula—which demands optimized vehicular and visual access along with singularity of use—no longer makes efficient enough use of land to justify its cost, particularly in the ever-more-desirable urban core. This new economic calculus—together with the growing neighborhood opposition that big-box development has recently been facing in higher density areas—presents a prime opportunity to introduce a new, more robust model of market-driven development, which Duck and Cover represents.

Looking at sites in three very different geographic contexts, Duck and Cover explores how the well-developed brand of one retailer may be strategically deployed toward the incubation of communities that, while privately sponsored, are nonetheless open and heterogeneous. In the case of Target, these originate in the social "cosmology" that appears on its own website, from which the identities of three imagined audiences posited in this project are derived: Target Green (all things green), Target Play (recreation, performance, gaming), and Target Town (urban life: car washing, commuter stations, post office/convenience store, gyms, workplaces, residential spaces, and so on). Each is sited in a geographic context that suffers from an undersupply of what it offers: Target Town sits at the exurban edge

(Tracy, California); Target Green is in an existing suburban power center, in parched but always sunny Phoenix, Arizona; and Target Play is on an urban infill site in open space–starved Brooklyn, New York.

All three versions of Duck and Cover exist on monumentally scaled, sloping surfaces that are literally and figuratively "branded" with a surface graphic that uses Target's eponymous logo as a form of two-dimensional primitive. Part billboard, part landscape, this surface blurs the categories of ground and facade, landscape and city, catch basin and catchment. It "pitches," both as signifier and as infrastructure—tied to economy through its role as a (newfangled) decorated shed, and to ecology through its role as a watershed. Using a different technique for each of the three scenarios, the surface of the slope is "thickened" in section, using the primitive as a template, embedding the brand with programmatic capacity and potential to serve as both bait and hook in attracting a wide range of audiences, without being prescriptive. The activated surface possesses a political and marketing savvy that exceeds that of its Venturian antecedents. An opportunistic version of the defensively minded berm-buffer, it is simultaneously a strategy of advertisement and concealment—one that aims to draw new audiences even as it purports to hide the big box in plain sight. The same device also ironically broadcasts and expands the retailer's visibility and presence beyond that of the ground-level experience of shoppers, to the elevated perspective of drivers on adjacent freeways or tenants in nearby office towers, and ultimately, the global audience of Google Earth.

Team Credits: Quyen Luong (project manager), John Chavez, Dustin Gramstead, Brendan Muha, Daniel Phillips, Daniel Poei, Ben Ragle, Stephanie Ragle, Amelia Wong, and Andrew Benson (renderings)

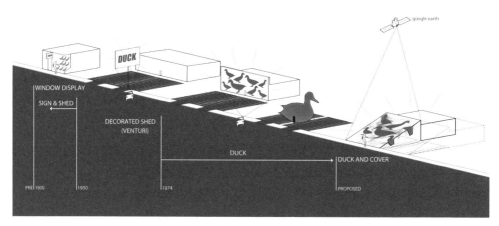

Window to Watershed: A short and future history of commercial display

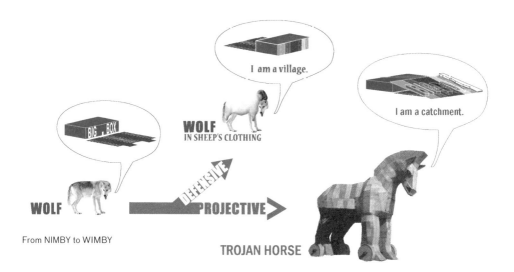

From NIMBY to WIMBY

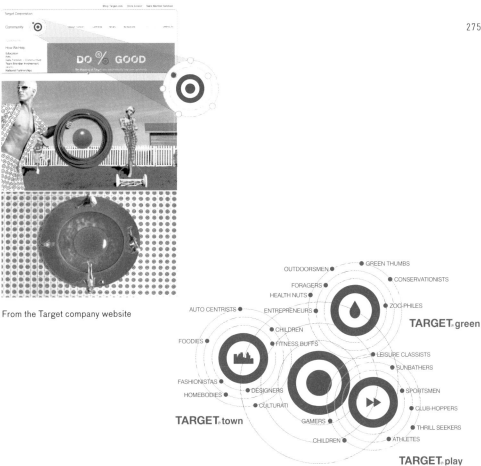

From the Target company website

Target(ed) Communities

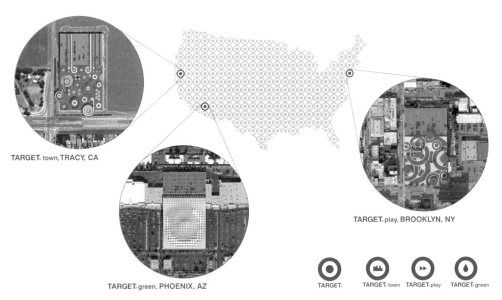

Target Nation

TargetPlay: Ground view

TargetPlay (Brooklyn, NY): Bird's-eye view

Transverse section

Section detail of the slide/wading pool/climbing wall/ shop kiosk

Pattern-to-program diagram

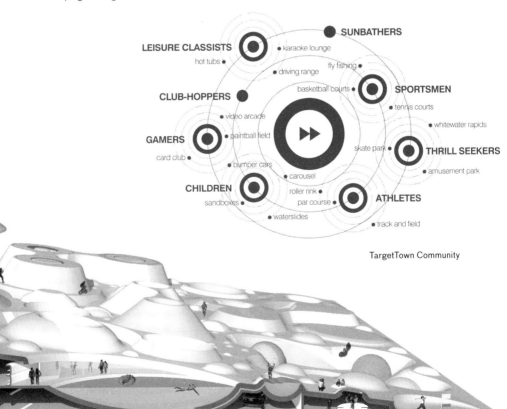

TargetTown Community

TargetTown: Bird's-eye view

TargetTown: Aerial view

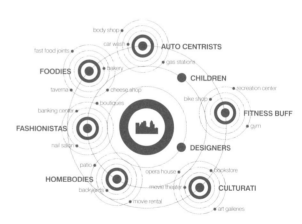

TargetTown Community

Transverse section

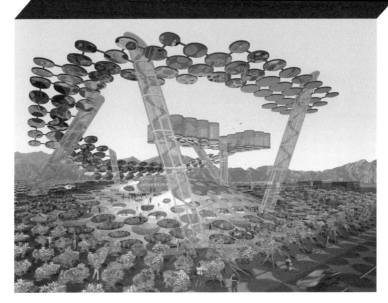

TargetGreen: Ground view

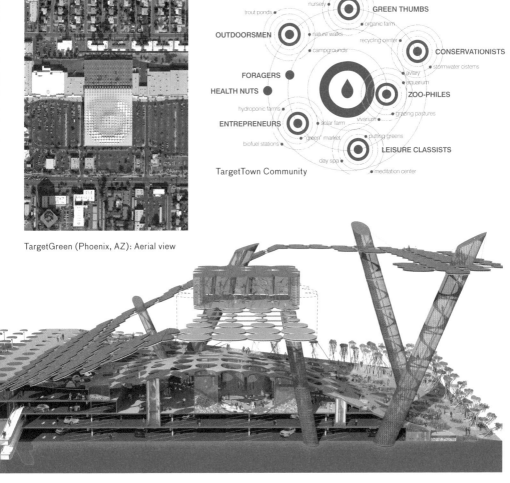

TargetGreen (Phoenix, AZ): Aerial view

nursery
trout ponds
GREEN THUMBS
OUTDOORSMEN
organic farm
nature walks
recycling center
CONSERVATIONISTS
campgrounds
stormwater cisterns
FORAGERS
aviary
HEALTH NUTS
aquarium
ZOO-PHILES
hydroponic farms
grazing pastures
ENTREPRENEURS
solar farm
vivarium
putting greens
biofuel stations
"green" market
LEISURE CLASSISTS
day spa
TargetTown Community
meditation center

Transverse section

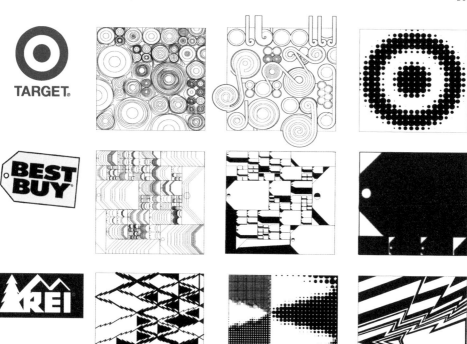

From brand to planning: Target and beyond

Screen still of *Logorama*, produced by H5, Paris, 2009

Image credits

Index